NIGEL KENNEDY

UNCENSORED!

NIGEL KENNEDY UNCENSORED!

Written in His Own Way And Words

FONTHILL

www.fonthillmedia.com
office@fonthillmedia.com

First published in the United Kingdom
and the United States of America 2021

British Library Cataloguing in Publication Data:
A catalogue record for this book is available from the British Library

Copyright © Nigel Kennedy 2021

ISBN 978-1-78155-856-0

Printed and bound in England

CONTENTS

WARNING

WARNING: Being 64 years old, the way I often express myself could be considered to be politically incorrect by today's thought police, particularly when I think I'm being humorous.

Please don't be responsible for ageism when jumping in to criticise my views by criticising the way I express them. My whole life has been spent breaking down barriers between people and the documentation is there to prove it.

Please don't worry, Be Happy! It's your choice....

DEDICATION

Dear Mal Summinkoruvver,

Thank you for your snide comments, and for thinking that you know so much more than me about political issues, terminology, boxing, music (!) and whatever else. I'm sorry that I can't resist taking the piss out of veggies, man made global warming alarmists (shit, it's hot in here) and political correctists. When you agreed to publish this book I really didn't know that you were all of the above and would get so wound up that you wouldn't publish me.

Your refusal to publish my book helped me realise I'd written a good one and reinforced my belief in every word I have written. You also helped me come up with a good title.

I remain faithfully UNCENSORED!

In the words of Chumbawamba: I get knocked down, but I get up again.

You are never going to keep me down or in the words of Ian Dury: There Ain't Arf Been Some Clever Bastards.

I would also like to dedicate my stuff to some nice people who don't have such a false sense of intellectual superiority … to Agnieszka, Antós, Ania and Huxley.

GLOSSARY

ARCM	=	Associate of the Royal College of Music
BABE	=	sweet person of either gender
BAD SHIT	=	not good stuff, very good stuff
BRO'	=	brother in spirit
BULLSHITOMETER	=	instinctive analogue sensory application which detects silliness, bullshit, stupidity or any other mental imbalance
CHOPS	=	technique on a musical instrument
CLASSICO	=	middle of the road classical musician
DAMAGER	=	Manager
DUMBFUCKTOR	=	conductor of an orchestra, not a bus
ELEKTRICKERY	=	Electricity
EXPERT	=	a wanker or person whose knowledge of a subject is vastly overrated, often by themselves
FLOWERS THAT BE	=	people with delusions of having moral authority over us
FUCKTOR	=	conductor (abbreviation)
FUKKA	=	an object, person or situation
FUKKIN'	=	fucking, a word used for emphasis or punctuation
GENDER	=	male, female or whichever of these you want to be. WARNING: I'm not prepared to count beyond 4
GOOD SHIT	=	good stuff
GROUND	=	Stadium
KAT	=	person of either gender, normally OK, or cat
KILLA	=	great, superb
KILLADILLA	=	even greater than great
KILLJOY	=	someone consumed by insecurity or jealousy who hates to see anybody having a good time and succeeding at something

KOOL	=	Good
KOOLKAT	=	good person of either gender
KUNT	=	the same as above, kunt-duck is another abbreviation
KUNT-DUCK-TOR	=	guy or whatever who waves a white stick at or against an orchestra
KUNT-TREE	=	a bordered area of land defined by its name and national characteristics, a type of music about truck drivers' love problems, term coined by Carlene Carter Rosanne Cash
MAESTRO	=	comrade or jumped up monkey, depending on the context
McSHIT	=	McDonald's
MONSTA	=	phenomenal, great, better than very good
MUVVAFUKKA	=	impressive, top level, exceptional, bastard
PUSSPORT	=	passport from a namby kunt-tree
REAL SPUTNIK	=	top class Russian geezer or geezerette
SHIT	=	Stuff
SHITUATION	=	a situation which isn't very good
SILVERY BOY	=	Jascha Heifetz
TO DWEEB	=	to talk a load of inane meaningless shit
TUTTI FRUTTI	=	a bit where the orchestra play without the soloist
TWO WEEVILS	=	two evils
WANKER	=	someone who is better off trying to recreate solo, unaccompanied
ZWEISTEIN	=	twice as bright as Einstein (DREISTEIN = figure it out yourself)

INTRODUCTION

Dear Friend,

Welcome to my book.

Please fasten your seat belts unless you feel that that would be an erosion of your hard-earned civil liberty and that in a worst-case scenario you've paid more than enough tax to look after the state hospital costs.

Once upon a time there was a beginning very near the start of my life …

A Beginning

From the vantage point of my cocoon there is light all around me but there is a permeating coldness which is increasing. From within myself there is also an increasing hunger. I am constricted by my cocoon so cannot move. All of these issues are just one overwhelming feeling. The coldness and hunger are now reaching an unbearable level. What can I do? Normally I would have warmth and milk by now. I know. I cannot move but I can scream and howl. I can feel the impending noise welling up inside me. It should do the trick, it always does … AAAAOOOOUUUUWWWW! … nothing … she hasn't arrived … no milk … she still hasn't arrived … cold … colder … no warmth … COLD HUNGER … AAAAOOOOO-WAAAA!!.... This is my earliest memory from the flat which we rented in Regency Square, Brighton when I was a baby of a few months old. My Mum had gone to teach piano or have a rehearsal in London. I'm not sure which, I wasn't there! She must have gotten late and forgotten that she'd left me in the pram on the balcony. A few long hours went by before she got back but—I SURVIVED! Nowadays that's called neglect but in fact what it did for me was give me a memory way earlier in my life than most people have them. It's very fashionable these days for over privileged people of all backgrounds to harp on about the "disadvantages" they previously suffered from in order to big up how momentous their achievements are. In these days of Internet lead information garbage overload exaggeration is the order of the day. In reality my no milk day was pretty tough but in the long run made no difference to me whatsoever... I don't even like milk anymore.

Since then life took an upturn and has been rich, varied and milk free. Starting from the seemingly narrow confines of The Yehudi Menuhin School and The Juilliard School (of artistic mediocrity) luckily things broadened out thereby embracing work with Robert Plant, Roger Daltrey, Pete Townshend, John Entwistle, Paul McCartney, Kate Bush, Jean-Luc Ponty, Stéphane Grappelli and of course many of the expected classical interpreters ranging from Yehudi Menuhin to André Previn.

I have also spent memorable times with the boxing and football fraternities including of course moments with the honourable and great fans and players of the club which originated football as we know it—ASTON VILLA FC. By Far The Greatest Team, The World Has Ever Seen.

For me, memories are not relevant to a book of mine unless they are amusing or confront imbalance. I respect balance as opposed to bullshit and the internal bullshitometer that I developed at a very early age has helped me create a more balanced environment around me, for my friends and colleagues within and outside the music world. The little battles I've had with record companies, the BBC, the Bavarian police, conductors and other self-appointed wielders of power have been all about that. It's a crime to let bullshitters of any type spoil our world. More specifics later!

Q. Nige, why are you writing this book for me to read?
A. Short question, long answer. Four years ago a fair few people offered me a fair bit of dosh (not enough!) to celebrate being 60. What an inane idea. 60 is a completely unnoteworthy age, too young to die but not young enough to win the unified welterweight championship of the world like Lloyd Honeyghan or Sugar Ray Leonard did. So my answer was "No way, muvvafukkas."

However, at the time of writing I am now (almost) 64 which is a much more amusing age. One year away from my bus pass and also in a position to be associated with a song by the most famous band in history. An age which while still having a future also represents a long enough life to have some potentially interesting reminiscences. I am writing this for you—a friend who might have been to one of my gigs or bought one of my recordings. Or maybe you've never sampled any of my stuff in which case please come in, sit or move around comfortably and try it. If you support the most significant club in world history to whom football owes everything including the league format there will be a whole chapter on Aston Villa.

I'll see you around the corner of this page.

EARLY DAYS

Early Days, Part I

It all started in Brighton, the year was 1956: Being born had to be done but life wasn't particularly easy for my Mum. Piano teaching was very poorly rewarded financially so in the absence of funding for a babysitter and being a single parent, my mother used to keep me in a crib under the piano while giving lessons to the students who came streaming through our flat. The owner of the house was a dentist who had his practice on the bottom two floors, we rented the top two which comprised a kitchen, a sitting room where the piano was and three very small bedrooms in the eaves of the roof (or do I mean in the attic?). The dentist didn't mind the classical music ebbing down through his ceiling while he drilled, hacked, gouged and cleaved his victims. The soporific sounds probably saved the dentist some of his sleeping gas bills and made the clients' tortures a little posher. My Mum had good enough taste not to teach intellectual music so there were no Hitchcockian film scores for the dentist to worry about.

This stowing of the baby / teaching situation was economical in three ways. Free piped music for the dentist, no babysitting fees and free musical education for yours truly from birth. From underneath the piano I was hearing Bach, Beethoven, Chopin and co. at Led Zeppelin levels with the inner voices of importance coming out nice and loud. I often get disappointed by a student or singer's failure to properly engage with their colleagues in the orchestra and the lifeless musical results devoid of much harmonic understanding of what the other musicians are playing. I end up thinking: "Where the fuck are they? In a fucking phone box? What about the composers and those other great musicians on stage? Where's their empathy for the situation, their colleagues and the audience? Man ... it's all so automatic."

It is then I remember that my time under the piano has given me an instinctive understanding of harmony and the bigger musical picture which these other kats never had a chance to get while solely developing their individual technical expertise. This lack of knowledge from the performer is why quite often classical music sounds impressive but as if nothing's happening. OY! Young kats! If you want the audience to really appreciate the music you are playing, and if you really want to appreciate the music yourself, my suggestion is to learn a bit of piano or guitar so that you gain the harmonic knowledge required in order to do the job.

The Yehudi Menuhin School

At the age of six years old I had been learning piano with my Mum and violin with a very good teacher in Brighton, Amina Lucchesi. I preferred the piano but was making good progress on both instruments. It was at this point that Miss Lucchesi informed my mother that Yehudi Menuhin had recently opened a specialist music school and that in her opinion I was talented enough to get into it. My Mum, like altogether too many other Mums in the world, thought that her kid was the next Jesus Fukkin' Christ Almighty so it was arranged that I went to the entrance auditions.

The audition was in London, my first time in Das Killa Kapital. I went into the audition room and three blokes were sitting behind a desk, they turned out to be Yehudi Menuhin, Marcel Gazelle (the music director) and Robert Masters (head of strings or something). No one put pressure on me to do well in the audition, so it was simply a new and interesting experience. Having only played the violin a few months I'm sure I wasn't a killa but my piano playing was OK. Gazelle and Masters were just strange suit wearing kats who happened to be there but I liked Menuhin. He was the one who talked to me and I had been given a couple of his albums for my fifth and sixth birthdays. It was like I knew him. First he asked me to sing back a phrase or two which Gazelle played on the piano. No problem. Then they played me a few musical phrases to which they asked me to make up the second half. I enjoyed that game and was good at it. I also, of course, played a bit of violin and piano to them. That was it. After the audition my Mum took me to London Zoo, I saw some giraffes, chimps, gorillas and got on an elephant. A good first ever day in London. After that it was back to Brighton.

Eventually my Mum got the news that I'd been accepted into the school. Although this was great because it showed that I had some talent, my mother had no means of income for the gigantic school fees required so it was GAME OFF. Classical music was obviously an exclusive game reserved for rich monkeys' kids. However, Menuhin talked on the phone with my mother and told her not to give up hope, maybe he could arrange something. Before long he informed her by letter that he had arranged a scholarship, The Menuhin Scholarship, which would cover my whole tuition and board for the complete duration of my studies at the school. GAME ON.

Apparently what Menuhin had liked was my ability to create the second half of musical phrases and also that I played the fiddle bang in tune with an attractive pure sound. It was going to be a bit of a wrench to leave the tutelage of Amina

Lucchesi, I liked her, she gave me sweets and I had just reached the level of being ready to join her pupils' orchestra. It was going to be exciting to finally play with other young musos from the area instead of practising on my own and having solitary lessons. She must have been a very fine teacher because a couple of years later she got two more pupils into the Yehudi Menuhin School. No other teacher had got more than one student into this very small select school. I had a great structure and set up with Amina Lucchesi which I was very happy in. I was going to leave all that and my home in order to take a giant step into the unknown.

The Yehudi Menuhin School was conceived when Menuhin became inspired, but also disappointed, by the example of the Russian specialist music schools. Apparently on a trip to Russia, Menuhin and his wife had heard products of such schools. One young violinist after another after another got up and played incredibly but with no soul or individuality, so Yehudi thought it would be useful and rewarding to set up a similar school in England but with the difference of a more humane musical agenda. He wanted to offer a more holistic and ostensibly more philosophical opportunity for talented young players. I concur with the thinking that you can teach any young monkey midget[1] to play the violin very impressively if it has the right number of hands, fingers and arms. The more salient point is once one has all that technique, does one actually have anything to say with it? Giving the monkey midget access to aesthetic considerations is more essential than making it repeat and repeat and repeat technical finger flicking.

In common with the Russian schools, though, the teachers appointed to their various jobs might have had musical or academic credentials but they had absolutely no idea how to deal with kids. The end result was a lot of highly talented, directionless, unhappy little bastards. For instance, putting a seven-year-old kid alone in a room to practise for four hours didn't exactly produce a lot of positives. My way of dealing with it was to do about 15 minutes practise after which I'd sit on the toilet for 30 minutes immersing myself in a science fiction book (a genre addiction I'd picked up from my fellow inmate, Simon Parkin) and waste away a decent proportion of the time that way. Some of us boys (girls didn't do this kind of thing, I'm sorry to be honest and factual, not sexist) developed violin dropping competitions. This progressed very well until the drop height extended above the top bunk near the ceiling. The objective was to drop the violin with so much expertise that it didn't break. This particular drop from ceiling height was more affected by gravity than expertise, and a valuable Gagliano (Italian) violin became the victim. The crunching noise and the twanging, zinging strings were great but its shape definitely wasn't. Creative explanations to the authorities were required. One thing was for sure, even the Russian schools never competed with us at that violinistic form of Russian roulette. Once we deemed this activity too much trouble and too risky, we took up roof climbing instead … (no safety net!).

---

1 This term doesn't mean I have anything against monkeys or midgets. Please don't cry, my sensitive flower.

The problem of young fukkers being unable to schedule, allocate or organise their own practise time continued. At some point The Powers came up with the idea of random practise supervision. There was one supervisor, Robert Masters' wife (Mrs Masters) who regularly dosed off, possibly because of my amazingly boring playing. I took advantage of this on a quid pro quo basis—if she couldn't be bothered to go through the tedious practise scenario nor could I. She was, after all, meant to be the professional one out of the two of us. Her head dropping was my opportunity to scramble out of the window, go somewhere out of sight and kick a ball around. I would have loved to have seen her face when she woke up to see my vacated space over and over again, but this never happened because of geographical reasons. It seems we had come to an unspoken mutual understanding. I wasn't doing my job, she wasn't doing her job, so nothing ever got reported. Maybe she was also dosing through other kids' musical tribulations because she was missing from the faculty the following year. I missed her for all the wrong reasons.

The world we lived in was Yehudi Menuhin's creation and was started with the best intentions, but the place was like a mixture of Gormenghast and Hogwarts. I haven't spoken with any alumni who remembered it as a wonderful place. I, for my part, am really grateful for Menuhin's generosity but feel heartbroken for some of the other pupils who were traumatised for the rest of their lives. Various issues are not relevant for me to go into because I came out of the experience completely unscathed but I stand by everything I said in a broadsheet interview after which, instead of trying to fix things, the school threatened a lawsuit against me.

There were some very good things and other slightly comical things about the school which I'm sure came from Menuhin himself. For instance, we were read a different religion or philosophy every Sunday morning which meant that there was no danger of any of us becoming fixated with the supremacist propaganda caused by religious prejudice. Our God is better than your God or there is only one God is such a loada bollokks. We all know that the only Gods are Aston Villa FC and we are plural. The Aston Villa Yearbook unfortunately wasn't among the various mind openers that we got little doses of but Buddhism, Taoism, Judaism, Christianity, Dostoyevsky, Tolstoy and suchlike all were. Music played a part as well. We sang Bach chorales and it fell to one of us each week to present an original work for the meeting. I was responsible for a fair few of those.

YOGA: Each time Yehudi came to the school he would be the enthusiastic victim of another fad which would then be imposed on us innocent kids. One time it would be Scholls—some clunky bits of wood which we would have to wear on our feet, stumbling around. Another time Bio-Strath, a disgusting brown liquid dietary supplement to spoil our breakfast. Another time seaweed tablets which would find their way into our pockets, turning the pockets into a kind of concrete by the time they'd been through the laundry. The worst, however, was YOGA. Lotus position was uncomfortable. It was all a bit silly. Then to make things unconscionably worse a big fat guru was delivered in and ended up destroying our table tennis table by using it as a platform from which to demonstrate all the silliness. The shape of the table tennis table was unalterably changed after the impossible challenge of supporting his weight. If there are three reasons why something is SHIT then it is normally SHIT so yoga is SHIT. 1) Uncomfortable; 2) Silly; 3) Fat Bastard table breaker; 4) Culturally appropriated as a substitute aerobics for lazy fuckers who, of course, dump the spirituality part down the toilet with their semi-digested KFC; 5) Menuhin fell from a supporting frame onto his head while doing yoga leaving his bonce and spine in worse shape than if he had never done yoga at all. There you go … 5 reasons … so yoga is SHITTER than SHIT.

Yehudi Menuhin with his yoga teacher B. K. S. Iyengar

SCRAMBLED EGGS! One night when we were rooting through the kitchen, I found the next morning's scrambled eggs pre-made and very economically watered down. Pretty disgusting and probably up until then an undiscovered but regular practice. Inspirationally I dumped another gallon or so of water into the putrid cauldron so that the eggs were unusable. The eggs were never watered down in future and the matter never became a big issue because leaving eggs like that was probably illegal or a severe health hazard. The staff must have figured out who was responsible when I signified my knowledge of the crime by offering to help them find out who the diluting master was who did it. We had beef sausages instead the next morning so it was a win-win shituation.

It was a bit weird going to this strange school, which was quite parasitized with lots of ambitious parents thinking their kid is the next Jesus Christ or whatever on the violin or the piano, and then come back to a completely different home life at the same time. It wasn't something great for a kid. My mum got remarried and we moved up to Birmingham. So, any friends that I might have had, they were way down back in Brighton. My stepfather was a doctor and was quite a bit wealthier than we were. For instance, we didn't have a TV in the house before my mum met him, and then we got a colour TV. Our new house was in the middle of a town, which is on the outskirts of Birmingham. It was three stories high, a much bigger house than what I'd ever seen before. Me and my stepsister would be up the top floor, our parents would be on the middle floor. I think it was two sitting rooms downstairs, it was a much bigger house. But it's better to be in a smaller house where there's no shit going on. I would have preferred that.

My stepfather was a bit of a wanker though, he was beating my mum. I remember trying to stop him one time when I was about nine or ten, and jumped on him. But I wasn't very big, and he was a big bastard. He ended up chasing me around with a knife. I went out and slept in the park for the night, I remember sleeping underneath one of the bushes and some people were doing some black magic, probably sacrificing something. I was less scared of that shit than I was of my stepdad with a knife, you know, as a 10-year-old, you don't want a fucking knife in your guts.

After that incident, every time he started beating her, I'd call the police. I don't normally call the police, but as a doctor, he had to maintain some reputation and I think instinctively I just thought "Well, fuck this!" He kind of stopped for a while, so that was at least a good result.

Going to see Aston Villa play was an escape from being in that horrible house on the weekends. In fact, football was a killer escape route. I was able to make friends with a few people and we'd go to the games and enjoy incredible positive energy. In them days, Aston Villa was in the Third League. But we had 48–50,000 people going. To know that we were all on the same wavelength was a great feeling. Having that big crowd around me was like being with extended family, replacing the one which maybe I didn't have.

FOOTBALL: The sporting curriculum was null and void in this school of precious hothouse flowers. With only about 15 boys of all ages to choose from it was pretty impossible to get eleven to form a team, particularly when the cultural disposition of almost half of them ensured that their priority was to prevent the possibility of their shorts getting dirty.

MUSIC AT THE SCHOOL: There was always music going on in the school. I remember breaking my finger playing football and being able to lie back on the lawn listening to amazing Debussy or Chopin coming from the various pianists practising in the downstairs rooms. What a fukkin' life!

At one point practise became a bit of an issue. This time some people were practising TOO HARD! In those days genders were very different from each other and there's no way that the boys would have been guilty of such behaviour. The girls started practising with pathetic diligence at all hours. It became like an epidemic and they were getting up earlier and earlier to practise before breakfast. Finally, when it reached the point where the lovelies were so desperate to get ahead that they were starting work at 4:30 a.m. us boys decided to take the piss out of the shituation. We arranged between us that we would all get up and start really early—so at 4 a.m. there was a literally unsettling pre-dawn chorus of braying, screeching, whining, scraping and wheedling violins disturbing the slumbering staff. The beleaguered teachers found it necessary to legislate against practise before 6 a.m. This had an almost immediate benefit for the girls who started looking far less grey under the eyes and ashen faced. I used to enjoy being able to reach equal levels to these overworking 'model students' by getting up just five minutes before breakfast. There Ain't Arf Some Clever Bastards …

JAZZ: The most stimulating aspect of my musical life during my schoolboy years was becoming interested in jazz and a few other non-classical forms. Garfield Jackson (the great violist from the Endellion Quartet) also had a passing interest in jazz because his Dad Sid could play jazz trumpet. My interest grew stronger as his waned but before he gave up altogether we were able to play for a few builders to celebrate the opening of the school concert hall that they had just finished. The teachers thought that the builders would prefer our jazz shit to Bartók's greatest hits.

This interest I had in jazz was strongly, no! … STRONGLY discouraged by all the music teachers at the Yehudi Menuhin School but I did have two very strong allies. Yehudi Menuhin and the spiritual/musical pedagogue Nadia Boulanger. Having played a lot with Stéphane Grappelli himself Yehudi could hardly get away with discouraging me, and anyway, he had shown a lifelong enthusiasm for folk music and Indian music as well as European jazz. To see if I was the devil child or not I was taken in front of Nadia Boulanger to play some of my jazz shit to her. No one normally had a one-on-one with this demigod but even though the teachers cowered a bit in front of her she never intimidated us kids. She sat there, the halo shining above her old head, and seemed really pleased that I wasn't playing something she'd heard before. She really encouraged me but it was a Saturday morning and I was very worried about missing the train up to Birmingham. Villa were playing, we beat Notts County 4–0 and I remember a stunning goal from Bruce Rioch. He only ever scored stunning goals.

SCHOOL CONCERTS: Musical highlights were usually the gigs we went to play as stunningly precocious young bastard pupils of the school. Most of the gigs have receded right out of the back of my head but I do remember my first visit to Paris with the school at the age of 13. We checked into a dark roomed hotel before getting ready for a rehearsal. I enjoyed the luxury of having a room to myself and thought:

"Kool, I'll have a crap right now in the luxury of my own bathroom." PRRRP…–…BRBR…BRB…SZZPLATT.

Mission accomplished. Nice soft toilet paper. I liked France. Even a shit was satisfying. Then it was time to flush away my good work but… what? No flush? There really was no flush. Imagining that maybe the French kept the flush mechanism under the toilet or somewhere else in the bathroom I gave the whole room an exhaustive search but my forensics kept on leading me back to my arrogantly glowering turd and toilet paper. There were two taps and a spout on the toilet but nowhere for my creation to go. There was a second toilet which looked more normal but it was too late now. While I had been making what I had made, however, I had been thinking:

"That's nice, if I had a girlfriend with me we could use the two toilets at the same time—and the two basins. Very nice." (I was extremely romantic in those days).

Eventually I realised that this turd of mine had exhausted all of my intellectual capabilities so I knocked on my mate's door to get his advice. I think it was either Simon Parkin or Felix Schmidt who came into my room to have a look.

"Hey, mate. How do I work this toilet?"

He looked while making sure to keep himself at arm's length. It didn't take long for him to give me the wisdom of his considered opinion.

"You've shat in the bidet, mate, you'll never get that out."

"Beee-day?"

"Yeah, the French don't like baths much so they just clean their privates in that. It's called a bidet."

"Beee-day. Disgusting. Oh dear."

"Yes. It's even more disgusting now. You better call Mr Norris. He might sort it out."

"Awright. Thanks, doctor. Good idea." I got on the phone. "Puis je parle avec Monsieur Norris, s'il vous plaît?"

"Quoi? Jeeurst spake Eengleeesh."

"Mr Norris, please… Ummm, hello, Mr Norris… fine… Ummm, I have a problem. Someone has shat in the beee-day and just left it there. I think I need to change rooms because I can't live with it … it's kind of disgusting."

The room change never happened but two offended-looking maids provided the woman power required to remove the offending article. One of them looked quite nice and I considered asking her to my gig but then I realised she wouldn't be captivated by my Mendelssohn trio. She would just be sitting there thinking about my bidet, what was in it and who had done it. First impressions were just too important, and her impression of me was… shit.

After the *la merde* scenario we went to see the Eiffel Tower. I guess the description of our trip there might be considered more suitable for a geezer who plays a bit of classical music to be writing about but you won't find it here. If you're interested you can check it out in Lonely Planet. Very, very nice Ozzie publication.

Friends And Influences: Stéphane Grappelli

There was a buzz of excitement going around the Yehudi Menuhin School that morning. It had just been announced that in the late afternoon the greatest jazz violinist of them all was going to come and play for us. I had already started to improvise, fiddling along to various jazz recordings and also played some rudimentary shit on the piano, so out of all the kids I was the one most looking forward to checking the gig. It was a win-win situation because it also meant Mrs Henderson's class was cancelled. She had the amazing ability to turn history into a series of completely forgettable dates and nothing more.

The jazzspieler's name was Stéphane Grappelli, and Menuhin had rescued his career from the doldrums when they had appeared together on the main British television chat show of the time—*Parkinson*. The combination of the two greatest and charismatic violinists from each of their musical styles fascinated people. Menuhin with his diligent, note reading vibrato-laden style and Grappelli with his smooth effortless violin playing singing like a canary (not one of those down the mines … don't be silly). And now Grappelli was coming to play to us little muso school bastards at Yehudi's invitation.

Grappelli's style in jazz was so effortless, compared to the rather grinding classical style we were being taught, that he was a revelation—and now we were going to be able to hear this legend from a few feet away.

Five minutes prior to the gig, Peter Norris, the Yehudi Menuhin School music director, had asked to speak to me. "What the fuck have I done wrong now?" I thought to myself as I went to meet him in the staff room. "I hope it's not about stealing that stuff in the kitchen, if the cook leaves it out it's gonna go." To be asked to go to the staff room usually meant something bad. I knocked on the door … "Come in, Nigel." I went in.

"You asked to see me."

"Yes, Nigel. I suggest you get your violin."

"But Mr Norris, I've done all my practise and the concert's about to begin."

"Well, you never know, Mr Grappelli just might ask you to play, and you wouldn't want to miss your chance."

Mr Norris had always been very annoyed when I played my rather uncouth style of jazz piano in the common room. This seemed an uncommon *volte-face* bearing in mind the face offs we'd had about that.

"All right, thanks Mr Norris."

I rushed off and got my violin which I put (in its case) under my seat for the gig.

"What've you got your violin for? Are you going to play?" asked my mate Garfield Jackson in his John Arlott voice. He was a nervous violin player but became one of the best viola players Britain has ever produced.

"I dunno." I said.

Finally it was time for the gig. Stéphane turned up with the great Alan Clare (piano) and Lennie Bush (bass). It was totally acoustic, no mikes, so I guess that's why he didn't bring a drummer. The music was fukkin' brilliant, the whole trio were blinding.

Stéphane came on in one of his paisley shirts (and trousers of course, clean up your mind) accompanied by Clare and Bush. Man, this was real music compared to the shit we were always listening to. Stéphane appeared very nervous playing to all of us precocious hothouse flowers. He didn't estimate that it was HE who was the master—loads of jazz kats used to have an illogical inferiority complex when comparing themselves to classical musos. Towards the end of the gig he bashfully addressed us in the audience.

"Dorz enivown varnt tio djjoin oooss?"

Almost before he'd finished the sentence I was up there playing with one of the greatest swing violinists of all time. We played 'Ain't Misbehavin'" and 'Honeysuckle Rose' by Fats Waller, 'Limehouse Blues' and 'Lady Be Good'. Stéphane loved it that a muvvafukka at least two generations younger was so into his stuff and could actually play it. His style was, of course, that fluid, effortless cascade of notes, which we all love so much. My more rugged bluesy style fitted in with him good and proper and our music benefited from me not trying to copy him. That day changed my life and from there on in, we had a long strong friendship.

Whenever Steff was in England, he would invite me to join him for his gigs on a Friday and/or Saturday night when I could get out of school. I was able to absorb and learn the music of greats like Kern, Gershwin and Porter the best way possible ... by ... PLAYING IT! We started off playing in folk clubs, then as Stéphane's career regrew he went on to concert halls etc. Hanging with Steff and his band revealed to me that there was a whole other musical life out there, other than the dentist's waiting room like atmosphere of the ivory tower called classical music. Jazz was played and listened to by real people with no airs and graces.

Apart from finding a musical world in which people just played great music without all the silly attitude, the positivity of the jazz world rubbed off on my classical music. I had now discovered that even though everything seemed written down anything could happen. For instance, the dead composer couldn't control whether it was a Monday or a Friday, raining or sunny, if there was a general strike, or loads of other random things. There were many, many factors affecting the transmission of the composer's soul, not just what was written on the page. Change was the only constant in life, so it seemed.

Another inspiration was that Stéphane always got the *crème de la crème* playing with him so there was a killa level all around the band. Musicians passing through the band were people such as Diz Disley (a serious Django disciple), John Etheridge (Soft Machine *et al*), Jeff Green (killa feel), Ike Isaacs (suave and Joe Pass-like) and Denny Wright (great rhythm and virtuosity). On bass there would be Brillo (hair), Len Skeat (rich, rich sound and always a solo on Satin Doll) or Jeff Klein (linear and fluid).

By the time I was fourteen or fifteen one of the highlights for me was playing with Steff at Ronnie Scott's Club, London. All the jazz greats had been on that stage and the magic was all around. It all went great apart from my awful jokes and bad haircut. Then another thing happened which could've changed my whole life path. Ray Nance had quit the Duke Ellington (big) Band in which he played violin and cornet. Duke Ellington's manager heard me playing with Stéphane in Ronnie's and offered me the job that Nance had left. The Duke wanted a violin sound in his band to replace that of Nance. Duke Ellington was one of the greatest (if not THE greatest) composers of the twentieth century and he wanted as many sound timbres as possible. It was a priority to be a quick sight reader, a good improviser and to have the right sensibility to replace Nance. A couple of years later after I'd moved to New York I remember going to a club to hear him play. He played killa violin and cornet, and finished the show tap dancing up on top of the bar. I certainly didn't have all those skills but I could produce a great classical sound as well as improvise—Duke with his original orchestration could probably have imagined using those qualities. So ... the whole caboodle had to be put before The Komintern which consisted of Yehudi Menuhin, my mum and stepdad and Peter Norris (the aforementioned school music director). It was obviously a big deal because I couldn't remember any other time when Menuhin, my parents and I had had a meeting. It was decided not to accept the offer, I think probably on two fronts, one discussed openly and one a bit more obliquely. Menuhin and my mum wanted me to become a muvvafukka of all time classical violinist (well, I've done that!). What they didn't discuss so directly was the picture I think they had in their minds of tour buses full of geezers holding brown paper bags containing bottles of very, very effective liquid. Being quite softly spoken and underage I had to acquiesce to their decision but to say NO to the greatest composer of the twentieth century was a lot to lose out on, let alone playing with all of the other geniuses (I Dream of Genii) in the band.

So, my life motored on towards being a classical soloist. Maybe I should change something now—it's never too late! Oh, wait a minute, I already did!

A year or so later, I was settled in New York studying with the violin pedagogue Dorothy DeLay. When I was having one of her very DeLay-ed lessons (always late!), I mentioned that Stéphane Grappelli was playing in Carnegie Hall that evening and was probably going to ask me to play. She said "I wouldn't do that if I were you, Nigel. CBS (now Sony, dear reader) are going to be there. They're interested in you recording Mozart for them but they'll ditch the idea if they think you're a jazz violinist." This was long before my career changed the little classical music scene. Before American Classicos wanted to appear as if they could play bluegrass or jazz, before European Classicos started throwing everything but the kitchen sink at anything! Now it's almost obligatory to do some cheesy crossover if you want to get a classical recording contract....

When I arrived at Carnegie I went to say hello in the band dressing room. Stéphane asked "Neeejgelle, veal you curm on et plaey Tigare Raag veeez urse ce soir?"

"Well, I'd love to Stéphane but my professor Dorothy DeLay doesn't think it's a good idea."

He took this ungrateful behaviour in a very humble manner.

"Velle, eeef yeou charnge your mayeend...." with which the band and Steff left to go on stage. Alone in the band dressing room just with my thoughts, I paced around kicking a doorstop in front of me as I went.

"I've just refused to play with the best violinist in the world."

KICK.

"How rude and self-centred can a precocious muvvafukka get?"

KICK.

"What was I thinking? I'm in Carnegie Hall and have said I don't want to play here ... and with the greatest violinist."

KICK!

"And I'm going to miss the fun of it too, how will I handle it after the gig when I've been too precious to play?"

KICK! The doorstop scudded over towards the refreshment table and at that point I saw the bottle of Scotch. Then I saw that I'd modified it to being two thirds air. "Fuck dis", I thought, "I've got my fiddle with me, that's a sign. I'm not an idiot. Stéphane is better than any of those Classico monkeys at Juilliard. I'm not going to miss this...."

I got my fiddle out of the case and went into the wings, waited for the right time to go on stage. When it seemed right I put my head round the door. Diz Disley beckoned to me and I walked onto the stage of the absolutely packed Carnegie Hall.

"Ah, Neeezzjelle, c'est vrai, you eeeez heeey-arre."

'Tiger Rag' was killing. Some of my friends in the audience talked about that gig for years and even remind me of it now.

The next week in my lesson with Dorothy DeLay.

"Well sugar, the people from CBS were at the concert you played with Grappelli. You played, didn't you?"

"Yeah ... and?"

"They thought it was very good and enjoyed their evening but they are no longer interested in recording you because they think you are the wrong type of musician."

Funny that if I had played jazz horrendously, like most classical musicians, they would probably have thought I was an amazing Mozart player.

"Well, if they don't like good music—too bad. I'm not interested either."

She was right, but so was I!

Talking of teachers, Stéphane Grappelli didn't need one. His style was self-taught (like Albert Sammons) and he was incomparable on his instrument. His example only fed my mistrust of teachers, toilet paper diplomas or degrees, or any school syllabus. Who was it, after all, who decided what we should be offered to know when getting further education? And were their lives so much better than ours that we could've benefited from them deciding this? There was a line beyond where this type of educational control bordered on propaganda and censorship. This question was pertinent to music, and also to history. Look, for instance, at all the countries sticking their dirty little mitts up when trying to take all the credit for winning the Second World War. Which syllabus should we believe? The English? The Polish? The American? The Russian?

Life was an arena, a real experience, not a theory borrowed from a piece of paper. Steff was a living example of what I felt. From my first gig with him in the Boggery Folk Club in Solihull (where a pre-fame Jasper Carrott was the MC and wouldn't let me in. I waited four hours on the doorstep until Stéphane ushered me in like a 13 year old fukkin' star![2]) to the last, he never played a bad note. His

---

2 Even though he's a Bluenose, Jasper and I became good friends until I chose to go and see Villa vs Man Ewe over doing a gig for him at the NEC. Sorry, Jasper—VILLA RULE OK.

dexterity and accuracy came from the fact he used very little bow and played very lightly. He always had the luxury of a microphone which meant he didn't have to physically project over the band. The louder you have to play, the more difficult it is to have that kind of speed. One's life as a soloist (without a mike) is spent evaluating facility versus projection. It doesn't matter how fast or clever it is if no one can hear it! Completely acoustic music and mike enhanced stuff are two completely different arts. Stéphane was the absolute microphone master, just as Sinatra and Mel Tormé were.

Stéphane's pre-war band with Django Reinhardt, The Hot Club de Paris was one of the first all string jazz bands, building on from Eddie Lang and Joe Venuti. The band was also the first really popular example of European Jazz. Everything before was a European copy of Amerikan style. The Hot Club became the most popular band in Paris and beyond so Steff always knew what he was doing in front of an audience. He knew how to communicate.

In regards to communication Stéphane was very pro-publicity (in common with my other mentor Yehudi Menuhin, who despite all of his other qualities was a bit of a publicity junkie). Steff said many times:

"Neeezzjelle, ennay pooblissataey izz gurd pooblissataey."

People with their little poootas and little Twitter accounts certainly believe that nowadays.

Another repeated saying of his which he would always tell me when he was going to play a popular song which I thought might be on the verge of being naff was:

"Neeezzjelle, but deess eeez gurd pour lest toureeestz ..."

He realised that he wasn't just preaching to the converted but was also playing for a new audience. He wanted to welcome newcomers into his musical world, not alienate them.

My last encounters with Stéphane Grappelli were connected with recording. Firstly, he agreed to record a song called 'Melody in the Wind' with me on my album called *Kafka*, a collection of songs about change. I had written this song specifically with his violin sound in mind. It was amazing that he agreed to do it but at the time of the session he was very ill. I thought it might be better to cancel the session, or at least run some lines up to his flat in Montmartre so that he wouldn't have to go out. (I liked his flat in Montmartre, by the way. Steff hated banks and kept all of his money in cash, stuffed in cracks in the walls. I dunno what happened when all of these currencies changed to the Euro—if he took all the money out of the walls at the same time I reckon the flat would've collapsed!). I suggested both of the options that had occurred to me. I particularly strongly suggested cancelling. But NO. He insisted on coming to the studio I had booked and recording the song. He didn't want to let me down. His violin sang like a bird but later, when I isolated his violin track, I could hear him coughing all the way through it. He obviously delivered his beautiful performance out of professionalism and maybe a bit of love. It means a lot to me, does that.

Around the same period of time three tenors who called themselves The Three Tenors, who all sang in the range of tenor and got paid more than a tenner, copied all of my and John Stanley's innovative marketing techniques even to the extent of copying my association with football when performing at the World Cup Finals in Rome that summer. Pavarotti's PR person at least had the decency to admit to me that they had carbon copied my approach. "Right", I thought, "I'll bury this lot!" I called up Yehudi Menuhin with the idea of doing The Three Violins who would also play for more than a tenor/tenner. He said in his saintly gentleman's voice:

"Oh, Nigel, what a wonderful idea. I would be absolutely delighted to play with you both…"

Great.

He was going to be the more difficult one to persuade but persuasion hadn't been necessary. So when I was hanging with Stéphane I told him about The Three Violins idea and asked whether he would care to do it, to which he exploded:

"I veeell nevaire play weeez zat peeeg ageen. Ee makes zeeez 'orreeeble meeestakes et zen leurks at moi azeef I deeed zem, ezree time mon cher, terreeebler. Non, I eam sorray. I veel plaee wiz you—you playee propearlay."

So The Three Violins bit the dust before they started. Shame—we would've had the tenners playing for a fiver as our support band!

Anyway, my experience playing with Stéphane changed my life. He was a completely unique character who had seen a lot of different eras and situations. It was also unique that his playing got better and better, like a fine wine. Thank you, Stéphane, for leading the way and allowing so many of us to play the violin in many different ways. You called me your musical grandson. It's an honour to be in your family.

Friends And Influences: Yehudi Menuhin

On one occasion Yehudi Menuhin chose me as being the most obnoxiously promising violinist from his school and the reward was to go play the Bach Concerto for Two Violins in D Minor with him in a gig in some place like King's Lynn or Norwich Cathedral.

We had done a good pre-show rehearsal and there were at least two and a half hours until showtime. We were in his dressing room with his wife Diana and he had just told me that I could address him simply as Yehudi instead of Your Most Worthy of Sainthood and of Godly Status Sir—this being rather a mouthful which, if used at the end of each sentence, could have interrupted the natural flow of any of our attempted conversations. Diana was making some lentil (mental) type of muesli stuff for Yehudi after having combed his hair. Yehudi asked:

"Nigel, would you like some of this absolutely delightful muesli? It's composed of the most amazingly healthy, finest ingredients with added honey and seaweed. One can find it very invigorating on a concert day."

Lauri Kennedy, a very early photograph.

Lauri Kennedy, a photograph taken in Hollywood, 1943.

Above left: Lauri Kennedy playing under the direction of Sir Thomas Beecham, a photograph taken in the USA. He was principal cellist of the BBC Symphony Orchestra from 1929 to 1935, and afterwards he was with the London Philharmonic and Covent Garden Orchestras. The photo is signed: "Good friend and colleague ... Laurie Kennedy with esteem and affection, Thomas Beecham Aug 17/43".

Above right: My grandfather Lauri Kennedy recording with the Fritz Kreisler quartet. *From left to right:* Fritz Kreisler, violin; William Primrose, viola; Lauri Kennedy, 'cello; and Thomas Petre, second violin.

My father
John Kennedy
in England
when he was
lead 'cellist in
Sir Thomas
Beecham's Royal
Philharmonic
Orchestra in
London.

Above left: Daisy Fowler
Kennedy (1893-1981),
Lauri's cousin and my first
cousin twice removed.
She was a famous concert
violinist, born in Burra-
Burra, South Australia.
She died at Hammersmith,
London.

Above right: Aged two at
Mum's piano.

Left: On the balcony of our
flat in Brighton.

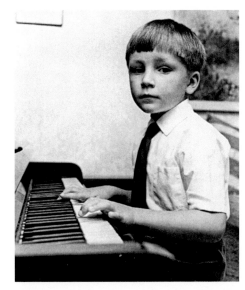

In 1964, after winning the scholarship to the Menuhin School.

In Nadia Boulanger's class. At the Yehudi Menuhin School but I did have two very strong allies. Yehudi Menuhin and the spiritual/musical pedagogue Nadia Boulanger. Having played a lot with Stéphane Grappelli himself Yehudi could hardly get away with discouraging me, and anyway, he had shown a lifelong enthusiasm for folk music and Indian music as well as European jazz. To see if I was the devil child or not I was taken in front of Nadia Boulanger to play some of my jazz shit to her. No one normally had a one-on-one with this demigod but even though the teachers cowered a bit in front of her she never intimidated us kids.

With Yehudi Menuhin and Robert Masters.

Above left: This is possibly another photo at the time of the scholarship, 1964.

Above right: At the Menuhin School. *Courtesy of The Yehudi Menuhin School*

Yehudi giving me personal 'hands-on' practical tuition.

Eight years old, on my way back to school.

The wedding photograph: Mum and Duncan in the middle, with Granny (left), Duncan's sisters and their husbands, and my step-sister, Jo, next to me. Granny appears to be focusing on me.

With Stéphane Grappelli; the nearest anyone got to being my idol. My experience playing with Stéphane changed my life. Thank you, Stéphane, for opening the door for so many of us to play the violin in so many different ways. You called me your musical grandson. It's an honour to be in your family.

In Gstaad, Saanen, Switzerland, for the Menuhin Festival Gstaad, August 1973. *From left to right*: Colin Carr, 'cello; Colin Twigg, violin; Carol Norman; Jacqueline Cole, piano; Susan Dorey, 'cello; Krysia Osostowicz; and yours truly, NK, violin. *Michael Ward, courtesy of The Yehudi Menuhin School*

Above left: At the Menuhin School, March 1974. *Courtesy of The Yehudi Menuhin School*

Above right: At the Charleston Manor Festival, 22 June 1974. Melvyn Tan and I played at the festival organised by Lady Rhoda Birley who lived at the house. I remember meeting Virginia Wade that day.

With Jimmy Lin Cho-liang at the Juilliard, New York.

"Thank you very much but if it's all right with you Your Most Worthy of ... Yehudi, I'll go down the pub and get a meat pie."

Diana: "Horrible ... that pie will take all the blood from your head to your stomach and you might not be able to concentrate. You don't know what's in it."

"There's beef, onions and nice gravy in it. If it's OK with both of you I'd prefer to see what happens. I think the pie will stabilise me for the concert."

To tell you the truth, I didn't much mind what Diana thought and could never understand how the best violinist in the world had got himself into such a seemingly pussywhupped shituation.

With that I bade them and their unsavoury looking veggie food a relieved farewell and hit the pub. I got the beef and onion pie which was delicious and everything was going well. Well, that is, except that that was the last thing I remembered until somebody was prodding my head with their foot, saying:

"Oy, closing time. It's past closing time and you owe us £55." (More like £500 in today's money).

That was going to take a while to pay off with my 25 pence a week pocket money. Then I remembered the gig with Menuhin ... shit ... I'd missed it.

"Oooer..." my mind creaked, "maybe I should've stuck with Mrs Menuhin's muesli ..."

It turned out that after I'd finished my beef pie someone had seen my violin case and asked if I played that thing. Apparently, I had got the fiddle out, played a bit of Irish stuff and had been bought a pint for it. Then one song led to another, which led to another drink and then to another drink which led to another song which led to another etc., etc., etc., and it seemed that I had bought everyone in the pub multiple drinks and cigars as well. I have worked hard at improving myself since then, but at the age of 13 I couldn't take my alcohol in a professional manner.

It was clear to me that I had to come to some kind of arrangement with the barman. After that I could worry about the equally significant problem of missing the gig. On my pocket money it would take four and a half years to pay the bill and that would be without tip. Then came my eureka moment. With a masterstroke I brought both the elements together, missing the gig with Menuhin and the huge bill.

"Please, can you send the bill to Yehudi Menuhin, No. 2, The Grove, Highgate, London N6? He will definitely pay it."

"Wot ... that violin geezer?"

"Yes, he's my teacher and I was meant to be playing ..." I bit my lip. Then the other bartender chipped in.

"That could be him. The other young violinist. One of the punters had been to the concert and said that the other violinist hadn't turned up."

With that I was allowed to leave. Someone had kindly put my violin and bow back in their case. I had three pounds I'd saved up so was able to get back to school by train. Everyone had left the empty and locked venue so I guessed that Menuhin's driver had my concert clothes.

Once back at school I decided that if I didn't mention anything the whole fiasco might just blow away. It was a ridiculous hope but the ostrich technique worked. No one mentioned anything and life went back to normal immediately.

About a week and a half later I received a postcard, very nice, and it was from Yehudi Menuhin. I have never been one for keeping mementos but I do wish I still had that postcard. On it he had written what I can almost remember word for word:

Dear Nigel,

I am so sorry that we weren't able to play Bach's Concerto for Two Violins together. I am sure it would have been magnificent.

You seem to have had a good time in the pub. I would like to remind you that although the occasional drink probably doesn't do one much harm, smoking can be really detrimental for one's health. Please don't smoke.

Yours as ever,
        Yehudi Menuhin

I have never before, or since, experienced such an attitude of humility. Even more remarkable coming from one of the greatest musicians in the world to a lowly student such as myself. Normally that type of humility at best is a little forced, particularly in the world of the Classico. He could have chucked me out of his school and that would've been perfectly normal.

A few weeks later I went to have a lesson with him at his home in Highgate. He opened the door himself and had a naughty schoolboy look on his face.

"It's wonderful you're here, Nigel. Diana's out and there's no one else here. Follow me if you would."

He sneaked to the kitchen and I followed in an equally furtive manner reminiscent of the Lavender Hill Mob what with my fiddle case and all. He opened the fridge and carefully pulled out four bottles of beer as if they were the crown jewels. We drank a couple of bottles and he really enjoyed it. Hanging out in a normal way. Surrounded as he always was by royalty, politicians and shockingly privileged people it was as if he was never allowed to do anything simple like that.

The last reminiscence I am writing for you is unfortunately rather different. Everyone changes and by the point of this particular recollection I was in my twenties, and establishing my own musical personality. I was no longer the 2nd Menuhin. I now saw classical music through my own eyes, not through someone else's rose-tinted spectacles. I had too strong a view and interpretation of what I was playing to be able to backtrack and copy somebody else, even if it was someone who had been my inspirational mentor for so many of my early years. I obviously hoped that Menuhin would feel vindicated and proud that I now had a personality and something different to offer.

Menuhin, on the other hand, was a fair bit older. People had been labelling me his heir apparent and in recent years his playing and conducting had received a fair bit of criticism. He seemed a bit resentful and definitely didn't want to pass on his mantle to me or anybody else. What he failed to perceive was that I didn't want his mantle, all I required was the nice glove I already had which fitted me personally. My opinion was that one Menuhin was a huge event for the twentieth century, he was still very alive, and to have another one would've been a gratuitous Menuhin overkill. I felt the same when hearing people cloning Jimi Hendrix. The first Jimi = mind-blowing, the second = mind-less.

The upcoming concert was me playing the Beethoven violin concerto with Menuhin conducting. I reckon it was in Chester Cathedral. We commenced work by me going to his new home in Mayfair (not half as nice as his old one in Highgate which I believe had been bought by Sting) a few days before the gig. It is normal for the soloist to be expected to render his specific interpretation of the concerto in question. The conductor follows the lead of the soloist and transmits the soloist's vision to the orchestra. On this occasion things were different from the start. In the first meeting I started playing to him the way I felt it and immediately he was jumping in, telling me how to play each note and even how to tune the violin. I was very disappointed in a man who on previous occasions had been so humble and inspirational and had always supported me being myself. To make things worse one of his sycophants was sitting there saying "vibrato, vibrato" all the time. (Long gone were the days when the vibrato knob was turned up to eleven for every note). After another 15 minutes of being prevented from playing more than two notes in succession a very clear course of action occurred to me. I knew what was going on.

"Tell you what, Yehudi, I've got the drift and I think I know what you're after. Let me go back home to re-practise the concerto and we'll see if it's better tomorrow."

When I got home I put on his recording with Otto Klemperer and played along with it over and over again until I could play the Beethoven exactly like Menuhin. Vibrato, slides, portamento, rubato, tone colour, tempos and dynamics all exactly identical. The technical and performance analysis that Dorothy DeLay had some-how got me to teach myself in New York came in very handy for this endeavour.

The next day I went back to Mayfair and played the Beethoven concerto to him again like a cheapskate 2nd class Menuhin made in 1970s China. (Probably hard to find after the Cultural Revolution!).

"Oh, Nigel", Yehudi reacted, "this is a wonderful transformation. You really understand Beethoven now, you have grown into his music spiritually."

"I'm sorry, Yehudi, but there's nothing spiritual about it and I have gained no greater understanding of Beethoven at all. All I've done is gone home and simply learned how to mimic your playing from your recording with Otto Klemperer."

"But it sounds so much better ..."

"But I am who I am and I've been asked to come and play my interpretation. There's no way I'm going to copy your recording in the concert. It's not at all honest to do so because I would be pretending to feel something that I don't... You're such a wonderful violinist, if what you want is a strict Menuhin interpretation of Beethoven why not play yourself? I am happy to stand down and get out of your way."

"But Nigel, you're advertised to play and people are looking forward to it."

"Well, if my name is advertised and people are looking forward to it maybe they'd like to hear what you and I bring to the music, not you and a clone. I'm not willing or able to be dishonest and pretend to be someone else, even if it's you. I can't help my DNA!"

"Nigel, please think about it overnight. I'm sure you'll change your mind."

"Of course I'll think about it, but I'll still be me tomorrow. If you want to hear the wonderful Menuhin interpretation of Beethoven I'm really happy to stand down so that you can play it yourself."

The next day was gig day and Menuhin hadn't taken up my offer that I fuck off. In the rehearsal things were a bit difficult for the orchestra. Who should they follow? Me with my more masculine, rhythmic forward looking view of the concerto or Menuhin with his enjoyment of stretching out every beautiful moment almost to a standstill? Basically quite fast or VERY slow?! The issue was not going to be resolved, it seemed, until the gig itself. Things didn't bode well but there was one reason I was pleased to be playing. My mother was coming and she would've been mighty disappointed if I'd have stood aside so that Menuhin could avoid our musical differences.

To make a longer story merely long, the performance was completely shit. Every time I helped the music gain some momentum Menuhin would drag the whole thing slower and slower. The orchestra couldn't read his beat and it was like trying to walk through quicksand, all of the energy was being sucked out of poor old Beethoven. Roll Over Beethoven—he would've done if he'd heard that performance!

Despite Menuhin trying to teach me instead of listening and making a musical partnership there was one redeeming factor which rescued the performance from falling apart altogether. Us musicians are trained with our ears, not with our eyes. The musicians of the orchestra were always going to respond to what they heard with their ears from me rather than to what they saw from Menuhin's baton. From my experience the orchestra musicians always prefer the soloist to the conductor. It's the choice between someone else who can play something and someone who appears unable to. Even though the orchestra were doing their best to follow me (while being shown the polar opposite by Yehudi's baton) it was still unforgivably embarrassing that people in the audience had had to pay their hard earned dosh to listen to that shit. At least, I suppose, the orchestra, Menuhin and I were professional enough to save the audience from being aware of our silly musical tug-of-war. Once Beethoven's body was no longer twitching we took our bows with all the normal saintly, gracious foppery and returned to our dressing room. Out of respect for Menuhin's wishes I didn't play an encore even though the audience seemed to want one. In my mind they deserved a decent encore after having to sit through all that dodginess.

Looking back on it ours had been a bit like a musical father–son relationship and, like many a parent, the 'father' can try to exert their will on their 'son' even when it's far too late in the day and the 'child' has grown up long ago. I had chosen a different path and that upset Yehudi's sense of order and seniority, he definitely didn't like it.

I remember trying, on occasion, to give something back to Yehudi who had given me so much. For instance, because he had started playing 'jazz' with Stéphane Grappelli I thought I'd help open up new vistas for him in this phenomenal art form. I turned up at his house with a (vinyl) record of John Coltrane. He hated it, in particular the drums of Elvin Jones which he said had no dynamic sensibility or feeling. Even though he said it in a very knowledgeable and guru-like way it was ridiculously ignorant. Our paths had diverged and I now knew and understood some things which he didn't.

Once in the dressing room at Chester I decided to have it out with Menuhin but avoided swear words because he was so saintly looking.

"Man, Yehudi, that was just dreadful, do you really think that was any good? I don't know what you were trying to do but you've ruined the Beethoven for me. I'm not going to be able to go anywhere near the concerto in the foreseeable future.…"

Before Menuhin (feigning surprise and obliviousness to the problems we had had on stage) could reply there was a knock on the door and my mother was shown into our room. Prim and proper but on this occasion with an unpleasantly obsequious and grovelling manner she whined:

"Mr Menuhin, that was marvellous. Thank you so, so much for all the amazing and wonderful things you've done for my son."

Menuhin hit genius level and immediately came up with the right response for each one of us. The grateful mother, the pissed off soloist and the self-righteous mentor.

"Nigel is so talented that whatever I've done seems to have come naturally."

That was brilliant! Even the turd of Beethoven just came naturally. A covert smirk of a glance unnoticed by my mother (or the flunky who had shown her in) was exchanged between us. That he could instantly come up with something so succinct and to the point but from both points of view yet again underlined that he was one of the great minds of his era. I was pissed off but now felt lucky to be there. A little humour is not a bad thing.

Yehudi Menuhin was a man far ahead of his time with his open attitude towards so many cultures miles away from the classical conservatoire. Also, as well as being very valued members of the Jewish community his whole family quietly and stoically supported the Palestinian people's human rights. He went to India and worked with Ravi Shankar before The Beatles knew that India was more than a type of rubber.

With his views on people and ecology one could say that Yehudi was a well-groomed, drug-free, classical hippy. I'm proud to have had such a unique and positive influence in my life.

Mugged Again—I'se a Muggin'

"Yo mofo, giss yer munne." I heard this form of address a fair few times as a seventeen year old in my second year in New York. Being addressed as MOFO obviously must have had a lasting effect on me because many years later I had a fan club which I called THE MOFO CLUB. Anyone joining automatically became an honorary motherfucker.

As it happened, by my second year in New York all of the scholarship dosh I had won in the UK plummeted down to 25 per cent of its original value because of the pound's exchange rate against the dollar. It had something to do with Edward Heath's relationship with the working people of Britain, or lack of one. Unlike the vast majority of Juilliard students my spoon was a lot less shiny, made of lead. The next year I started busking and also formed a funeral quartet which took care of things financially but for now I was without funding. As well as eating macaroni cheese for a year (don't get me wrong, I love the fukkin' stuff) I had to find sub-zero finance accommodation. I found a very good size couple of rooms (not in great condition) on the borders of Harlem and Spanish Harlem. The rent was almost non-existent and there was no problem practising because my musical noise could never compare with all the other constant shit kicking off in the area.

To get down to Juilliard and back I took the subway each day which involved walking to and from the subway station for a couple of blocks. I was on the way back to my room to cook my tried and tested macaroni cheese when, for the third time in a couple of weeks it happened.

"Yo, mofo, giss yer munne...."

"Fukk this", (I thought to myself. I was walking past the basketball courts where my previous two excellent muggings had happened. It was the same four experts who were confronting me this time) "surely they realise that I don't have any money by now. Whatever happened to third time lucky? This must be because I'm white. They've already had my watch. Maybe they're pissed off that after I ran for it they found out it didn't work." Loadsa shit like that was going through my head. They were now blocking my path. I showed them my asthma inhaler to let them know it was all I had. They'd seen it before.

TALL: (*he was the tall one*) Wossat geetar ffinng?

Squat, Spider (*spidery looking guy*) and Muscle were crowding round me.

ME: That's my violin, you can't take that, it's my living, mate.

SPIDER: Teehee. Dat's funnee—aksunt, moyte.

SQUAT: Open dat fing.

MUSCLE: Yaiyer, open dat.

ME: It's my violin (*I opened the violin case*).

SPIDER: Wassat lowng white teeng?

ME: That's the bow.

SPIDER: Teehee—bouw legs.

TALL: Dat's no geetar. Fauw strin' wood, man.

ME: No, it's a violin, man.

SQUAT: Wo'it do?

ME: (*Thinking I had nothing to lose*) It does this.

I quickly wound up the bow and started to play some semi-bluesy Jimi Hendrix type stuff, a bit incongruous, one violin on the street against the odds.

MUSCLE: Huh?

SQUAT: D'white thang mae sown ... (*fair play—even a lot of Juilliard students didn't realise that and thought it was the left hand which did it!*)

I carried on playing because it seemed the only way to delay the inevitable. After all, with no fiddle I would merely have been Fiddler on the Sploof ...

TALL: Wo' dat call?

ME: It's my violin—check...

And I played some desperate mix of Irish and blues.

TALL: (*while I was playing*) Huh, veee-lon.

SPIDER: (*as if he were coming up with an amazingly innovative social programme, and it is the words he used which I still find memorable*) Hmmm ... Maw peep' shu' doo dat....

I stopped playing—my most high-pressure least rewarding lowest attended busk ever but at least some cats had heard and seen a violin for the first time.

SQUAT: Yaw aw-rite—seen yo' roun'.

TALL: Veeeol-en ...

MUSCLE: Veeelon.

ME: Yeah, violin. Can I keep it?! There's loads more of these if you want them at Juilliard on 6th and Amsterdam ... and they're worth more than mine (*I wasn't lying*).

MUSCLE: Due-yar.

ME: Yeah.

TALL: Yaw-rite. We do Due-yar. You be look-ow ... You wid us. We do job ...

SQUAT: Yeaar, you bring dem Am-stamm. We do it.

ME: Sorry mate, can't do that. I ... got asthma you see (*showed my inhaler*). The pressure makes me nervous and I can't breathe. Then you'd get caught, mate.

SPIDER: Teehee—dat funnee asssunt ... moite ...

I don't think they ever did Juilliard, never saw them around there but from then on I was the funny guitar playing guy and apart from the odd smirk as acknowledgement they left me alone as I walked past the basketball courts ... and I had learned that from our little ivory tower sometimes it's too easy to forget that some people have had a very different life and don't even know or care what a violin is. The next year I got my shit together, left the area and never saw them again playing basketball all day.

Life wasn't all bad. However, many great musicians were playing in the clubs in those days. The sessions were after hours, all the kats were there after jobs and were there for the music and not the money. It was a great hang despite the fact that I was deemed by many to be from the wrong social and cultural background. It became a bit known that there was this pale violin kid who was a protégé of Stéphane Grappelli. That got me thru' a few doors (literally) and on the nights I'm on about Helen Humes, Joe Williams, Ellis Larkins and Major Holley were all there and I got to play with all of them. An inquisition at the door was a small price to pay. Getting to jam with these world class musicians was a far greater learning curve than attending Juilliard—and needless to say the late hours completely fucked up my morning attendance record. I learned musical prioritisation early, and that good music can also mean/be a very good time. I took this attitude into my classical playing and to this very day I'm still more prone to a smile than a grimace.

THE WORST GIGS I'VE EVER 'AD

Whilst not quite comparable to collecting lobsters from Jayne Mansfield arsehole I've done some jobs which weren't all that fantastic. It might seem strange that shit gigs stick in the mind so much more than the good ones but I suppose it makes sense. If you've planned to do a great gig a surprise departure from that plan is more noteworthy. Also, good gigs help us to respect ourselves but bad gigs help us learn about music and being a human being who makes mistakes.

Of course, I've done gigs like Polish Woodstock or the Singer's Jewish Festival in Warsaw[3] where the promoters were just slime balls but promoters of that type can be overcome in order to give the public the great concert they've paid for and deserve. What follow are different. Unknown unforeseeable factors made sure that each of these three gigs was at least a mini fiasco. They appear in chronological order:

Snap, Cackle, Stop (British Embassy, Washington DC)

In the early '70s there was a wee bit of noise in England and Scotland about a young talented violinist fukker who had passed his ARCM (Association of the Royal College of Music) with record marks, 100 per cent in every category, at the age of 15 to 16 years old and was now going to study at The Juilliard in New York. Oh yes, ladies and gentlemen and other types of people, I was verily a well and truly talented muvvafukka! An echo from the British chattering classes must have reached across the Atlantic.

The English Speaking Union, who had given me £500 to survive in New York for a year (deffo 500 shitters better than nothing) forwarded a request that this young classical wizard play some shit in the British Embassy, Washington. To this

---

3 This statement is not anti-Semitic. Whatever race they were from they were disgusting slime balls.

very day the British classical violinists are shitter than the Yanks and Russkis—maybe the Embassy glitterati wanted to show that at least this time the Brits had a winner. The gig was for diplomats and kats doing very, very well off British and American taxpayers' money. After the expenses of my pianist, no, I said PEE-YA-NISST, the travel for both of us and some sandwiches for the trip I'd make a profit of $200. That was kool and would pay the rent of my nice cheap flat in Harlem for two months.

I decided to play the last movement of Brahms D minor sonata (aggressive and severe, but majestic), some Bach for solo violin (spiritual) and some beautiful short form Fritz Kreisler songs to reward the poor listeners for checking all the preceding serious heavy shit. I believe it was Peter Orth who I played with but if I'm wrong it was someone proper classical anyway.

We took the train (Amtrak) from Penn Station at about 9 a.m., the gig was at 4 p.m. Then we were going to be able to get a train around 8 or 9 to be back in NYC around midnight. All good.

We rehearsed for half an hour in the embassy from about 1:30 p.m. to 2 p.m. The venue was an ornate ballroomish looking place (with chandeliers, gold leaf chairs all set up for the audience and a plush red carpet down the middle dividing the seats like an aisle). Posh. Or at least opulent. The piano was a schweinehund and probably cost less than one of the gold chairs. Nevertheless we were ready and cleared out of the room so that the rich kats could go in and parlay, hob-nob, grovel or whatever else took their fancy.

Four o'clock prompt we were told that everyone was ready for the gig to commence. Walking through the corridor towards the ballroom I made a very conscientious geographical note of some tables with hundreds of ready poured glasses of wine on them.

Even though I'd had a go, the audience were probably thinking "Quite cute, this young English guy from Beatles-Land must be very talented because he's not very smart looking." We bowed to the pseudo-cognoscentis' knowledgeableish applause and launched into the severe rather barbaric movement of Brahms. Crescendos, diminuendos, dynamic contrast, rhythmic pacing, it went brilliantly for at least three minutes even though my very accurate gig radar didn't detect any particular enthrallment from the audience. More like "Oh dear, fuck me, how long is this going to go on ...?"

Not very long as it turned out. A few more seconds and ... SNAP!!

A nervous CACKLE from one member of the audience.

And STOP, because I had no option to carry on.

My top string, the E string, had broken. "Excuse me, Ladies and Gentlemen, my string has broken. I'll just be a second while I go and get another one."

I could sense the audiences' disappointment. "Oh no, I wish he didn't have another one ... does he really have to go and restring it ...? ... Oh my gosh, he's probably going to start it all again from the beginning when it could've been almost over by now..."

I stalked off the stage and down the corridor, downing a glass of white on the way to the dressing room, my violin case and my spare strings. It was then that the little angel under the employ of the bourgeoisie hoi polloi cast its magic spell. It was a muvvafukk of an embarrassment but there were no spare strings in my fiddle case, they were back in Harlem. Fukkin' amateur … the audience definitely weren't going to wait expectantly for seven hours while I went to get the strings. They already couldn't wait to get out. Having left my fiddle in its case my two very dexterous hands now had a purpose. I downed another white and re-entered the stage with a tray full of them. A sense of expectancy rose from the audience on the sight of the tray (which I put down next to the piano) and a sense of relief that the violin hadn't reappeared. Instead of the music I quickly improvised a speech suitable for the verbose pseudo-cultural occasion.

"Laydeeez and Genteelmenzz"

"You will be euphorically deeelighted to know, as you verily do in this unsurpassably wonderful kuntreee of freedom, human rights, education and qualitee of life, that this concert of yee oldee music is well and truleee by the blessing of Gawd, prematurely terminated. Like in the life in Amerikaaa you, after hard work and incredible striving, finally get what you aspire to and therefore deserve. You are now well and even more truleee … FREE(E)!"

"I am honoured to present to you what has been decreeed by democratic and general consensus the reeeal highlight of this afternoon in the popularity contest the results of which have been instinctiveleee cast, at this very uniqueeee, very greatest of most higheee moments in the nowww …"

Having delivered my speech in the true Amerikan style (my name isn't Kennedy for nothing) I started doling out the wine to the front row. Brahms was well and truly forgotten and my audience liked classical music a lot more now they didn't have to listen to it.

Lots of free wine later I managed to relax with the highfaluters and have a great time.

We got the train back to New York.

I still got my $200. Yeah.

N.B. I played the same music a few years later in Malvern which was interrupted by the piano falling through the stage so things could've been a lot worse.

– Pop – Pop – Pop Muzik
The Juilliard Orchestra, Alice Tully Hall, NYC

In my second year at The Juilliard School ("of Musical Mediocrity") I was having a pretty good time—but not within those corporate walls. The City of New York had far more to offer, any time, anywhere, any place. My embryo involvement in the jazz scene had picked up and the young white kid from Eeengulurnd was getting a bit of a reputation (a good one, you fukker) in a couple of clubs. I was learning music in a bigger sense of the word but Juilliard still unfortunately made some demands on my time.

The school had a horrible classical symphony orchestra which I was meant to attend. The main point of good orchestral playing is to lose your ego for a while, display some empathy and become part of the greater whole. The violin sections in this orchestra unfortunately were unable to do this and were inhabited by wannabe soloists with their violins screeching acerbically like a Cat on a Hot Tin Spoof, Fiddlers on the Fukkin' Goof. I transferred to the viola section hoping that the instrument's incongruity might just open the door of humility for some of its players. Also, playing one of the lower, inner voices was going to give me a new perspective in the philharmonious sounds of an orchestra. Pleasantly enough the piercing soloistic violins would be on the other side of the stage.

AnyhowasIwassayinit, I was having a good time in the jazz world and had been up all night having a corker as well as learning more than one could in the fukkin' 'lliard. That evening it was the orchestra gig night and I was late… which wasn't exactly very good. The gig began at seven and it was already six by the time I realised it was Mission Impossible (the series not the film, because the shituation was going to go on and on). My viola was in my Juilliard locker so that was OK but my classical flunkery gear was way uptown—any attempt to get to my place and back would make it Mission Implausible. I decided to see if my friend in the drama division costume department would lend me some flunkery on the sly. I went to her desk and asked her.

"You're not much of an actor though, are you?"

"Well, I can drive a cab or wait tables, and anyway no one wears flunky shit in real life so that should qualify me. At least for Laurel and Hardy."

She went and got me some bang average flunkery.

"You've absolutely got to bring all of this back by five latest tomorrow. Don't get the shoes dirty or people will find out. I should be charging you."

"Let me return the compliment. You can have a ticket for tonight's show for free", all tickets were free of charge, "and there'll be a decent party after."

"If I wasn't working…" (—and this was prophetic) "I'd come and have a look at your show."

"We're playing music, you know. It's a concert, not a show—and the idea with classical music is that you listen, not look. The idea with a bottle is that you drink it, not look at it."

"Alright, I'll join you for a drink tomorrow."

I went to my locker, changed into the drama wear and rushed to the backstage of Alice Tully Hall. Shit … too late! Just too late! The kuntducktor had just walked on stage to kuntducked the overture. The door closed behind him. I paced up and down cursing myself. The orchestra manager approached me and didn't improve things.

"You lose your credits for being late."

"If you don't give me the credits I'm leaving now. What will that make you look like? It'll be all your fault."

I didn't give a fukk about the credits. What piece of toilet paper ever got anyone a job in music? Oh yeah, it was really important. Where would John Coltrane, The Beatles, Marvin Gaye, Howlin' Wolf have been without their doctorates? As long as I didn't get chucked out of Juilliard I could carry on living in New York on my student visa. If my scholarships got terminated I could get by on the dosh from busking and the odd jazz club appearances that I had started doing. In fact I'd have more time to spend on good music rather than the puerile garbage I was being taught at Juilliard. I could also sleep on a few sofas if I was too short to pay rent. My professor of violin, Dorothy DeLay, would always teach me for free because she liked me. I wasn't diligently sycophantic and she liked our discussive arguments. These thoughts were running through me.

"After the overture go on stage and sit at the back of the viola section." And with that the orchestra manager walked away. He didn't want the kuntduck to associate him with my lateness by seeing us together. It would make him look like the amateur that he possibly was.

As it was I had just hatched a plan. If I could get on stage without being noticed then maybe my whole attendance problem might not be registered by the kunt, and then my credits blah bla blah might not be an issue at all.

The overture finished with a bang and a wallop and the kuntducktor exited the stage into the wings with the normal smug look on his face. I was hiding well out of his sight which wasn't difficult because he was completely absorbed by himself. Now came the difficult bit. The kunt was going back on stage to do a lot of bows in order to desperately garner the adulation he thought he deserved.

Espionage like I stealthed one and a half metres behind him (far enough for him not to hear me (do kuntducks have hearing?) or smell me but close enough to avoid his peripheral vision). I was in a crouching position, following him between the first and second violin sections to the mid-front of the stage. I hoped the audience wouldn't see me. This was a miscalculation because the auditorium was raked meaning they could easily look down on my furtive activities, metaphorically as well, most likely, the superior bastards. Of course the main thing was that even though everyone else was aware of my impression of a tortoise on speed, the kunt wasn't. He was busy lapping up the few drops of rather restrained applause he had earned, which was tinged by a certain amount of amusement at my outlandisch and inexplicable actions.

Having got that far I looked up from my Quasimodo-esque pose and saw that those horrible, acquisitive, ambitious little viola Gollums had appropriated my front seat. An empty chair was glowering at me from the back saying "come here, you Limey bastard, none of those mentally challenged bastards are going to vacate your seat." Well, I wasn't having that so I got all the fukkin' violas to get up and move back one seat in order to vacate my rightful place. There was no way that I was going to play behind those ill co-ordinated talentless fukkers.

Grudgingly they obliged my wishes and slowly stood up. I re-assumed my hard earned place but by getting the viola section to stand up I had started the catalyst for another fuck up. Noticing the violas standing up the whole orchestra stood thinking they had probably been beckoned to do so by the dumbfucktor. Traditionally it is the fucktor's prerogative to ask the orchestra to stand so that he can look good in front of the audience by pretending to want to share the acclaim which he is really trying to take for himself. Either that or a fucktor will do it as an obsequious move so that the ork like them enough to give them another job or even an artistic directorship—precious! On this occasion the dumbfucktor had had the opportunity for such milking of the shituation rudely taken away from him. He visibly, for a second or two, took a shit load of umbrage and turned round beckoning us to stand again. This gesture didn't elevate him to Zweistein level in anyone's opinion because we were already standing. I could see him momentarily clocking something different about our viola section (namely me suddenly appearing in it) but he couldn't tell what it was. He ponced offstage looking a bit annoyed that the orchestra had rudely stolen his thunder and made him look a bit of a dullard.

Now I could relax. As was customary the whole orchestra sat down again. We were going to await the fukktor's return to conduct the symphony. My borrowed trousers felt a bit tight around my crotch and I thought:

"This is uncomfortable. I hope these strides stretch a bit."

The dumbfukktor came back on and tested his already questionable power by getting us to do the rigmarole of standing up again. What a kunt, cunt. My trousers were too uncomfortable for all of this. Then, in a final gesture of Simon Says, he got us to sit down once again. That's when it happened …

Uu POP – POP – POP MUZIK / – POP – POP – POP MUZIK

Shubydooby-doowap – – Shubydooby-doowap – – – –

Nick nack paddywack

My trousers had kind of exploded

Talk about – – – POP MUZIK Talk about – – –POP MUZIK

– POP – POP – POP MUZIK　 – POP – POP – POP MUZIK

And from that point on I was left scraping the viola in the normal orthodox viola position between my legs thereby protecting my dignity and the audiences' innocence. All my trouser buttons had POPPED off the fly area and one by one had landed spinning on the floor. Not being a pant wearer I had to preserve my modesty. Didn't want the show getting too interesting à la BBC.

Proper POP MUZIK.

Needless to say, there was a talking point after the show and it wasn't the particular dick with the white stick, it was another one belonging to me.

Brahms Trouble
A Juilliard CONcerto CONpetition

It was announced at Juilliard that there would be an immature shoot-out over Brahm's most mature orchestral work, his concerto for violin and 'cello. The winners would get to play this concerto with the Juilliard Concert Orchestra (which featured in the last subchapter). The concerto is referred to as the Brahms Double in the classical music world but after the following fiasco I have always called it the Brahms Trouble.

Quite a few of my fellow Juilliard sufferers were thinking of entering this silly competition and Dorothy DeLay wanted me to go in for it because I had such a strong relationship with the music of Brahms. In what is meant to be a collaborative and spiritual art form I've always thought competition to be particularly stupid but I was in New York to learn about violin from DeLay so her opinion mattered. I had won my ARCM diploma with 100 per cent playing Brahms' music and in addition I was the natural successor to Menuhin regarding his mastery of Central European music. If I was adjudged not to have won at least there was going to be some juicy scandal to enjoy. Also, what with my late night jazz stuff making mornings impossible, my school attendance record was atrocious so toeing the line and doing the silly competition had its merits.

The next day after the previous day I met up with Pierre Djokic who was by far the best 'cellist in the school, at least in my opinion. Pierre was unlike most other 'cellists in that his playing was effortless and his intonation impeccable. This certainly set him apart from all the other Juilliard 'cellists. He was also a calm, good natured, debonair example of a person. He asked me if I wanted to take part in the competition saying that he thought we would have a great chance of winning it. I was really happy and agreed on the spot, after all, with Dorothy DeLay's desire for me to sell my soul (sorry, I mean to do the competition) this was a really fortuitous development. Anyway, if we felt 'fukk it' at any point we could always pull out. We decided to go for it and play the music our very own way. We were two bad muvvafukkas and we were Ready To Rummmbuuul. Other contestants were warned.

> If you're looking for Trouble
> You've come to the right place
> If you're looking for Trouble
> Just look right in my face
>
> We've never looked for Trouble
> But we've never ran
> We don't take no orders
> From no kind of man

Our taking part in the competition had an outstandingly negative affect on it—to the extent that every other contestant withdrew because they didn't want to lose to the Menuhin kid and the school's best 'cellist teamed up together. I guess another reason was that Brahms was a DEEP composer, so that if one only had had a good technique with no insight things could've turned awkwardly embarrassing.

The work and preparation that Pierre and I did went well and it seemed we had a special interpretation to offer towards what was Brahms' last great orchestral masterwork. This music is stuff I've moved on from at this stage in my life but at the time and with a colleague like Pierre it was a privilege to be involved in the ebb and flow of such a unique symphonic work.

Of course, it's so stupid to turn the aesthetic and altruistic form of good music into any type of competition but, to be honest, Pierre and I had nothing much better to do. We were below voting age but there is no valid excuse for turning a spiritual activity into a competition whatever age you are. The only extenuating circumstance that got us off the hook is that it was NO LONGER a competition. All the other competitors had run away!

Despite the lack of opposition the jury of the CONpetition (most of them failed players) said we still needed to compete in front of them to win it. The jury lovelies couldn't play decently themselves but still wanted to tell us muvvafukkas whether WE could play or not....

Pierre was Croatian and understood the value of some decent red wine so in civilised measures we enjoyed our work, particularly because Brahms' qualities are rather like a mix of red wine and fresh air. Brahms has a depth that Mozart will never have. Red wine has a depth that white wine will never have. Brahms and Châteauneuf-du-Pape, Mozart and Riesling. So, fukk off Wolfie.

After a couple of weeks the day arrived when work finished and play started, so to speak. We had fukk all to compete against but were faced with the strange situation of still having to go on stage to 'compete' for the jury. That's when the strange process started us thinking a bit weirdly. What the fukk were we doing?

PIERRE: What if we lose and it's to nobody? That'd be far worse than losing to a real person.

ME: Yeah, you're right mate. That would be shitter than shit. I hope we don't lose.

PIERRE: Yeah, we'd have to play especially shit if we were to lose this one.

I opened my violin case and my violin looked up at me.

MY VIOLIN: Hello, you bastard. You neglect me all the time and then expect me to help you out at a time like this. Well, you'll get no help from me today.

ME: (*a little nonplussed at my fiddle's rebellious attitude but speaking to Pierre, I don't talk much to my fiddle*) Well, let's do good stuff and play well enough not to lose.

PIERRE: Alright, let's do our best. We shouldn't lose.

He opened his 'cello case. His 'cello looked in a right bad mood.

PIERRE's 'CELLO: Well, I'm with NK's violin on this one. I'm tired of being exploited ... and never any gratitude or credit when I sound good. Just fukkin' performers slapping themselves on the back all the time. I've had enough. Today I've decided to sound like a mix of cow with elephant turd.

Unaware that we had such a serious rebellion on our hands we walked onto the stage fairly optimistically. We were going to let music do the talking through our instruments. A bad misjudgement. The Brahms Double Trouble is a conversational discourse between 'cello, violin and orchestra. The 'cello starts but the conversation wasn't very, very nice.

The supposedly profound and beautiful music commenced.

PIERRE's 'CELLO: Groowwl, ... whieieie..ien, schleeeewee w-e-e-e-e ...

MY VIOLIN: Bl-eeeet, ssscrape, wh ie ie ie ien, schleeee w e e e e ...

'CELLO: S-s-s-slap, sssscrap, hack, grrrrind

VIOLIN: We-e-e-e-ah-t-t-t-t eee-e-e

HEAD OF JURY: Thank you (*sounded a bit sardonic*) second movement please...

VIOLIN AND 'CELLO: (*in octaves*) B-L-e-e-a-a par-r-r-p, ping – shlaaaehr......b-l-l-e-e-e-a-t

HEAD OF JURY: (*tersely*) Third movement please.

VIOLIN: Schling – digga bum – digga, bum-digga schlong-digga bum-digga, bum-digga schlong-digga bum-diggadiggadigga.

'CELLO: Prrrr-r-r Schling-digga bum-digga, bum-digga schlong-digga bum-digga schlong-digga prrrp-digga chiggachigga shit-digga gold-digga crap-digga prshlzirgggg digga.

HEAD OF JURY: (*interrupting and taking a deep breath*) Clap ... CLAP ... that's more than enough ... ssssss (*intake of breath*) ... you can go now while we deliberate the result.

We walked off having felt as if we'd lost against ourselves and the rest of the world. Our instruments had also contributed having been in a very vengeful stubborn mood. I felt like swinging my churlish, selfish violin against the wall to show it who was boss. Who the fuck did it think it was? I got the better of myself.

ME: Man, that was bad as in as shit as shit, mate.

PIERRE: Yeah, man. That was horrible. They will probably disqualify us.

ME: Fuck the stupid judges, who gives a shit what they think? If there's one lot of fukkers who would've played even worse than us it's them lot.

PIERRE: However shit they are won't make our performance any better.

ME: Fukkit mate, we've lost. How did we do that?

PIERRE: This is really bad. We're going to be the first anywhere to lose without an opponent.

ME: We've really fukked it. At least in the Olympics if the opponents don't turn up you get a gold medal if you finish. I reckon our medal is a lead balloon. We're shit.

PIERRE: Yeah. Lead, man, we're shit....

The longer we waited for the judges' deliberation the more certain it seemed that we'd lost. If we'd have won, surely they would've told us immediately, the maths weren't that difficult after all. Half an hour passed, an hour passed. After an hour and a half we were called back in. We moped back onto the stage.

JURY SPOKESPERSON: Congratulations, and enjoy your performance with the orchestra.

Congratulations for playing like turds but being the only option available. The following week we went on to give a great performance but if I'd have been spokesperson for the jury I would have pronounced:

"GUILTY!! Life imprisonment or ... THE CHAIR!"

To celebrate winning the CONpetition we went to hear some REAL music at The Village Vanguard and had a bottle of wine on the way downtown.

"Regret is mostly caused by not having done anything." Charles Bukowski.

Worst Gigs Outro

So there you have it, Laydees and Genteelmen ... THE WORST GIGS I EVER 'AD.

You don't have to be Columbo to figure out that these three fiascos have a common denominator unique only to them—they all happened when I was 'attending' The Jewelliyard Skoowal of Mewzick. I need SAY NO MORE.

CLASSICAL MUSIC

The following chapter goes on a bit and is about my involvement with classical music.

Classical music is a feeling. A feeling which in many cases was felt many years, even centuries ago. That it has been notated doesn't mean that it is any less about emotion than any other type of music. The only type of music to be free of emotion would be that which was written by something not belonging to the human race. Whether we want to pretend to be dispassionate or not, as human beings we are all influenced by things as small as getting out of the wrong side of the bed. It's probably little things like that which are responsible for some of us pursuing idiotic synthetic formuli rather than the truth of the human soul.

It is my purpose to instinctively and emotionally understand the feelings felt by the composer (in many cases long ago) and convey them as a live entity HERE AND NOW in the modern day. In the field of classical music, it is my ability to do this which has set me apart from others who cling desperately to technique or theory as an end in themselves rather than means to an end.

My frequent returns to classical music (which is only a fraction of my output) have been devoted to nurturing these feelings and finding the best ways to convey them. This hasn't always been as simple as it sounds or looks. Many opposing forces have confronted my simple and honest objectives, ranging from business bastards to being the only one not adhering to the status quo. I was, though, secure in the fact that if some jumped up kunts dumped me out of the music business I could return to busking which, anyway, was far more fun and remunerative than doing gigs for the BBC, British classical concert promoters and suchlike. Some of the people I had to work with or against were such a pain in the posterior that the only reason to put up with that shit was to be able to share beautiful music with a larger number of deserving people.

The following chapter might or might not explain how I found the emotional core of music. It certainly will explain how I fought to maintain the right to be myself, which is the only premise one can use to truly be a musician. GOOD LUCK!

Early Days, Part II

Classical music was the first type of music I ever heard because my mother and grandmother both taught classical piano at home. There are a few things which make classical music unique which, depending on your viewpoint, are either major strengths or major weaknesses.

It was the first music anywhere at any time to be written down by notation. This meant that someone could read and thereby play the correct notes without hearing them first. It also meant that generations way down the line would be able to read and play the exact same notes without idiosyncrasies and Chinese whispers (Oops! I hope the BBC don't consider the term POLITICALLY INCORRECT … relax guys, it's just a term) changing them. However, with the written notes becoming more and more specific the freedom to improvise became more curtailed through the centuries until disappearing altogether in the seventeen hundreds (except for the cadenzas in which the majority of classical musos are nowadays too lame at improvisation to create anything new on the spot).

Another benefit of notation was for the composer, who could write for numerous musicians to play simultaneously, enabling them to achieve his exact musical vision without random fuck ups. These advantages of musical planning are obviously balanced by a certain loss of spontaneity still to be found, for instance, in jazz, world or folk music. Jazz has developed its own style of notation which is possibly superior because of its accuracy, spontaneity and spirit as well as the importance of the character of the guy reading it.

But don't worry. Classical music is not completely dead and when played well can have a far greater dynamic contrast of volume than any other type of music. Quiet moments can be very personal and sometimes almost inaudible, while loud moments can be very loud, particularly when played by the huge orchestras of up to one hundred players employed by composers such as Stravinsky. If you've not heard it check out Stravinsky's The Rite of Spring to see what I mean. In my opinion the best recording is conducted by Antal Dorati. No other type of music uses that many musicians simultaneously apart from the Holte End at VILLA PARK in full song. Also in our favour is that us Villa fans are not hampered by an overload of musical technique.…

Another interesting thing … playing gigs of any type of music and getting paid for them by a ticket buying audience is all down to our classical brethren of a few hundred years ago. Classical music was the first to stage concerts for a paying audience in the late 1600s. This way of presenting their music eventually enabled classical musicians and in particular composers to turn their back on being employed as glorified lackeys of either the church or the court. Musicians no longer had to create background music for these dubious institutions and an equally important development was that larger social circles were able to enjoy listening to the great composers playing their own music. Who would have thought that musicians from every genre owed so much to classical music? But they do … every penny and every freedom.

One last thing … classical music like jazz, world or folk music, is a REAL LIVE experience, never the same twice (unless played by a soulless formulaic performer!) People may ask what is improvisational about classical music. ANSWER: Dynamics (within the composer's requested parameters), rhythmic pacing, tonal colour are just some of the avenues open to an intelligent instinctive classical performer … and this doesn't even take into account the necessary response to each unique audience and the acoustics one encounters in any particular hall on any particular night. Welcome to the potential world of classical music!

My Way—Sound And Attitude

Quite early in my career I figured that if I was going to represent/perform music to an audience or on record in an honest manner doing it MY WAY was going to be THE ONLY WAY for me.

I've had some fantastic mentors and been inspired by phenomenal musicians along the way but being the second Menuhin, Stern or Grappelli, while being an easy option, was going to be (in the best case scenario) only the second best Menuhin, Stern or Grappelli. More likely than not, despite having some of the best ears for copying in the business, there would've been someone better at mimicry than myself in which case I'd be third best (or I might've been outclassed by a mynah bird).

Being the first and best Kennedy was always going to be better than being a pseudo Menuhin or any shit like that. As myself I was going to be able to give colleagues and audience something unique. Not just a copy.

Now that there are so many of my epigones doing one or many of the things I did while (from within their groovy clothes) professing to be "bringing classical music to the masses" like little mini-Kennedys, looking back I must have been doing something right. There weren't any mini-mees saving classical music from obscurity when I first went round the block. Now that violinists can tog up how they want maybe way back then I could have said "That's one small step for a violinist, one great leap for violinist kind." But I didn't. They're both great but I'm even more into Satchmo than Neil Armstrong.

Of course, an artist should always be in charge of their manager, one doesn't want the tail wagging the dog. At the moment, though, primarily in Britain, but also in Europe and the USA, there are some exorbitant claims being made and phenomenal coverage being given to artists who are decidedly mediocre and it's got to be the sodding managers. OY! MANAGERS AND RECORD COMPANIES AND THE BBC! STOP SELLING US FOOL'S GOLD!

Before all of this, there was a short period of time in my career when I tried taking on board all the sage-like 'wisdom' of classical agents. At the time there was no other advice to listen to. I didn't really enjoy travelling around like a cheap prostitute doing the bidding of agents and conductors pretending "Oh d-a-a-arling, isn't this wonderful" in order to get another job, but at first I couldn't think of a way out or a different approach.

I had long been aware rock, soul or popular albums that I liked had between ten and twelve short tracks on them, each track not being much longer than three minutes. I also knew that some of my favourite classical artists like Kreisler, Menuhin or Casals also reached a lot of 'normal' people with three minute record-ings during the age of 78 rpm recordings. It's also worth noting that only an intellectual idiot would assume that these beautiful pieces were inferior to an endless heavyweight symphony because of being concise.

People in general don't have time in their lives to enjoy an endless turgid 15 minutes long track. We do housework or other boring shit when listening to music and need something concise to give us a bit of pep. Having played Vivaldi's IV Seasons quite a bit it struck me that it fitted well into the formula of 'pop' music. 12 tracks, all short, with beautiful accessible melodies and vibrant rhythmic impetus. No one has to think about the meaning of life to get through three minutes of Vivaldi, it was just energetic music with good contrast. No one could've felt bad when they were listening to that stuff. I went into EMI hoping they'd get the idea … and they did!

By the mid-eighties, there was a new regime in the record company of Simon Foster and Barry McCann who worked under supremo Rupert Perry. Can you imagine a great German record company such as Deutsche Grammophon (of Herbert von Karajan fame) not promoting German artists? Well, before Simon and Barry got their jobs and did their stuff with me that was the story at EMI Classics. The beach must have been their favourite place because they would promote anything which moved from across the shores. They would've promoted a wave or a deck chair (made in France) above myself. "EMI are very, very, VERY proud to announce the imminent release of the incredible new concerto La Vague No 1 written, played and bullshitted by Maestro-issimmo Monsieur Chaise Longue … blah, blah, BLAAAH…." If my name had been Nigolai Kennedyev it might have been OK. "EMI are overjoyed to announce our amazing 500 record deal with the incredible Russian failed abortion violinist Nigolai Kennedyev. We haven't heard him yet but believe him to be unsurpassed when playing repertoire from Siberian gulags and the steppes…" (in fact, that sounds quite BBC-ish doesn't it? I better give them a call-skyev).

We changed all the above bullshit with a release called The IV Seasons.

Suffice it to say, Rupert Perry, President of EMI Records UK introduced me to a proper manager, John Stanley. He was very different to those glorified agents, who call themselves managers, from the classical world. The main drift is that John went into EMI and in particular told the classical employees, "If you want to sell records you'll have to sell Nigel for who and what he is, not try to change him into something he isn't. His value is in who he is." John then entrenched himself in the EMI offices in Manchester Square, marshalled the troops. And the rest is history not just for me but for all the others who benefited from the work

John and I did in the front line. When one paves the way, one first has to get rid of the shit and deadwood. We received a load of jealous criticism for what we did because the particular shit and deadwood we were removing were entrenched, Old Etonian archaic attitudes and our success embarrassed those responsible for holding the classical world back.

It was not a virtue but I was proud when John pointed out to me all the positive spin offs we were responsible for regarding the marketing of classical music. Positive developments such as Classic FM, The Three Tenors, Vanessa Mae, the rise to prevalence of so many young British soloists and the fact that listening to classical music on the radio no longer meant being one of as few as 300 people listening to BBC Radio 3 (I am being too kind there, at one point they got as few as 250 people listening in the whole of the British Isles!)

In fact, I remember my career was so different to everything else that was going on and there was so much bitching about me from the chattering protected classes that it actually got discussed in Parliament. The discussions ended with my beloved Labour Party (the real one, that is) passing a motion that my career and what I was doing was good for classical music.

I still have very good hearing, and my ears are open, so I am looking forward to hear the magic words "Thank you, Nige" (no need to say professor, maestro, exalted one or any other over obsequious shit). Any younger classical performer contending that they are innovatively bringing their music to a wider audience should at least thank me for making the tools available with which they can pursue their (or more pertinently their manager's) aim. Oh well, I can't hear much coming my way so I'll do it myself. "Thank you, Oh Exalted and Virtuous One, who is Original And The Real Deal, for delivering us from evil Laura Ashley record companies and Old Etonian agents...."

VIV—The IV Seasons

Whenever I was going to Villa, I noticed that all of my friends either were completely apathetic to what I did, or they actually disliked it. Sometimes they'd say it was nice out of pity for me because they didn't want to upset me, but they actually didn't really like my shit at all. So I was just thinking to myself: "Man, it would be really nice if some of my friends could actually listen to some of my shit." What if, instead of saying it was "clever", they actually enjoyed it? If I had been playing Motown and Soul Music and Ska, they wouldn't have minded. They'd have liked that and they'd been coming to the gig. But with this Beethoven and Brahms stuff? No way that they were going to sit and listen for 20 minutes for one movement of a concerto.

The reason I came up with the idea to record The IV Seasons when I did was not to dominate and change the classical world, it was to counteract the sad way it was played at the time. There were two schools, the boring, one energy level of the 'modern' school and the boring, one energy level of the arrogantly and falsely named 'authentic' school. Both schools were pretty smug and it was time for something less complacent and self-satisfied.

When taking stock of the Baroque period within which Vivaldi was writing, it's necessary to take stock of his contemporaries to understand the qualities he had which were unique to him.

Bach is obviously the greatest, with his longer more developmental forms, evolved sense of harmony and counterpoint. His whole effect is a kind of cosmic meditation.

Handel was a great linear craftsman and relatively benign.

Scarlatti was harmonically and decoratively complex and adventurous.

What Viv had compared with these lot were memorable melodies allied with comparatively huge dynamic contrasts.

I have a natural gift for understanding melody but what I had to think about was how to help people perceive and enjoy what were huge contrasts in the time in which they were written. After all, people in the '80s had already heard Zep, and John Cage's 4'33" of silence had also been written. People were not going to feel the dynamic contrasts if I played Viv's music all at one volume like everybody else. Being aware of the problem was enough to help me portray the quality of contrast I was looking for. I was also aware that, in music and when listening to it, no one likes cleverness apart from the kat who thinks they are being clever plus a few half boiled intellectual sycophants, so I avoided gratuitous poncing like the plague.

Another affirmation of my thinking was the opinion of my friends who didn't like classical because it all sounded the same. All the po-faced cleverness also got to them. What helped my album do well is that I do actually like people! I liked the audience, was grateful that they spent time and money coming to my gigs, so was genuinely audience friendly in the literal sense of the words. I didn't put myself above anybody else except the classnerdicals who were and still are welcome any time to get off their high horse and join me. Having a brain's not a problem, it's how you use it!

The result of my thinking was that I did fast tempos fast, slow tempos slow, loud passages as loudly as the orchestra could manage and quiet passages intimately and almost inaudibly. Not too many crescendos or diminuendos and there you have it. I got the contrast we required.

My recording of The IV Seasons was meant to be an antidote to the prissy self-satisfied interpretations of the so-called authentic period music school. It certainly was that time of the month for those foppers when my album came out! I also wanted to provide an escape from the cloying, complacent heaviness of the then current school of well-known virtuosi. Both sets were as appalling as the other and no one was doing poor old Viv any favours. It's a bit ironic that quite a personality cult grew out of my album even though the other guys' albums were more about their personalities and my album was more about Vivaldi's.

For the 'record', I didn't intend to take over or change the classical music world when recording The IV, just to offer a fresher less boring alternative. Luckily I'd had a broader musical experience than the other current soloists so I had the tools to present a new more energy giving approach. I'd been to India, I'd been a regular fixture in the jazz world, I'd been a regular busker (before one had to have a licence!) and been through living in the underbelly of New York so I was ready—and I had classical chops second to none. "One of the best pairs of hands in the business." Isaac Stern.

The recording sessions were fine. I think the English Chamber Orchestra were pleased to be playing with a British director/soloist for a change. As I said before, before my career altered things the violin soloist scene was completely dominated by kats from across many shores. Kennediski or Kennedberg, Kennedanya, Kennedy-Wu, Kennedenko, Kennemoto might have been alright but Kennedy would've been a good name for a bus conductor, not a classical conductor.

Obviously the energy was good in the studio but the only thing that might be of interest to you would be the moment when we rehearsed the second movement of Spring during which a barking dog is sonically portrayed by a solo viola. Normally it is played in a very namby-pamby way with a diligent classical technique resembling a dead sloth. To circumvent that problem I reminded the violist that he was going to be portraying a dog, not a stuffed gerbil, and asked him to portray it brutishly. A snigger went round the orchestra. My instruction was completely surplus to requirements, viola players have a well-earned, well cemented reputation for playing like that naturally and inadvertently.

Although I wouldn't say that Vivaldi is the best composer in the world there's an electricity when I play his stuff and his slow movements have a confessional aspect to them when in my hands. It just happens. These qualities were yet again completely missing in a diligently correct and boring Proms performance I heard last year which was billed as exciting. I suppose the grass grew at Villa Park during the performance and the groundsman might have been watching it. There's still a long way to go before we get younger fukkers understanding the real magic of classical music. Taking a risk every now and then might have something to do with it.

When the album came out it changed my life completely. Huge sell-out gigs everywhere under my name. I'd book the orchestra rather than the other way round. The bestselling classical album. Chat shows. This Is Your Life. Recognition on the street. The biggest outdoor classical gig ever to have been held in Britain. And most valuable of all, my Villa comrades singing the first movement of Spring (don't be cretinous, not all of it!) pretending to play the fiddle, as we walked towards and into the ground.

Yeah, that ugly fukker Viv changed my life.

John Stanley—The Modern Diaghilev

I've had an amazing career with one highlight after another really since the age of about 14. This chapterette is going to set the record straight against any of the killjoy know alls but its primary objective is to focus on the vision, understanding, organisational powers and leadership qualities of John Stanley, without whom the seismic shock of my musical approach on the classical world would never have happened. In order to give perspective on his work (and mine) it's necessary to start a little bit prior to our involvement together. Once we got going he was going to become the Diaghilev of the modern day.

Before I met John I was already working with the world's leading orchestras and jazzers getting rave reviews wherever I went and, like always, doing it on hard earned merit. I'd also recorded Elgar's Violin Concerto, sold 60,000 copies and won every award imaginable. I didn't have any PR and was only getting performance opportunities because I played some hot shit better than all but a very few of my contemporaries. In some repertoire I was unsurpassable (Central European classical repertoire and swing pre-bop) and in other repertoire they were unsurpassed. My advantage was/is that I can relate deeply to many types of music.

After that initial kind of success I'd played The IV Seasons a few times in Spain and really enjoyed its fresh energy and the immediate rapport that it allowed me to establish with the audience. And as I said before, I also noticed that, in common with popular chart albums of the time, it comprised of 12 tracks/movements all short enough not to tax the mind and time of any casual listener. The music wasn't overcomplicated and was just as easy to listen to as anything done by the British '80s glamour bands. Listeners would just have to survive without the poofy[4] hair.

I went into EMI and described my idea to the guys. Rupert Perry and I later became friends and I remember going to Swindon–Villa with him (he supports the other team) and there wasn't much to choose between the two teams in those days. At this point, however, he appreciated my idea and thought of John Stanley as a manager for me. He explained that without a good manager nothing would be achieved and that it needed someone to interface with the record company. He fixed that we should meet.

John was, and still is, a well-dressed bloke without being ostentatious. It could well have been that the cost of what he was wearing on the evening we first met exceeded my whole clothing budget for the previous five years. He was well turned out enough for me to worry about how he would survive sitting on my dirty overused wall couch in my pigsty of a garden outbuilding flat. I concocted something to drink and he wasn't at all put out by my haphazard environment. I remember he had a complete picture in his head and he warned me that if

---

4 Whingers…NO! You're not getting away with that! NO! Absolute NO! Just a term to describe hair. Absolutely NOT derogatory to anybody.

what we did worked out it was almost inevitable that I'd face a backlash. His correct sizing up of the shituation was that the way that classical people were doing things was indeed clarse-farce-ical and that many people would be jealous, confounded or embarrassed about our success and that I might make enemies for life. People might try to discredit me. Mystic Meg's surname must've been Stanley! I didn't give a shit about those turds and didn't mind aggravating a few tossers. I certainly couldn't see myself enduring the classical world as it was back then for very long. It was change it, re-arrange it or get out altogether.

While John meticulously materialised his master plan with EMI, I went back into the studio to re-record a few of the slow movements of my already recorded IV Seasons in a more improvisatory and atmospheric way. Now that I had a reason I wanted the feel of the music to get through to my friends, not just self-estimated connoisseurs. Most of my friends didn't like classical music but with this album they would at least be able to put up with it!

Finally the album was released and SLAM! BAM! BOOM! FUCKKIT BIGtime we were doing damage.

Rewinding a bit, John had got to work. To start with he had told EMI that I could carry on selling 20,000–30,000 copies of whatever (6–7,000 counted as a sucksess in classical!) if they wanted to sell me as the second Menuhin–Milstein–Old-stein–Clone-stein blablahstein, but that they might have the possibility of selling millions if they sold me as the first Nigel Kennedy.

Having persuaded them of that he went into EMI's offices and oversaw everything. So many managers I've worked with blamed the record company when there was a fukk up. "The record company didn't do this, the record company didn't do that, the record company fukked this up, the record company fukked that up...." If the best you've got is retrospective blame then the only successful thing is blaming successfully. I delivered on the violin and as a communicator, John delivered as a muvvafukka manager of all time. It didn't interest either of us to be sitting around doing post-mortems on what went wrong. John went into the record company and controlled everything whether people liked it or not. Easier said than done.

A large record company was like a brontosaurus, it had a huge, huge body and at the far end of a killa long neck miles away was a pea-sized brain unable to send messages to control the body. John took his large brain into the middle of the body and controlled it. (Now record companies still have the pea-sized brain but no body).

EMI possibly viewed John as a Svengali, the classical music business should have viewed him as Jesus Christ fukkin' Almighty, The Saviour. No chance of an EMI fukk up or any slacking off. Another important thing I noticed which seems obvious is that John didn't try to get decisions made by lower cats because they didn't have the autonomy to make them. He'd talk to the fukker who could make the decision. He also engineered it that the decision makers waited for him, not the other way round. You'd be surprised how many managers spend hours a day talking to people who have no ability to make a decision.

Meanwhile I just got on with being myself and the success just seemed to happen around me. It didn't take long for the mental midgets to try and look intellectually a bit taller. Here are some of the fabrications they came up with.

My 'look' was fake, created by someone else, probably John and/or the record company and was a fabricated 'image': WRONG. John had instructed the record company to let me be myself and what with my attitude nobody would have dared to tell me how to look or behave unless they were mentally challenged. For better or even better I've never had a fukkin stylist or any of that airhead shit.

I was merely a product of marketing and not the real deal: WRONG. The more purist success I'd had in my earlier years was impossible to deny, it was on record literally and metaphorically. That talent doesn't just disappear because of a jealous egghead. My hotshit fiddling and respect for my audience whatever their background made me unique and the ONLY real deal around. More proof of the veracity of my words—I could go on but fukkit, I don't even have to answer to those mental misfits.

Some kunts didn't like me and were jealous: CORRECT. Fair enough. That's the price of success. They had a lot to be jealous of!

I was bad for classical music: WRONG. The public voted with their feet and walked into my gigs. Thank you for that. The Labour Party proposed the motion that I was good for classical music and it was passed in Parliament. PRE-TTY G-O-O-OD. Thanks for that too!

What John gave me was to have received career and promotional opportunities considered absolutely normal in more popular forms of music.

There is no manager I've met who has John's vision, inspiration and keen intellect. Some of EMI's employees whinged quite a bit when John got the credit for masterminding my success. What did they achieve for my albums without John? Whatever they did manage was on the foundations he built. The other proof of how good Gandalf was (sorry, John Stanley, they look rather alike) is how many artists and damagers have copied verbatim what we did, either knowingly (the unoriginal scoundrels!) or unwittingly (the witless scoundrels!).

John's a bit of a da Vinci character so who knows what he's been up to, but for the time being 5 or 6 million sales later, cheers Gandalf … sorry … John.

My Way—The Punk Violinist Is Born

Robert Masters was my first violin teacher at the Yehudi Menuhin School of Music when I was about seven years old.

MASTERS: (*shows me some Shakespeare*) Now Nigel, read this … good … now tell me, what do you see between the lines?

ME: … ummm … (*using all of my seven year old intellect*) … well … (*and then with a flash of inspiration*) … I see the white bit between the lines of words where there are no words written … ("*that should do it*", *I thought*).

MASTERS: (*a flicker of displeasure crosses his face*) Try again.

I look at the book again trying to see if the white bit between the lines is actually a slightly different colour, like pink or light blue or something.

ME: (*after studying it really hard*) … is it really a different colour? It still looks white between the lines … it could be a bit of a yellowish white.

Mr Masters was a nice bloke but a hopeless teacher for a seven-year-old boy. I was doing shit at the school, making absolutely no progress academically or musically. I hated it there and would have loved it if I had justifiably been chucked out. I could then have moved up to Solihull and started to try fitting into the new family my mother had just married into with my drunken and abusive Stepdad doctor or whatever he thought he was.

Back at school, in an attempt to save the shituation, I was moved to a different violin teacher. It was the fearsome tyrant otherwise known as Jacqueline Gazelle. She had been a pupil of the great Romanian violinist, composer and conductor Georges Enescu at the same time as Yehudi Menuhin. Her hot-headed tyranny scared the shit out of all her pupils and there were loads of tears (some credit her with ruining their violin playing and careers) but somehow her bullying style brought the best out of me. I had something to fight against and I fought back for the first time in my life. Having her as a teacher learned me how not to be a victim and my violin playing also progressed in leaps and bounds. (It's funny but the number of professional victims I've met in the UK, which is apparently the fifth richest country in the world, is just unbelievable. These blamers are not short of a bob or two but think they can get what they want without contributing anything. It's always someone else's fault. Victimhood is shit and real victims don't broadcast it all over the place. I'm happy that I've been neither a pretend or real victim. If I see a pretend one then pretty soon I call them out).

Anyhow, refusing to be a victim and the improvement in my violin playing helped Gazelle appreciate me. Her bullying all but disappeared.

Mrs Gazelle had a strict dress code for her violin lessons which involved cleanliness and stuff but I was even allowed to challenge this. I could turn up straight from football, a trail of mud falling from my legs, boots or whatever else all over her nice posh carpet. As long as I played some sweet violin all was OK. THIS WAS MY FIRST AFFIRMATION THAT IN MUSIC THE SOUND FAR OUTWEIGHS THE LOOKS IN IMPORTANCE. It's amazing how few people in our music business realise that even now. What's the matter with them? Even a ten-year-old boy knew that.

I guess looking the way you want to is simply an extension of yourself as a human being—and it makes you wonder about the inner personality of a person who feels the need to wear get up which makes him look like a semi-human walking bat. DRAKUL RULES OK. Although this is also not exactly rocket science it seems to be way beyond the comprehension of a fair few people (especially in classical music) who seem to think that the clothes maketh the

BAT, sorry! ... MAN ... or to reminisce about Tyson Fury—BATMAN....[5]

Meanwhile, back in the Yehudi Menuhin School I had reached the historical age of about 12 years old. There were a few silly discussions about my hair which was getting longer because I refused to get it cut. There then followed another incident in my learning curve. As one of the more precocious brats of the school I had been chosen to play a few numbers in the Yehudi Menuhin School pupils' concert in The Wigmore Hall, London. I was to play works by Brahms and Ysaÿe.

I'd found a nice paisley shirt a bit like the type Stéphane Grappelli wore, that's why I liked it. I also had a fairly decent purple tweed jacket but when wearing it I couldn't move my arms and felt like Worzel Gummidge in a straightjacket. I believed in the very humane announcement issued by the Trotsky Propaganda Department of the Politburo of Russia prior to the Tchaikovsky Workers' Party Competition in Moscow—"Comrades, WHEN PLAYING THE VIOLIN IT IS IMPORTANT TO BE ABLE TO MOVE YOURS ARMS—PRAVDA." My plan was to play without the jacket so that in a good Russian violin playing tradition I'd be able to move my arms. Rumour has it that violinists in other countries also need to be able to move their arms.

Having seen me preparing to go on stage without my jacket Jacqueline Gazelle suddenly appeared like a dragon on speed.

"Where's your jacket?" she shrilled at me "You're just about to play. Put it on and get on stage. If you don't put it on you don't get to play."

My parents were attending and had come all the way down from Brum so I had to play really.

ME: My jacket's too tight....

GAZELLE: (*interrupting in a shrieking voice and stamping her foot*) Do you want to play? Put it on.

To the accompaniment of a few titters and mirthful glances from the other kids waiting backstage I dutifully squeezed into my jacket. I entered the stage and Gazelle closed the door behind me. She could see part of what was happening on stage through a little window in the door but I was now invulnerable to her commands. I could do what I liked. She couldn't stop me without being involved in a horribly embarrassing scene which would make her look stupid. Teachers don't like looking stupid.

I calmly put my fiddle on the ground and then removed my horrible 'strait' jacket, rolled it into a ball and threw it onto the floor under the piano where I hoped it would be out of Gazelle's sight. The audience thought the Laurel and Hardy-esque routine rather irregular and semi-hilarious. I then played my stuff really, really well with no mental or physical inhibition. After acknowledging

---

5 This is not sexist against women, just against men which doesn't seem to matter. It just so happens that it's men that have to wear the silly stuff. Women can wear exactly what they like but maybe shouldn't push it as far as hot pants and mini-mini dresses unless, of course, they want to, in which case they can.

the audience with all the bowing and scraping expected of me I picked up my crumpled jacket. I put it back on to a little crescendo of applause before exiting, trying to appear to Gazelle as if she had nothing to pull me up for. She hadn't and she didn't because I had played fukkin' good. I was called back quite a few more times by the enthusiastic audience. I had something and I knew it. The audience enjoyed hearing some pretty good sounds played by a free spirit and classical music didn't need to suffer from 'lack of jacket syndrome'.

The last and final nail in the coffin of wearing flunky gear was in The Royal Festival Hall, London, a few years later during a period when I had been advised to wear the bat gear again by the condescending wannabe gentry known as the classical music business. I was going to play a concerto (probably Brahms not Liszt) and all the rehearsals had produced great results, the orchestra and I were really enjoying our music making and everyone was ready. I also was just as prepared sartorially. All the finery necessary to look like a poncing underpaid butler trying to maintain appearances in a fading and crumbling house of fallen nobility was hanging (bats do that in the daytime) ready to put on. Or so I thought.

It was gig day so I opened my concert clothes hanging bag in order to hang the elements of bat gear separately in order to get out the last crinkles. They would also be ready to don after the morning dress rehearsal so that I could practice a bit getting used to playing in that inhibiting foppery junk. Anyway, as I was saying, I opened the bag and was confronted by ... NOTHING. The empty bag looked very seriously and knowingly back at me. I would say the bag had a disturbingly insolent attitude. I had forgotten to put the gig clothes in the bastard bag and they were still hanging nice and vampirically in my New York apartment.

This was a bit of a situation because it was a Sunday, everything was closed, so I couldn't rent any of the stupid stuff. It was in the era, by the way, before that devil ghoul Thatcher had replaced society and community with commerce. Is Germany any the worse, compared with Ingulund, regarding living standards because of giving people space to think about something other than money on a Sunday? Ummmm ... NO! Not exactly!!

I digress. It was Sunday and I had a gig that night but no fopping finery. I had to sort something out. After the dress rehearsal I got a cab and went straight to the only place I knew of which was open. Camden Market. In Those Good Old Days it was kool, cheap, with quite a lot of English punters and none of that I ♥ LONDON claptrap. This was well before the suspicious fire and redevelopment of the place to facilitate the commercial ethnic cleansing[6] known as tourism. My objective was to buy black stuff because that's what Classicos wear in general apart from female soloists who seem to be allowed to wear all kinds of flouncing upper class prostitute stuff. Get out the whip, baby![7]

---

6 Before getting het up look up ethnic cleansing in Cambridge dictionary. I might be persuaded to use the term cultural cleansing next time, though.

7 This is not sexist, just my observation and reaction of a 64 year old codger. Don't be ageist, please.

It quickly became clear that the only clothes I was going to be able to get were punk stuff with chains and a gothic edge. I got all togged up for under fifty quid.

I'm not sure if you know but in old fashioned classical concerts the soloist is merely a guest of the orchestra, it isn't his/her show. Backstage before the gig I was a bit worried what my colleagues would think about the new get-up. The conductor raised an eyebrow but didn't seem to mind, although what with him in his flunkery and me in my punkery we must have looked a bit of an odd couple strolling through the orchestra to take our performance places front stage. There were quite a few sardonic grins exchanged amongst the orchestra who were happy to see me as challenging the system. The audience also exchanged a few "What's he up to now?" "What'll it sound like?" and "Is he going to fuck it up?" looks.

Most importantly the performance went killadilla. I always save my best playing for the gig, when there's that unique synchronicity of energy between the audience and musicians. Everything before that point is mainly preparation but when we are free to live the music and that magic moment of NOW, everything transfigures inexplicitly into a much higher level of consciousness.

With the gig having gone so well and the orchestra and I having enjoyed sharing the magic moments which only happen in live music I wasn't too worried by what people thought of my £50 Camden cock up. As normal, I was just ready to have an after gig piss up with my friends and family. That's when the strange thing happened from the enthusiastic line of after gig well-wishers for whom I was pouring drinks and signing autographs.

"Nigel, that's wonderful what you are doing, bringing classical music into the twentieth century...."

"Nigel, it's wonderful that you are rebelling against those awfully boring classical conventions..."

"Nigel, your clothes breathe new life into classical. You breathe new life into classical music." (*The second half is true!*).

"That's amazing punk classical innovation...."

"When did you become a punk?" (*This afternoon for fifty quid*).

"Thank you Nigel for saving classical music...."

"You're a PUNK VIOLINIST...."

And there you have it. THE PUNK VIOLINIST WAS BORN! When getting back to New York I got some paraffin, went up on the roof of my building with a couple of friends and did a ceremonial burning of the bat suit. It was the best it ever looked. Since then I have always played in whatever I'm comfortable with. This has resulted in better music for the audience, my musical colleagues and myself.

Contrary to the sneering conclusions of some lovely little pseudo intellectual killjoys my 'look' or 'image' was never (and never will be) a cosmetic superficial business move. Being comfortable with who I really am is paramount—if this causes discomfort for a killjoy or two that's their problem and they'd best go to an analyst. I would wager that the vast majority of those who are or have been rubbed up the wrong way by me already have been getting professional psychiatrists' help—they certainly need it.[8]

This of course leads onto:

Risk Taking

I've noticed that in successive years we have been living in a world which has become more and more obsessed by qualifications from studying rather than gaining life experience. This closed attitude allied with a pandemic of addiction to computers has led to us drowning in an ever-increasing swamp of inane unrelated facts completely devoid of context or original thought. Copying seems to be more popular than creating, quoting seems to be more popular than thinking. This observation applies to how people mistake theory for practice. The result is a regurgitation of theories and statistics with no practical application. A kind of risk-free sheep politics is evident in which expressing a slightly different idea leads to one being identified as a black sheep and being dragged off to a pseudo-intellectual slaughterhouse. This really sums up most of today's fashionable ideology which seems to be built on pitifully faulty foundations therefore making its advocates horribly insecure. So insecure that they fly off the handle or brandish censorship if someone expresses a more thought-out idea than the chattering classes' mundane status quo. It's only when one has a sneaking suspicion that one might be wrong that censorship or bleating over an opposing argument might seem attractive, or when one's quoting a prevailing opinion without having thought it through oneself.

I mention this because music and 'real life' reflect each other to a certain extent, but in my opinion, music should be opening a few doors emotionally which might be closed in 'real life'. That is why I find it so sad that this pathetically earnest flock-like mentality still pervades in what should be our special and unique world of musical freedom.

It's time for the young pups to realise that as a soloist one is guilty of negligence if one doesn't employ creative thought. Creativity co-exists with risk. Boring plagiarism co-exists with safety. Only pretending to be original co-exists with shitness and naffness. It's our job as musicians (with individual names and fingerprints) to offer something to our audience that people don't already have, otherwise we are merely offering people a mundane musical equivalent of mass production. Mutton dressed as lamb (to continue the flock analogy—in fact, if you want to check some original violin playing listen to Jerry Goodman in The Flock or later in The Mahavishnu Orchestra—loads better than this politically correct soft-core shit called violin playing that we see nowadays on the desperate BBC).

---

8 There is no stigma attached to psychiatric care and going to an analyst doesn't mean you are a killjoy. It just happens that most killjoys are fucked up, that's all.

Even though this ineptitude of thought is more endemic to classical music one can see that it has also crept into jazz, the music which is synonymous with originality and creativity. Jazz, within 100 years, has developed at breakneck speed into the most evolved and original form of music available to mankind, so why so many Coltranes? Why so many Charlie Parkers? Why so many Kenny Dorhams? Why even, so many Norah Jones's? Isn't one of each maybe enough?

This brings me to a literary side road which is nevertheless relevant to mention because it was a risk worth taking, it redefined my whole career.

I personally love the kats who come up with their own original approach and don't worry, ladies and gentlemen, there are plenty of them if you look deeper than PR led media.

For want of a better description I'll call my approach The Kennedy Formula! This is how it happened....

THE KENNEDY FORMULA

As I was saying earlier, when I chose to pursue my career in a more responsible, less class orientated manner I was very excited about the prospect of sharing some beautiful classical music with people (including some of my friends) who had never experienced it before.

With my experience from busking in New York I had played my brand of music to all kinds of people across the board. I was now going to try to completely change the music business and be the very first person to bring classical music to anyone and everybody regardless of their financial or ethnic background. To do this I was going to take an approach which was in many ways the polar opposite to the very exclusive private club that the classical music world was at the time.

To achieve this objective, as opposed to the idea just being a Kennedy pipedream (I do love a good pipe), my manager John Stanley had me working with music business kats (outside of the stuffy Old Etonian and Laura Ashley world) who made their living by getting great music of all kinds over to the public at large in a real way, rather than surviving off sponsorship from the closed world of Arts Council grants and posh buffoonery. It was a relief, much more exciting and God forbid, fun to find a new way which completely bypassed the fuddy-duddy world which previously dominated classical music in such a self-indulgent way.

It was, of course, a completely untrodden path. John Stanley who allowed himself to be addressed as John—I called him John, other colleagues and friends called him John, his wife called him John and I will hereon in refer to him as John—alright John? Ummm ... JOHN alerted me to the potential risk of treading my own path:

(i) The risk of alienating the snobs who ran or wrote about classical music, their little minds might think that popular meant bad. This proved to be the case in a fair few cases and quite a few little shits squeaked out of their metaphorical backsides.

(ii) The risk of embarrassing the snobs who ran classical music and were doing a shit job, who would try and cover themselves by talking bad of me. John was also prophetic on this one. There was a fair amount of malicious slander emanating from the jealousy and envy inspired by my efforts to get one or two people to listen to my music, something that my sour little adversaries had so abjectly failed to do.

(iii) The risk of alienating snobby musicians. Luckily this didn't happen much. Having one's ears open is the nature of the beast as a musician and it was fairly obvious I could play, knew about the music I was playing and was bringing something special to it.

(iv) The risk of losing my living by failing and getting no more concert fees from the snobs. Not such a big risk in truth. Proper concert fees for British soloists didn't exist before my career had its impact. I remember the £50 fee the BBC paid me for my first radio recital which took about two months to prepare. I earned far more than that every time I went busking for a couple of hours on Fifth Avenue. Basically, if the shit really hit the fan (no reference intended to my West Midlands Police chapter!)[9] I could revive my busking career which was real, enjoyable and more than paid rent and food. There was also a significant risk that the classical division of EMI would get the hump because what I was going to do would shake them out of their complacent lethargy, disturbing their cosseted and cobwebbed ivory tower. Strangely for an English classical record company, EMI used to ghettoise artists from the United Kingdom putting them on a lesser sub-label only available in Britain. They treated us Brits as passport holders of The United Serfdom of Great Britain. As I mentioned earlier, it's hard to imagine Deutsche Grammophon ostracising all German artists or Motown refusing to release recordings by American artists, particularly if they were born in Michigan. So, in fact, not a lot to lose from EMI in that particular case. A good old Irish name wasn't going to hack it.

It was a real eye-opener to work with a manager of such exceptional vision and knowhow as John Stanley. The picture he could see was so much bigger than the tiny private school alumni microcosm that I'd been faced with before. In retrospect the work that I did with John, who marshalled the forces at EMI, certainly changed things. My goal was to bring absolutely top-level classical music to more people who deserved to hear it. I hadn't reckoned that media and record company executives would grow cloth over their ears at the site of a dress or something, or that they would necessarily have to believe the fake and exaggerated claims of artists' managers and regurgitate them to those of us who comprise the long-suffering public. I guess generating work and opportunity for anyone who plays music, bogus or not, is better than having done nothing. One can't really blame managers, A&R men or reviewers, to tell the truth. If they didn't have cloth ears, they'd be doing my job, not theirs. So, my friends, having possibly brought you into classical music I have to reassure you that there will be many occasions when you will be listening to something that the BBC or some other 'learned institution' will have described as exciting, brilliant, or even worse

---

9 This hypothetical reference is to a specific horse riding individual in the chapter mentioned.

politically correct. You will wonder why it sounds boring, dull and even worse sufferingly correct. Why? Because it is! Don't blame yourself for not getting it. It's probably shit. What might have been described as a Rolls-Royce could well be a Fiat Uno in disguise with a nice dress.

More important than any number of second-rate media soloists are all the people and audiences around the world who I am so proud to have brought into contact with classical music for the first time.

After all the gassing above I'll return to The IV Seasons. It is that composition and my interpretation of it which lead to the marketing model which so many people in the ensuing years have copied TO THIS VERY DAY (thank you Dillian Whyte). If I can't think of anything else to write about, I'll write about how part of my life became inextricably linked with The IV Seasons. I might just tell you how this amazing set of concertos always gave me, the audience and the orchestra such exceptional energy and how I was able to channel my own special brand of energy back through the music and to audiences around the world who became my musical friends.

Suffice it to say that once John, I and the record company ascertained that my interpretation of Vivaldi and my performance style were actually worth marketing and had something relevant to offer the public at large we all got to work.

In addition to the joy of communicating my music with so many people, which reaffirmed my belief in myself, this musical adventure drastically changed my financial situation. All through my Juilliard education and my earlier career I had been surrounded by rich privileged people but never had any money myself, I just had an overdraft following me around. If there was money to be had from this campaign I was glad to take it, reckoning that I deserved it just as much as anyone else involved. I also had no doubts that I deserved the pay just as much as other posh looking artists who were eating up taxpayers' money from their vastly inflated fees (subsidised by the Arts Council and suchlike), playing music which had no relevance at all to these self-same hard-working taxpayers. I also didn't fail to notice the haughty attitude of some Classicos trying to dismiss my work as too lowbrow. I later noticed that when having the dollar temptation of similar campaigns dangled in front of them these same twats jumped at them like lemmings over a cliff of iniquity. I was Midas but they were Judas![10]

My focus was that a lot of classical music is so beautiful that everybody deserved the chance to hear it. My aim was to open the doors of the snooty private club who thought they owned these beautiful sounds whether they liked it or not, and let everyone in. WE MANAGED! It might have been a bit much to expect everyone to love the classical stuff but the hitherto private club had been nationalised and everybody could now at least see if they liked it. Some of the over privileged and complacent club members resented this and tried to discredit me in various

---

10 I use the name Judas to signify love of money. No other context should be inferred.

ways. It was too late though. Despite their efforts to close the doors again their posh horse had bolted....

LATER ... In addition to loads of young pups desperately copying The Kennedy Formula my encounters with record companies and other music business drones (excuse the double meaning) were at least as amusing. There's many a time over the last few years that I have been sat across the desk from some male or female pisshead who, with a condescending look and with a "my boy, this is the way we do it" or "this is how it's done", have quoted me exactly the formula that John Stanley and I invented. These ignoramuses have thought they knew so much but didn't even know their own field enough to know who invented the formula to which they owed such a comfortable living.

To tell you the truth the classical music business is so full of shit and shitters that it is truly ... shit ... there are luckily a fair few exceptions which prove the rule.

Luckily my colleagues, my audience and the music itself make all of the idiots above worth putting up with. There is no substitute for one of those magic nights when everyone is lifted as if by a divine inspiration and all the morons are well forgotten. That's why I am involved with my beloved music and am still improving every day, even now.

Letter to A Young Artist

"My dear little young folks,

"What makes no sense at all, and what all too frequently happens in 'The Arts' is an institution trying (and all too often succeeding) to institutionalise an individual. If the circumstances the institution believes in actually still existed these self-elected despots might be acting rationally—but when dealing with a free-thinking individual these circumstances DON'T exist because the individual has moved on more quickly than a monolithic organisation and evolved a new reality."

"Fear is prevalent in music, but no one does good by fear. All of this development of killer techniques from jazz guitarists or classical musicians, it's a kind of protection device. You impress people by how quick you can move your fingers so that they don't look beyond that into your heart. I don't mean you can have too much technique, but concentrating on technique to stop anyone making a musical judgement on you, that's you just blinding the audience with technique. We want something to liberate us and to make us feel like we're flying. The element of fear doesn't do good for music at all. It's shit."

"A lot of the things I was hoping for have actually happened, like the comeback of live music or the demise of record companies. I've been hoping to see them go down for the last 30 or 40 years. Not to see people go out of a job or nothing, but at least people sitting behind a desk can no longer tell the musician what to do when they are completely ignorant themselves. People can listen to so much more music than they used to have access to. The segmentation of it through levels of society is not so strong as it used to be. Overall we artists have more autonomy now."

"Play only the music you love. Choose your own repertoire, choose the stuff you relate to, so that you can actually give something unique. You are unique, no one else plays like you. No one else feels the same when they hear that melody which you are going to play. There's one and only one person who can play it the way you do. Enjoy sharing the music with other people. Because that's the most beautiful part of it, whether it's with colleagues or an audience: value the moment. Don't be frightened, you have got nothing to be ashamed of, the audience is your friend. If anyone fucking turned up to see you, they haven't turned up to judge you. The audience have turned up to be transported into a beautiful realm, and you are completely capable of doing it."

A LIFE IN THE SPIRIT OF
LAURIE KENNEDY

Now that the molecules of my body have dispersed for so long and for such a great distance I can see physical and metaphysical reality from a far broader perspective than a mere organic sentient biped. My body has risen up into the clouds and beyond and also descended down low into the ground. I am part of the water, soil and air which feed the Earth's vegetation and therefore the rest of the existing species. My molecular body has spread further outwards than the eye can see through an intergalactic telescope and further inwards than the most powerful microscope can detect. From my vantage point I am not in two different worlds but one endless one. I can see cosmic reality outwards and inwards as the universe or an individual molecule. Both are now inseparable. The fact that I am communicating through words is because I am using my grandson Nigel to express myself to the earthbound. He has asked me to do this and I am happy to oblige. I should point out that where I am now has no geographical location point and that communication is just one infinite entity—so please don't write to me in Australia! I am, what is known in your organic world as DEAD.

That is not to say that I don't remember fondly the small details of my physical life, and some of these details are what Nigel is asking me to recount. I have many cherished memories of my time spent as part of mankind. Memories of music are particularly important because it opened doors to the spiritual world that I now inhabit, long before I left the physical for the metaphysical. After my metamorphosis I at first maintained direct contact with your world through my son John and now through my grandchildren, one of whom is facilitating my reaching to you through the writing of his book at the present moment. Your moment, that is. Time is an invention of mankind, in reality there is the infinite. We all know this where I am but there are many artists and far fewer scientists who know this where you are.

One thing I've seen is that even when living within the physical realm, the Kennedys have, for many generations, had a portal through which to reach the metaphysical. As well as being intelligent intuitive musicians this ability is at least partially connected with our Irish heritage. We Irish have always had the ability to co-exist with the physical land as well as travel to reach other worlds or realities. Us Kennedys have always used music to open the door to the world which is beyond the physical. As well as mere knowledge (which is available to any half-wit from the chattering society) we have something far more important. Soul. Of course one can teach knowledge and our Kennedy clan are of above average intelligence. But just try and teach soul, empathy or wisdom. Impossible, they can't just be reeled off like a parrot. My grandson has battled against the doctrine of syllabus orientated thinking all his life, I never encountered a syllabus, and musically we have both occupied the world of the soul.

Kennedys have always been travellers. I remember my father, Samuel Kennedy, telling me how our family had left Ireland to go to England and then to Australia.

The Kennedys left Ireland because it was a completely unsuitable place to even try and live under English rule. Under the English survival was not of the fittest but of the fattest. Like Darwin, my father theorised about Australia but along different lines. What he realised was that the 60 per cent survival rate on the boat was far better than the 10 per cent survival rate at home. Staying in England long term was also not an option because the no blacks, no Irish, no dogs mentality was around long before the 1950s.

Up here above I can unfortunately still hear the chattering classes who seem to have multiplied like rabbits since my day. They are interrupting my train of thought right now. Just as rabbits were once a plague upon Australia these chatterers are a plague upon any intuitive empathic thought (and I mean real thought) in the so-called Western world. At the moment they seem to have a psychosis about something called global warming (let me tell you, when I was a child Australia was much hotter) and something else called woke, that seems to be a lot of white people and some black people culturally appropriating a word from a specific segment of society in America. These people are ruining any chance of a philosophical encounter with true reality. Oh, what a relief, they've stopped for a second so I can carry on with my story.

Back before the proliferation of these chattering classes my father, Samuel, used to tell me constantly of his journey to Australia and how lucky we were to be in a position to build a new life. He told me of the endless months on the boat with a diet of millet (on a very good day, the policy of the shipping companies being to spend as little as possible on food), and of the less fortunate people who perished on the way. Travelling steerage, he said, meant he was lucky to be alive, and that if he had died I wouldn't have existed, so I was lucky too.

Work was the name of the day building this new world. Originally he came to Australia to try commission agenting but while this business idea was showing itself to be a dead end he came up with the idea of promoting (or exploiting) the musical talent of our family. The Kennedy Troupe was formed. We had a horse pulled wagon with 'The Kennedy Troupe' painted on both sides in capital letters and we would travel nomadically from town to town. I heard so much music, mainly vaudeville—popular songs of the day mixed with one or two more accessible examples of classical music, that it all came naturally to me.

There were far more important things to do than spending extremely valuable time on a formal, orthodox education. We learned about reality and it was work, work, work, the old fashioned way, to build something of our lives. The palm to the forehead stuff was an irrelevant and self-indulgent luxury we simply weren't interested in and couldn't afford. Whatever education was considered necessary was given to me by my mother Bertha, my father, or by various members of the troupe. I am very grateful that my mind was never confined by the narrowness of preconceived learning and teaching. I have seen my grandson's success in avoiding being limited by curriculum mentality and wholeheartedly approve. My son John also had the same healthy Kennedy attitude. Upon finding out that he had won a scholarship to study 'cello at the Royal Academy of Music he wisely dropped his law studies at Balliol College, Oxford University in order to pursue a proper life in music. His decision was vindicated. Within four years he was lead 'cello in the Royal Liverpool Philharmonic and within eight years was lead 'cello in Sir Thomas Beecham's Royal Philharmonic Orchestra in London.

I very much regret having disowned John. From his 'cello playing it was obvious that he was my son and that he had inherited my talent but I, thinking he was the love child of my wife with the great tenor John McCormack, abandoned him to being brought up in London by a rich Catholic woman, Mrs Atkin-Swan, who became his adoptive parent. In an almost mirror image mistake John abandoned Nigel, leaving him in England, returning to Australia with another woman, a singer. At least Nigel was with his real mother who loved and cared for him deeply. I know they had problems surviving on the £5 a month John sent them but Nigel wasn't unhappy. Nigel was then himself subject to a form of abandonment when at the age of six he won a scholarship which resulted in him being put in the rather strange confines of The Yehudi Menuhin School of Music. This, though, is a mistake any mother could or would have made, sending a talented child to the school of one of the most charismatic, important violin pedagogues in history.

Looking back on it from where I am now I can see that John and I have left Nigel with a legacy incomparable among his contemporaries. I would call it genetics but DNA seems to be the fashionable term for it in your present world. In addition to pure musical ability Nigel inherits the ability to entertain and cross genres from my vaudeville background, and the desire to be inclusive and share with his colleagues, from his father. This mix in addition to an intelligent and diligent approach to his preparation is very, very potent, and is probably why so many people love his music and how it communicates with them. These people range from the most recognised musicians in every field to people who have never heard whichever genre my grandson is playing. This DNA, as you like to call it, puts Nigel far, far above the level of one or two deluded types who think they might have a better idea of how he should go about things. These scholarly ignoramuses would be better off not trying to grasp above their true station and instead should help people at large have the chance to hear my grandson's unique, all embracing talent. This would produce much more beneficial results than their bogus moral 'thought policing' patrol of the arts. This grandson of mine knows about music not only intellectually (which is the easy way) but also in his eternal soul. He towers above all moribund theorists and I am proud of him. What his travels watching a team called Aston Villa involve or what purpose this endeavour has I will never know, but as my life testifies, it is good to be involved in different activities.

Even if I say so myself, I made outstanding progress in music at a very young age. As a small child I was already being stood on a chair to play bagpipes or sing for the audience, and by the time I was ten I was a fully-fledged member of The Kennedy Troupe. I had become pretty good at piano and was just commencing 'cello. My dad had picked one up very cheaply in Newcastle (New South Wales). Who would've known that a while later I would be playing on the most important classical concert stages all over the world and playing with the leading classical geniuses of the day.

My life changed, possibly for the worse, when I took a boring music conservatorium teaching job in Melbourne. This job was far better than what a former vaudeville artist would normally have expected so was impossible to refuse. It guaranteed steady income and a pension, nothing to be sneezed at by a family of nomadic Kennedys. People might find it difficult to imagine a world devoid of the infantile chatter of your computers, or even telephones, but in those times being settled and seeing the same people day by day had a certain appeal. Playing in India, South Africa, New Zealand and all over Australia with The Kennedy Troupe was my normality. A boring job and not travelling ceaselessly were something new to me. Overall, though, there was something missing but I couldn't identify what, or what to concentrate on to fill the unexplained void. It was the great singer Dame Nellie Melba, a household name around the world, who changed and refocused my life.

Dame Nellie was a far more universally recognised soprano than any of the ones you people are listening to currently. When she came to sing a gala concert at the music conservatorium where I taught, she sang with piano and 'cello. I was drafted in to play the 'cello part. Whether she was impressed (being an older woman) by my Rudolph Valentino looks, my musical ability or both, I will never know ... but she made it clear to me that I was so talented that I had to, absolutely had to become a touring artist so that the world could hear me. She engaged me to tour with her, many people became engaged by my playing and I then became engaged by them! I continued a long musical association with Dame Nellie.

My musical kaleidoscope expanded with a six year period of touring with the wonderful Irish tenor John McCormack. More recently you have maybe heard a tenor called Pavarotti. McCormack was better and even more popular than this. It's a shame that my wife Dorothy, who was playing piano on these tours, thought he was even more wonderful than I did. Our touring with McCormack took us all over the world with long periods of time apart in America. People in America loved my playing and were eager for me to live there—I later did.

From then on there were endless musical adventures. These included inspirational partnerships with Feodor Chaliapin, the greatest bass singer even until the very day you exist in. Fritz Kreisler, he was loved in every household. I played with this God of violin Gods frequently and recorded his poignant and wistful string quartet with him, violist William Primrose and second violinist Thomas Petre. I see that Nigel also recorded this string quartet as a tribute to his favourite violinist and myself. Well done, my grandchild. Your recording is almost as good as mine! All right, I admit I did have the advantage of recording it with the great Kreisler himself. I saw that Fritz became your favourite violinist even before you realised there was a family connection. Very good taste, my boy. Far less cliché than Heifetz or Oistrakh, for instance, even though Oistrakh was a subliminal artist. Heifetz, despite his great technical control, never made truly great concerto recordings, which require more than great violin playing. Partnerships with the conductor, for example, are a prerequisite far more than just admiration from other violinists. Collaborations with Jascha Heifetz, Arthur Rubinstein and Albert Sammons all followed and took me to heights approaching the spiritual world within which I now exist.

After that Arturo Toscanini, the frightening but great conductor, invited me to join him and lead the 'cello section of his NBC Orchestra in America which was the best quality orchestra and the best paid orchestra in the world. Playing in this wonderful orchestra meant I lived in New York. Despite the cultural firmament of New York I preferred the West Coast with its open spaces which were more reminiscent of Australia. I lived for quite a while in Hollywood playing in film scores. You can hear my solo 'cello on Walt Disney's cartoon Fantasia and also on other films from that era. Contrary to accepted belief cartoons (or animated pictures) were originally made for adults. Then, with Tom and Jerry and suchlike they became kids' entertainment. Fantasia was an experimental masterpiece set to classical music, the quality of which is unlikely to ever be attained again. Many would say that the computer graphics you have nowadays are unequal to the moving cartoons painted by human beings in that they have less pathos or feeling.

With the proceeds from my time spent in America I bought a hotel in Taree, New South Wales. My wife and I had great plans for the place but lost out to small-minded local councillors. What I wanted to bring to Fotheringham's Hotel were a beer garden, a rooftop garden, an extra bar and beer available every day instead of just three days a week. Unfortunately, Taree wasn't ready for such earthshattering changes, except for beer available daily. Dorothy and I gave up after 18 months, there were too many brick walls apart from the ones which comprised the structure of the hotel. I returned to concert touring after that frustration and then bought a pub in Sydney.

Having had a wonderful life, free of the limitations imposed by formalised education, I can honestly say that schooling was the best thing which never happened to me. I can see that my grandson also doesn't overestimate education. He has spent time meticulously unlearning strictures imposed on him during earlier years. I have always subscribed to the established theory that of what we have been taught by others, only 20 per cent, maximum 30 per cent, is of any relevance if you want to involve original creative thought, that is. Nigel has also been lucky to have had teachers who encouraged him to find his own solutions rather than impose their own opinions. Of course, this approach would leave weaker students completely at sea.

I know that Nigel is writing a book which, amongst other things, is transmitting my thoughts. I'll be reading it and might drop in a comment or two during the course of his writing, unless I have something more important to do up here existing in the cosmos … for example, at the moment I'm watching the BBC looking down at Uranus. One last message to you, Nigel … Who is the best judge of what you are doing? … It's you, my boy. How many people could possibly be qualified to have a relevant opinion about your musical directions bearing in mind the pedigree that you have inherited from your Kennedy ancestors? The shape of O (found twice in nobody) points to the answer. Goodbye for now.

CONVERSATION WITH LUDWIG VAN BEETHOVEN

Prelude

Look at the Second World War. Poland think they won it! Britain think they won it. Amerika think they won it. Russia probably did in fact win it and at the greatest loss. The 'truth' seems to be tailor-made in hindsight, to support whatever political agenda is dominant at the time. A statue or street name gets toppled in order to be replaced by another tin pot demigod who will also be toppled or replaced in a few years. This intellectual posturing, by the people with the time and money to do it, all goes to show that music and art are the only forms of communication across the centuries, which aren't altered in retrospect for political convenience. Beethoven, Bach or Jimi Hendrix express the same sentiments now as when they were alive.

The prevalent mentality at the moment (if the media is to be believed!!) is to find dirt on yesterday's heroes and drag their status down towards the cesspit. I doubt this is very character building, at least not in a good way, for the younger generations. Surely, in order to bring up optimistic considerate future adults it's necessary to concentrate on the positives in people of history rather than only the negatives. I'm sure there's dirt to be dug up on even Mahatma Gandhi or Nelson Mandela but would it really help anyone now or in the future to try and do that? I'm sure someone has done it already but that's not relevant to the point I'm making. Passion, tolerance and compassion beat ambivalence, intolerance and hate any day and aren't those more appreciative qualities the ones that we should be teaching our children and natural successors if we want to have a more productive and positive society?

Whether it's Ludwig Van Beethoven, Miles Davis or James Marshall Hendrix compassion and communication of the truth are what still reach us from their music today and that's why I can still communicate with them now, so long after they passed on to other worlds. I have opened the channels to Beethoven's spiritual being many times when performing his music and my conversations with him became possible on that basis. I should add that Ludwig Van chose to communicate with me first, not the other way round. I communicate with Jimi Hendrix in the same way and will relay a conversation with him later, at least if we cross spiritual paths while I've got the pen in my hand.

Beethoven hardly spoke English at all during his lifetime but in his metaphysical state language is no longer a barrier.

Conversation

ME: Oy, Ludwig, are you around?

LUDWIG VAN: I've been near you all the time, Mr Kennedy, you just didn't realise it while you were writing to your friends.

ME: Forgive me the limitations of my earthbound senses, Ludwig, how are you?

LUDWIG VAN:

not well at all not big not small

ME: But surely, Ludwig, it's impossible for you to be unwell as a spiritual presence in the cosmos … big? … small? … I thought you were all-encompassing now, like in your music in which you miraculously bring the elements, nature and mind all together into one immeasurable existence.

LUDWIG VAN:

But it's ve - ry ve - ry ve - ry sad, it's ve - ry

bad, it sends me sad, it's ve-ry ve - ry ve - ry ve - ry

bad, it makes me sad, it's all a fad.

ME: What makes you feel bad or sad when you lift so many people with the amazing reach and pathos of your music?

LUDWIG VAN: Mr Kennedy, do you mind me talking at length? I would like to communicate my thought with you and your readers.

ME: We would be honoured. Of course I'll be your faithful servant with my pen just as I am with my violin when I play your music.

LUDWIG VAN: Mr Kennedy, I feel as if all the work I did at the start of the Romantic period was in vain. There have been great interpreters of my music. Furtwängler was deep, Karajan was natural, Menuhin and Brendel spiritual, Kreisler radiant and they all opened a door to my music in the same way that you do now. But I worked so hard to gain musicians their independence and I feel that any advances I made have been frittered away by self-serving careerists who are happy to sacrifice our creative rights for their selfish gain. Herr Kennedy, you must wake these people up! You are the only one not programmed by the same outside influences I fought against as a composer, conductor and pianist. Please don't stop or give up furthering my work, sometimes a lone voice can be the strongest and you have to root out the chaff. Others might make the right noises but they are fakes and sycophants. I was surrounded by those types in my day. Even though he said he was a friend, Spohr was just such a type. All serious gesture and no substance. You have this picture service now which shows these fake scoundrels all the time, they like the sanctimonious types of vacuous artist, I believe they're called Beeb Bea Sea or something like that.

And why do so few people need so much more money than all the rest of the world put together? I stopped working for royalty almost 200 years ago and established musical independence but what has happened? Musicians are so much more sycophantic now, tugging their forelock and curtsying constantly. What's wrong with them?

ME: Yes, it's all very shallow and the music sounds very automatic to me. Where did the depth of your music come from? There's a simultaneous groundedness and stratospheric exaltedness within your music. What was your inspiration? Maybe this is one of the answers to today's problems.

LUDWIG VAN: I'm inspired by nature which is, after all, where everything comes from. The earth, the flora, the fauna, the aviary world, rain, sun, wind, day and night. The interdependence of life, its endless cycles. The depth and poignancy of the interrelationship between everything. The vastness of the cosmos. They are all one thing and they channel through my music. I've noticed that you and that unusual gentleman Jimi Hendrix channel the same things but in different ways. That's why I keep an eye on you and have many conversations with Mr Hendrix.

My approach to music and its development means that I don't understand or condone the divisiveness of people's culture nowadays. Having expanded and augmented the orchestra in my time to free music from its shackles I'm disappointed in how closed minded and compartmentalised music still is. What interest would a musician have in playing just one tiny part of it? The only reason could be that they just don't love music enough. My 'Ode to Joy' and Schiller's beautiful literature were not created to divide people into sad little cliques, in fact the opposite of that kind of silliness is what we were trying to achieve. Why are people still only worried about themselves (and a few people exactly like them)? If our human race is going to be at least equal to the animal kingdom we have to do things together, celebrate not criticise each other's cultures and ways of thinking. I am neither white nor black[11] and can see the futility of these racial groupings. Everyone in your time seems obscured in a cloud of their own petty subdivisions. Whatever happened it has relegated to nothing the great ideas and hopes I had for humanity and music.

ME: Yes, I have always subscribed to your ideas but even in my small life I've received criticism almost bordering on hate for playing different types and styles of music, for trying to share music with people outside the limited social circles it was previously played to. Much as you did in the early 1800s. And this is JUST MUSIC I am referring to—with these attitudes towards artistic expression it's no wonder that people are unable to respect each other in even broader aspects of life.

LUDWIG VAN: Herr Kennedy, forgive me for saying, there's absolutely no such thing as JUST MUSIC. Music represents the only life force which can unite us all, the whole human race and all the multifarious species. It might be that you have problems in England because the vast majority of the gentry and intellectuals actually have quite a Philistine attitude towards music and musicians.

ME: Yes, I know you experienced that yourself. There was a conductor from after your time, Sir Thomas Beecham, who summed it up nicely when he said "The English may not like music, but they absolutely love the noise it makes." In my experience the authorities only tolerate music when it comes to taxing the musicians.

LUDWIG VAN: Those might be your specific problems, Herr Kennedy, but in general there are too many people talking, and talking on and on about music instead of listening to it or playing it. They will never better themselves as human beings if all they can hear is the ceaseless drone of their own voice. Kennedy, you and the very, very few like you have to change this. If you succeed all men shall become brothers, wherever one's gentle wings hover. Whoever has been lucky enough to become friend to a friend, let them join our music of praise. Every creature drinks in joy from nature, even the worm was given desire.

You must use your unique gifts with music and people to help everybody away from talking about themselves and to help them use their ears. I should know about this problem having spent so much of my life in agony without the ability to hear. Listening is a gift which the world has forgotten they've been given.

You must use your gift, Herr Kennedy, to help everybody stop talking. I am happy that my music is a conduit through time and space for the spirit of life...

---

11 Beethoven might have said white before black because he was probably white during his terrestrial life.

but in reference to superficial people's reaction to everything about you apart from what is important, remember the vitriol which came my way because of my making the orchestra bigger, maximising dynamic contrast, opening channels for more primal forms of energy through music and for turning my back on being a musical slave of the centres of wealth represented by monarchy and church. In your era it seems that these two evils have been replaced by equal parasites that you call record companies and media. These two representations of superficiality are not as powerful as they think they are, so Herr Kennedy, sei ein Mann and do not be controlled by them. Remember my colleagues, all of the same mentality as myself, spirits such as Herr Johannes Brahms, Herr Hendrix, Herr Curtis Mayfield, Herr George Clinton, Herren Miles Davis and John Coltrane, Herren Led Zeppelin. They all communicated the spirit of life through music despite the small-minded self-appointed authorities, not because of them. These gentlemen are your lineage.

ME: This is an amazing lineage, and when Yehudi Menuhin introduced me to your music, little did I think that later in time I would be lucky enough to be the one to continue it. I'm sorry that the people of my time have wrongly categorised you as 'classical music' and will take a certain satisfaction in putting them right!

Why do you think the world of written down music is so disgustingly sycophantic and predictable? Is it the fault of Laura Ashley or Margaret Thatcher?

LUDWIG VAN: Very funny, Herr Kennedy, but in fact your question is very serious. Looking at your world now I am faced by more questions than answers. For instance, why do so many people think only about themselves? Why are people's thoughts led and shepherded so easily like sheep? Why are almost all people so cowardly at the moment? Why does someone like you, Herr Kennedy, stand almost alone? And where is the courage, nowadays, that I showed in the 1790s? I very much dislike what you people would call smooth operators and am very unhappy that they still prevail today. There's not one of your contemporaries who puts the music before the safety of their career or the approval of some over privileged employer. Even the segregation of my music into some snobbery induced ghetto called 'classical' is something offensive and against all my beliefs. The term 'classical music' is prejudicial against, not in favour of my music. When I was writing music this ugly term didn't exist and if it had I would have quickly and firmly disavowed it. This type of classification and generalisation is insulting and has nothing to do with my music at all. In addition to which, Haydn and Mozart were from the 'classical' period, I am not. I created a new more extended more virile kind of music.

ME: Why do you think those that are called 'classical' musicians today are so gutless?

LUDWIG VAN: Firstly, never trust someone who displays all the correct etiquette, Herr Kennedy, they will wait for your back to be turned and while displaying all the correct etiquette will stab you in it. But to answer your question more directly, perhaps the term 'classical music' is partially responsible for the moral shortcomings of those who play it. They seem to associate the written note as being a finite, repeatable occurrence instead of the note itself being an infinite gateway to endless emotional and intellectual possibilities. Because, to them, the notes are already there on paper, not much thinking and feeling have to be done.

These musical mongrels build a technique on their instrument and play within its (and their) capability. Real musicians build a technique and push it to breaking point, risking mistakes to find or learn something and enlighten their colleagues and audience. The heart and mind control the technique in the hands of a real musician, not the other way round. You must try to help these famous but weak musicians to overcome their moral and emotional disabilities. You should also try to let them know that a performer is not there to teach the audience. He or she is there to share a journey of true discovery with them. Sanctimony has no place in real music.

You must also, Herr Kennedy, help these poor automatons find out that music is ALL or NOTHING. Music is not a convenient and safe route from A to B, it's a previously untold and uncharted journey of the soul.

ME: Yes. Music is not something to automatically repeat because it is written down and the page looks the same the next day. One can see that from great jazz music.

LUDWIG VAN: Yes, I admire and love the work of people like Charles Mingus, he has the earth in his music, or Coleman Hawkins who has heaven in his harmony. In my time improvisation was important but as soon as our music became described as 'classical' the art of improvisation was lost. Unfortunately many lesser jazz musicians today are equally straitjacketed and limited by the preconceptions and definitions forced onto them by academia. It's too easy for them to live in past definitions instead of creating future parameters of their own.

ME: Do you have any other advice or encouragement for me?

LUDWIG VAN: Herr Kennedy, you now have a lot of epigones, male and female. I suffered from the same type of people copying me. Take no notice of these people apart from trying to get them to actually think for themselves. If they engaged their own brains they would have a far more rewarding life in music. After all, who do you think had the higher spiritual life? Rembrandt or the unfortunate plagiarist who made the 500th copy of his work? So yes, either ignore them or help these poor people.

I also see that you are the first man since Fritz Kreisler to create original cadenzas for my violin concerto. Thank you for this. One or two other violinists have taken note of your cadenzas and followed your lead. I see that you were also the first since Herr Kreisler to do this for my friend Johannes Brahms. You couldn't have chosen a better fellow to write for. He started off being my musical disciple but then truly found his own great voice. He was born about 20 years after I died but we are very close spiritually now, as we always have been.

I also see that you are writing a violin concerto dedicated to me. I am pleased and consider it very fitting, particularly in view of you being described as a modern day embodiment of me because of your rebellion against the pseudo-authorities. I am glad that you are not directly copying my style but are respecting my use of melody, harmony, enharmonic change, and rhythm. I see that you are writing it for my 250th birthday, which has already passed, but I'm sure you know that your work is more important than the number.

(As Beethoven receded from vision I felt struck by his unremitting, ever increasing, intensity. While finding this inspirational I was left wondering what on earth (literally) has happened to the performers one hears today. Why have radiance, desire, depth and inspiration been replaced by this bland, insipid, sanctimonious professionalism? It's a lack of respect for the composer and audience. Here's to the next gig!)

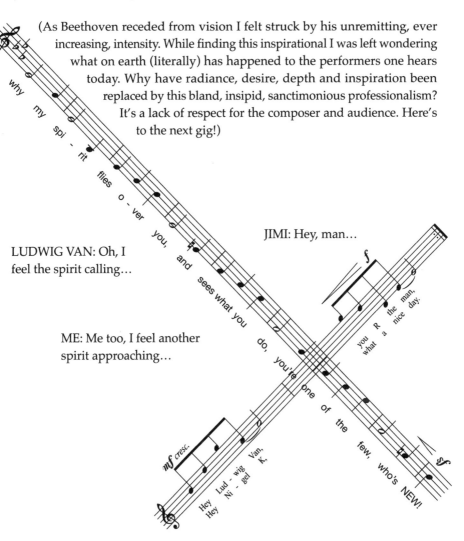

JIMI: Hey, man…

LUDWIG VAN: Oh, I feel the spirit calling…

ME: Me too, I feel another spirit approaching…

CONVERSATION WITH
JIMI HENDRIX

JIMI: Yo Nige-yawl, you gettin' on fine with Old Ludwig. He sometimes gets' bit depressed y'know.

ME: Yo, Mr Hendrix.

JIMI: Call me Jimi, man. We're all on the same wavelength here.

ME: Cheers, Jimi. Yeah, Ludwig Van talks a lot of sense. He's been through a lot of battles so that the rest of us can express ourselves without being faced by financial tyranny or manipulation.

JIMI: Yeah, I hear you, man. It's a shame that so many musicians still subjugate themselves and are told what to do.

Hey, just wanted to let you know, it's a bit funny having a thing called Hendrix Foundation named after me but I'm glad they came after you to play my shit.

ME: There are some composers that I seem to know fully even before I really check their shit, and you're one of them. When I play your music it's like we have the same fingerprint or we're brothers or something. It was that Alan Douglas geezer who approached me. When your foundation asked me to play your stuff that was the final endorsement I needed. I realised I was a rightful interpreter of your musical legacy and it all clicked.

JIMI: Yeah, rightful…and righteous, man! I like the violin, I tried to play one once. It was all strung up wrong for me 'coz I'm left handed.

ME: I think I've got the photo of that … fiddles aren't totally symmetric so it's hard to string them the other way round. You need to get one specially made. Where were you then?

JIMI: We were in the BBC in Maida Vale. The bloke who owned it had left it there on the chair and when he turned up again he looked bad nervous when he saw his fiddle in my hands. Thought the mad guitarist was gonna break or steal it…!

I'm glad to hear my music done on the violin though, man. Especially by a fiddler who has guitar consciousness. It's a different sound with the same drive.

ME: What about style, mate?

JIMI: People copy my riffs 'n shit and that's fine, but I prefer to hear another dimension. I'm always looking for a broader view, man. You know I like symphonic and jazz so I'd like to hear influences but obviously more from the vibe, not from those actual genres, dig? I'm not after the type of orchestra where they have no rhythm and make a sonic slush and not the type of jazz, man, which has more noodling than China. Be yourself, you know. If, later, you're gonna die, then you're allowed to live your life the way you want it.

ME: Nice one, stuff it to the moral thought police. Which other versions or interpretations of your music do you like?

JIMI: Your two kindred Irishmen did great, man.

ME: Rory Gallagher and Gary Moore?

JIMI: Yeah, that's them. Gary Moore really feels and knows his feedback. I also liked hearing that string quartet Kronos during my Purple Haze, interesting, but maybe they forgot how important a part of The Experience Mitch Mitchell was. You know, my music isn't just an idea, it's the whole thing, drums are part of it.

I like what you're doing, man, because you're a bit reckless. Freedom, man, that does it—playing carefully with all that due diligence shit just doesn't do it—no way.

Extending all my songs is kool, man, that's what I want. Sayin' it in three minutes is kool too but if we're there to play we might as well play. Anyway, you know I'm into extended forms like jazz and symphonic too, so it would be proper good if you can use your instincts that way, from your knowledge of music but with that fantasy you have. Hey, your grandad was big in symphonic, wasn't he? When I was a kid in Seattle I heard him in that film Fantasia. Kool sound, man, you got it in your blood, mate.

ME: Do you think it's funny to say 'mate' because I come from Ingulund.

JIMI: Yeah, man. You're doing kool because you're bringing so many elements together that I love, through my music…mate.

ME: Alright, mate, what do you think and feel about me realising your music in a way that is mainly instrumental?

JIMI: It's all kool, you know. Less words, more meaning. I don't use many words anyway.

Sometimes I feel that maybe my guitar playing and my antics overshadowed my songwriting—in my mind they are all part of the same thing but in other people's mind, you know. It's outasight that you are focusing on my songwriting instead of my guitar playing.

I've noticed you're different from all those around you. Sometimes when an animal is a bit different the rest of its species want to kill it, with humans this might only stretch to metaphorical, man. I think, primarily, they see the difference as a possible evolution which in the future might threaten their own existence by leaving them behind and making them redundant. We all know the cliché about keeping the gene pool strong by killing the weak ones. But this is the opposite, you know, the gene pool doesn't like it if a stronger better one is going to put them out of business—nor does an individual. That's what happened with you and that BBC guy from the Bleeb.

When I was around I did somethin' with the guitar and even though I'm softly spoken and humble I was portrayed as aggressive. Some aspects of society couldn't deal so easily with me being different, and the fact that I didn't conform to their stereotype made them feel embarrassed and uneasy. I've seen you get the same shit from the classico and rock guys. The not very good ones get threatened by someone who can take it further than they can. The Classicos, I've seen them, they will try to dismiss you in a superior dismissive kind of way. Don't worry, man. They've never been lucky enough to even be able to think of, let alone do what you're up to. The shit rock ones will come up with some blah bla about you not being hardcore. Man, I've even heard them talk about The Beatles like that and anyway, your Crosstown Traffic will shut them up.

And, you know, I also rose above that black-white thing which is currently flippin' the wig of so many of your socio-politicos on the Blurb Bleeb Sea. What's happened to your TV man? It's all gotten really uptight, you know. When I was on the Third Stone there were uptight racists on both sides. There were the Black Panthers on one side and the rednecks on the other. A lot of my black brethren didn't think I should be playing with white musos or playing to white audiences—but Mitch and Noel gave me that rocky thing and understood that psychedelic stuff which goes so great with my astral blues stuff—and when you close your eyes everybody is every colour, don't you think? I learned a real lot with the Isleys and with the Jimmy James stuff and all that but I evolved and became myself when I came to England. I suddenly was neither black nor white, or both, dig man. What you're doing is OK man, not being put in little boxes means you can use fantasy to show different sides of reality. The good stuff is not a schooling thing, it's out the box, man.

ME: I get you, man. Tell you what. I'd like to ask you about what you imagine hearing in particular songs of yours.

JIMI: Sure man, but you know, my music is open, be yourself. The only way for me to be bored is if you did my songs my way.

ME: Thanks mate, I don't think I'll be able to help leaving my fingerprint on your songs. I feel them deeply….

And this is what Jimi said about each song, in his words from our conversation:

Hey Joe

Do what you want, man. My version is nothing like the original. You don't need to do it like the original, you don't need to do it like my version. Do it like you, like your version.

Third Stone from the Sun

This is our planet seen from inner space and outer space. Every type of music is kool for this song, man. Expansive symphonic, Celtic, Indian, didge, rock, jazz fusion. Explore, man.

Voodoo Chile

This is, as you know, heavy, man. Rock it mate. If there was an orchestra they'd have to stand up or something, get involved, and it would need loads of the drummer to keep it together.

You gotta blow your chops off too Nige-yawl—don't take no prisoners.

Drifting

I dig the way you got the water represented by 'cello, man, and the flow at the end. Maybe the verse could be played by oboe, man, that would suit the vibe.

Crosstown Traffic

This is another rock number, man, but with a bit of Isleys and Mayfield too. I dig the Zappa Gumbo Variations thing you put in the middle. Nice one, man, you remind me of Sugarcane. Rock out, rock on, mate.

In 1983 A Merman I Should Turn To Be

This song is definitely a symphonic one of mine and it can be extended BIG time, man. This is a long story and do whatever's necessary to tell it. It's an epic journey and can go through folk, classical, jazz, Indian, rock. You name it, go where you need to go to tell the story. Time has passed but I would still like this song to sound cosmic/personal, futuristic/historic, all-encompassing, mate.

ME: You like saying 'mate', if you're not careful it'll become habitual.

JIMI: Yeah, man, that's the objective, mate.

Purple Haze

Man, this one is rock and space, primal but out there. This is the song which captured the imagination of the Hendrix Foundation when you played it during that kids' show on the Bleeb. Loadsa drums, mate, and go for it.

ME: Alright, mate.

The Wind Cries Mary

This song is about couples, argument and reconciliation. This represents my arguments with girlfriends, plural, dig man? I think your violin can represent the feminine side of the song. Also the high harmonic shit you do can represent the wind. The Db chord is the climax of the argument and then immediate reconciliation. Your violin stuff really suits my song good, mate.

ME: Cheers, man.

And with that Jimi floated off to his heavenly business and I went about my terrestrial business thinking what a humble, intelligent person he is.

If you only judged the cover, you wouldn't need the book.[12]

---

12 If you're reading this stuff I guess the cover was alright...

THE ROCK ARISTOCRACY—
THE IMPORTANCE OF THE STORY

Sometimes when we listen to classical or jazz music we too often become aware of the performer and also (if it's in a modern genre) the composer rattling off a lot of notes at us, not for our benefit but for theirs.

I've noticed that when classical musicians listen to jazz or Romani music they are always impressed by the note rattlers rather than by a musician who has pathos, content and feel.

The Classicos and the Jazzos for the most part can't believe that there is something more important in music than system and complexity. What we get from them because of this are emotionally stultified performances. We then have to put up with listening to performances which are obsessed with technical detail and completely devoid of any bigger picture. I remember, for instance, going to a London gig in which a very talented colleague of mine played a formerly beautiful Cole Porter song. It was an over cultivated massacre. He took a perverse pride in burying the song's inherent qualities in hyperactive harmonic changes and flicking around with the right hand to the point that the song was unrecognisable. The Classicos in the audience (and some jazzers) were very, very impressed but Cole Porter must have been turning in his grave. Roll-Over Cole-Porter!… Dying once is inevitable but drowning in a sea of gratuitous harmonic substitutions and superfluous passage work is surely a fate worse than death! After death! … I think this collective fallacy comes from the prioritisation of curriculum over the spirit of the individual, rampant verbosity over life knowledge and the spouting of superficial facts over a deep reality. Yep, this observation stretches beyond the realms of music—people calling on endless facts without knowing anything!

I have been muvvafukkin lucky to have been able to spend valuable learning time with people of REAL individuality and talent. No textbooks or preaching were involved. These people have been born with the qualities that one can't learn at school or university, not the predictable parroting or mimicking but real cognitive intelligence. They are the ROCK ARISTOCRACY!

I'm using the term 'rock' very loosely in some of the following examples but what they all have in common is that they are one-off unparalleled composers who invented their own genre instead of getting it out of a book or from a teacher. They are reachers without teachers—gifts from way outside the realm of boring curriculum.

What I learned from these guys was gold dust, qualities which couldn't be taught but were essential if music was not going to merely be loadsa self-indulgent notes. Whether the composer was Bach, Beethoven, Benny Goodman, The Beatles, Bob Marley, Billie Holiday, Bentley Rhythm Ace, The Beat, Bachdenkel or Bhujhangy Group ALL MUSIC HAD TO HAVE A NARRATIVE.

The story is even more vital today amongst all the pre-categorised shit we have shoved at our ears. If there's no narrative integral to the music it will be, at best, mediocre and theoretical. And you don't need to go to school to know that this power of narrative applies equally to composers whose names don't begin with the letter B! (Like Bozart, Bed Zeppelin, Bank Zappa, Bick Drake, The Bolling Bones).

Another symptom so many Classicos display is the fear of playing something wrong, this fear has also crept into a lot of second level jazz. The curriculum definition of what is correct has become so narrow that it is almost impossible to get it right without being insufferably boring, and that narrow curriculum mentality is preventing the majority of Classicos and Jazzos from discovering endless possibilities in music which are obviously right, and beautiful into the bargain. The unique moment of NOW is so important in both of the above forms but it is being forsaken in order to worry about past practice and other people's opinions. It's no wonder that, as listeners, after a short burst of interest we become bored and disinterested by inflexible technique motivated by fear.

What the following ROCK ARISTOCRACY all have is something way, way above the mainly average note spielers and churners. They have the ability, without any unnecessary preamble, to create a canvas, paint a picture and tell a story. These kats approach music with a far greater, more natural intelligence than the fabricated performing parrot spiel-monkeys which are manufactured by the music college conveyor belts.

The great thing about having met these geniuses of music is that whether playing classical, jazz, rock, my own music, Jimi Hendrix or any type of fukkin music I have learned from them and realised that the validity of storyline applies to every note in the universe. You will never hear me play without a spiritual narrative, and I was given access to that essential element because of sharing moments with the following masters. These masters pretty much appear in the chronological order that I met them in.

S'Paul McCartney

When I met the man it was soon after my first "classical" concerto album of Elgar came out. In the clarse-ical world I was getting a reputation as, if not the greatest, at least the latest. That I'd played a lot with Grappelli and had musical abilities beyond the boxes somehow had brought me to the attention of Paul McCartney, hence him asking me in 1986 to come and play on 'Once Upon A Long Ago'. 'Once Upon A Long Ago' was a single which was to be the only newly recorded song to go along with a compilation of his greatest hits.

This genius is one of the greatest musical storytellers in history. Vivid imagery, rich harmony and charisma are all part of his normal musical world. He also knew from the very beginning that serious doesn't, I repeat DOESN'T mean solemn, sanctimonious or sad—those are for wannabe-serious wankers who think they've seen serious leaving Tesco's last week.

S'Paul is mega multi talented. Songs equal to anybody from any genre. You don't just hear a McCartney song, you get transported, you see, you smell, you feel the time and place. In the same way that Fritz Kreisler or Django Reinhardt/ Stéphane Grappelli transport you back to the '30s, Macca transports us to the '60s. The great thing is that he's alive and well so his songs from today will transport us back to this time from the future.

What an honour to be asked to go and work with one of the greatest composers of the twentieth century! In addition the song was being produced by Phil Ramone and mixed by George Martin. Muvvafukka BOOM!

I'd listened to the song quite a bit so I was relatively prepared when I turned up and entered Abbey Road Studio No. 1. The song was a typical McCartney beauty. Undertones here and there of The Beatles and overtones of McCartney as the individual writer he is.

Being a bit early (don't tell anyone!) I had my fiddle unpacked and ready to go, with some charts of the song I'd written down put on a music stand. The room of Studio 1 is huge but I was in a kind of ceiling-less booth they'd constructed for me down the far end from the control room. The lack of ceiling would give the violin sound some space while the booth would prevent too much room character affecting the fiddle sound so they could add and control the reverb later.

I'd got my bearings, headphones working, violin sound OK etc. and Paul came in. It was immediately apparent that he was a bloke who cared about the people around him and that he wasn't desperate for me to treat the thing as a whole big deal. His demeanour meant I could relax and we got down to it.

My part was going to be improvised so I had to come up with something.

"I'm well into your song, mate. What type of stuff do you want me to play?"

"I know you can play any style. I dunno, man, something kind of romantic, I guess … do what you want Nige."

They rolled the tape and I played something I thought Macca might have meant by romantic. It was horribly Classico romantic, Hearts & Flowers-ish and infested with vibrato. I knew immediately I'd done a bummer and that it was the wrong shit. Macca hadn't invited me in to play schlock all over his stuff. I waited like an ashamed dog who has soiled the floor and is waiting to see if the master has noticed.

"That's very nice, Nigel. Can we have one more take? What I'm really after is something romantic, you know."

"Right, man. Give me another go...."

I quickly thought about what the fukkk Macca meant by ROMANTIC. Then I thought about it from his point of view and the beautiful guitar lines of George Harrison came to mind, and also the work of Robbie McIntosh.

"Do you want something like this? I've got an idea."

They played the track and I played my shit, no Hearts & Flowers, no sickly vibrato, just real expression, not automatic. I reckoned I'd done all right and that in another couple of takes I'd give them a really good one.

"Give me another couple of goes and I'll get it, man...."

"That was fantastic, Nige. We don't need any more takes. That's the one. That's exactly what I want and we don't want to spoil it. I thought you'd crack it, man. Thanks, Nige. Great."

Shit! That wasn't exactly a hard day's work! I guessed it must have been all right if Paul and the guys in the box liked it. Just as well I hadn't paid too much attention at music school, otherwise I'd never have found a way into that song.

"Nice one, Nige. Thanks, we love it. You're a two take wonder!"

With that I was back off home to celebrate having done a good take (and a bad take) for one of the most important songwriters of the twentieth century.

Within a few days Paul's kats had called up my mouse to see if I would join him for a couple of other things, the shooting of the video and a live transmission to Japan which was a bit of a laugh.

The video shoot was a bit of a problem schedule wise because I was playing Prokofiev violin concerto for a week with the Oslo Philharmonic at the time. Luckily there was a day off between gigs which coincided with Macca's filming and he sent over his private jet to get me there and back. No concerts were missed and my life was perfect, doing stuff with Macca and playing Prokofiev Concerto No. 1. The posh mode of travel was bearable too.

In the hotel the night before the shoot there was a small jam and Paul's phenomenal qualities as a muso were obvious. Wonderful keyboard player, wonderful bass player, a killa positive vibe and charisma in everything he does.

Because I had to piss off back to Oslo there wasn't time to film every second of the track. I shot the thing (my solo) in a hat and coat and for the rest of the song a stand-in geezer wore the same hat and coat. He looked better than me, the bastard.

Linda, Paul's wife, was on the shoot and I remember how lovely, relaxed and very together she was. There was a lot of creative energy and a buzz around but she was totally chilled. She was the perfect partner in life for Paul.

Finally, a week or two later we did the live transmission to Japan. What I remember about that is the shirts. For some idiotic, stupid reason a dolt of a stylist had issued us with horrible Hawaiian shirts. Maybe she didn't realise that Hawaii and Japan are actually different places with just slightly different cultures.

I got my shirt out and thought "Oh, fukkin no." It was naffness personified, black with a giant pink rose on it. "Fukk dis", I thought, "I'll only wear this shit because Paul's a really good bloke." Then, as I watched everyone else put on their shirts it started to dawn on me how lucky I was. Keith Airey had a blue and red shirt which looked like a furniture design from a '50s American airport, Stan Sulzmann had a green, pink and red shirt and Paul had been issued with a brown and orange one which looked like the carrots hadn't agreed with someone. To think that Paul or someone was paying this stylist, it was like paying for your own assassin.

We were sitting around like a load of fukked up parrots waiting for the transmission to begin when I saw Paul eyeing up my shirt from the other side of the room. Before long his PA came over and said to me:

"Aren't you lucky? Paul's going to give you his shirt."

"That's so kind, but this one's bad enough, it's hardly as if I need two."

She might've been the idiot who ordered the shirts and made us all look like pillocks, I didn't know. She started to try and plain talk me.

"You know what I mean. This is his show and you're lucky he's giving you his shirt."

"Well, this is my shirt and Paul's lucky I'm not giving it to him. I definitely don't want the puked carrots on shit one."

A nice abbreviation is in order. Paul gave me a present and I gave him the shirt. I look like shit most of the time so wearing a shit shirt was not so shit as it shitting seemed and all the shirt shit wasn't more than just a shitting shit shirt … shit!

When I was leaving the hotel I went to thank Paul for a great time but he'd left already. The maid had another present from Paul so I left with two presents. Not a bad reward in addition to a shit shirt. When I celebrated by burning the shirt I bet it was hot in Hawaii…

Planty (S'Robert Plant)

First Meeting

My girlfriend Jacquie Turner was a good friend of Planty so when he needed me it wasn't hard to get in touch.

In 1992, Planty was recording his album *Fate of Nations* and he had some Indian kats playing some violin lines and various stuff on his single 'Calling To You'. There's a well-worn cliché about Indian music being so much more advanced than the Western stuff. In this instance it wasn't the case. For the record, I love

Indian music and my mentor Yehudi Menuhin was friends with Nehru and Ravi Shankar before The Beatles realised that Indian wasn't some type of rubber. I'm sure the Indian geezers who Planty had got in were really good but apparently they just couldn't get their head around what Planty wanted harmonically or rhythmically, so were unable to hack it.

I've got to use his real name once even though it doesn't come naturally, here goes: Robert Plant called up Jacquie and said something like: "That Nigel boyfriend of yours plays all kinds of music, doesn't he? The Indian guys that I got in haven't quite done it for the song I'm doing, can Nigel come in and have a go?"

By the next day I was in RAK Studios. This place has probably produced more hits per square metre than any other fukkin' place. It was owned by Mickie Most, an incredibly positive bloke, who probably produced more hits pound for pound than any other muvvafukka. The studio is still owned by his family and they've kept it absolute top crème de la crème to this very day.

Anyhow, the kats were playing me the song and it was opening out in my mind as was the situation. Here I was, on the verge of making music for one of the most influential singers ever. Singers hadn't only copied his voice or his genre, they'd also copied his look. I remember talking about it with him. He didn't mind the copying that much as long as they weren't shit. I didn't have any epigones yet at that point, my footprints were still too risky to follow. But were little fukkers and fukkerettes from Britain and America crawling out of the woodwork to go through the doors of perception that one has opened ... to discover something and develop? No ... to earn some dosh by being an inferior plastic copy—MERCY! I know what Planty feels like but he's had it even worse, man! One thing which will always set The Real Deals apart—real versatility versus fake versatility. Plant is The Real Deal.

It was time to start having a go. What I've learned is that it's always OK to make the first mistake. Muppets who don't want to work with a human being can fukk off. If no one tries anything you have a stalemate before you've even begun. Everyone was chilled and very patient—I could've listened until it was dark and the cows came home which would have been a pretty strange sight in St John's Wood.[13] It was time to do damage. There were some specific orchestral things that Planty wanted doing so I decided to do them first, get them down and nailed, so that I'd be even more into the song by the time it came to doing my more freeform solo.

After a while I'd done the orchestral parts (on acoustic violin) and it was time for the electric solo. I'd started playing electric at the age of 16 when I went to live in New York. The realms it opens out take you away from the typical clichés one expects from an acoustic violin and it's then possible to create a totally original sound identity. Having met Jean-Luc Ponty in those days gave me the wings to fly—he had shown me all his effects pedals and had been a gigantic inspiration.

---

13 Dear political correcto, please don't cry. I am NOT suggesting that all rich wives are cows.

Planty's song 'Calling To You' was a monster pagan world rock thing—fantastic. Michael Lee's dark, heavy drumming was particularly effective and gave the song an incredible momentum. The song was primal but stratospheric. As far as I remember the electric solo came together pretty quickly. Three of four takes max. One of the great things about recording electric is that you can be in the control room with the producer and hear your playing within the real context of the track through the big speakers. A greater than great producer, Chris Hughes, was producing this one. I learned something off him. Up until that session I had been using the wah wah pedal as the name would suggest, using the wah to go wah or even wah wah, or wah wah wah, or even WAAHH! What Chris showed me was finding a magic spot on the wah and just leaving it there as a sound character rather than an effect. Simple, but a revelation! Thanks Chris! Robert was very laid back in the studio, wise and content enough to just let things happen. My part got done with no angst and everything came out great.

Sensitive Americans

Fisons was going to go on tour with his newly created repertoire and as was his custom he was doing a relaxed warmup gig in The King's Head, Putney. It's a kind of famous tradition of his. He invited me to join him and his band to play my solo in 'Calling To You'. It was great crack, full of Plant and Zep fans getting the one in a million chance to see the muvva of all muvvafukkas in a real intimate gig of the type Planty hadn't done since the '60s. A killa evening.

In the soundcheck I went in and started having a go. It was going to be a great experience to play the song live with Planty's overdrive vibing. Planty's a proper channeller. There were a couple of Americans in the band and at the beginning of the soundcheck I was getting my electric fiddle sound right. I'm not sure if you know, but contrary to the vibe and image of rock there are many stars and stripes boys who for some reason want it all squeaky clean. The sound through my Mesa Boogie combo had starting sounding good but immediately one of the Yanks went all namby and whined:

"Hey ma-a-a-a-n, couldya turrrrn it deeoouwn a bid, my e-e-e-e-a-a-r-r-rs-zzz."

And the other incredible Yank heavy rocker bleated in:

"Ya-a-a-ah, ma-a-an, yeeou bedderrr turrrn id-deeayooon...."

I wasn't into turning it down. What was the point of an amp? To not be heard? Was it invented by American mice? Planty came up and I thought:

"I better turn it down, I suppose."

But he announced:

"Turn it UP, Noige. This is English rock!"

The Americans obsequiated themselves back into position and behaved a bit more like what they were. Guests in our country—and bombed out by a … violinist?

As I said before, playing with Plant was and is one of the highlights of my career. He summons something from astral planes and the core of the Earth. He's got muvvafukkin' ears too so is always responding to the musical situation while leading with his 100 per cent commitment and power of charisma.

The New Age Travellers

The next time I saw Planty Jacquie, Carmen (his daughter) he and I were having an afternoon/evening together near Kiddy. It was summer so it was lovely and we were in a pub. Suddenly the girls started talking dweeb, not a word wasn't wasted. Babies, children, clothes, holiday destinations, it was merciless. Plant and I had to take emergency evasive action. We quickly but politely took our beer outside (Banks's of course, we were in Worcestershire) and heard some music coming from somewhere. We followed our ears and were taken across the road to what looked like a little sports hall.

"Shall we check what's going on, Fisons?"

"Alright, sounds OK doesn't it?"

We entered the hall through the front door and found ourselves in a kind of lobby. The stale insidious smell hit us like a typhoon in the face.

"Phew, that's pretty strong."

"Horrible, Planty. Let's get out of here before it's too late."

Planty turned round in a hurry to sneak out and I made to follow him but before we could get out the door some uniformed jobsworth caretaker type of guy didn't want us to leave until he had had the chance to chuck us out with all of his unrivalled authority. He hurried to stop us leaving so that he could say:

"Oy, what are you doing? We don't want your type in here. You're not welcome. Get out!"

Now he really was somebody. He'd managed to chuck a couple of strangers out of his stinking dance hall.

"We were just leaving", Planty protested, towering over the jobsworth as if he were a little Jack Russell puppy.

"Well, you are now", the jobsworth said, unbelievably satisfied with himself, his power and his cleverness.

"Thanks for your hospitality."

We went back to the pub. Planty had been very humble and I couldn't be bothered to make any trouble either. We both just wanted to enjoy our pint, and possibly another after that.

We headed towards our table hoping that the girls' dweebing had run out of steam. Somehow the incident got reported in *The Mirror* or *The Scum* the next day: "Robert Plant and Nigel Kennedy chucked out of dance hall mistaken for New Age travellers."

The Wolves Phantoms

The next incident which happened with Planty wasn't, in fact, with him at all.

I got back from tour and found my gates sprayed in claret and blue from the cans I had been using to spray paint my Jag. (If you get a Jag it's essential to correct its colour if necessary). The graffiti lacked the refinement and cultivation that one finds in London or New York and it was fairly obvious who'd done it. There were references to Wolves but in our colours because of the beautifully limited colour scheme I had chosen for the car. Wolves are a team of great history and are bullshit free as a club but my life hasn't brought me loads of Wolves fans as friends. It had to be Planty and his kid Logan. It wasn't great artwork but any artwork by the Plant family in claret and blue is OK with me so I left it like that. It was like my very own Banksy but better because it was in Claret and Blue, and painted before anyone had heard of him. It was, though, probably created under the influence of a pint of Banks's.

It was quite a long time later that Planty told me he'd popped round to see me, found the gate and front door wide open, rang the doorbell to no response so went in and found … nobody … a ghost house. He then turned off all the lights, locked the front door behind him, locked the gate and left.

It turned out I'd left for the tour and forgotten that closing doors, gates and turning off lights is quite a good idea and very traditional. Lucky it was in Malvern and not in London, mind you, did the same thing there too and no harm done there either.

Just no Rock God to shut up shop on that occasion.

Kashmir at The Royal Albert Hall

At the time of writing, the last music Fisons and I made together was a memorable performance of 'Hey Joe' and a barrier breaking version of 'Kashmir' as part of a Bubbly Jubbly all creatures great and small fukkin' gig I was doing at the Royal Albert Hall in 2017.

Planty and Jean-Luc Ponty were my mega guests. Ponty from my jazz background and Planty from my muvvafukka background. Ponty played an amazing set with me, my violin God is playing blindingly as well as ever and I love playing his space age trance fusion classic with him, aptly named 'Cosmic Messenger'. Right now, though, I will not digress and will tell you about the inspiration of working with Planty.

Planty's approach to 'Hey Joe' is stunningly original and is like the calm before the storm. His two Bristol monsters, Justin Adams and John Baggott, were fantastic and helped sculpt massive sonic canvases for us. Somehow, in Plant's version one really gets an angle on the meaning of the lyrics, which hit home far stronger than in anyone else's version including Jimi's. He also veers away from all that heavy guitar shit that everyone's done over and over and over.

The version of 'Hey Joe' was Planty's arrangement whereas the arrangement of 'Kashmir' was going to be mine. Our performance of 'Kashmir' was historic. It was the first time that Plant had performed it without the involvement of Jimmy Page. I didn't realise this until after the performance which was lucky. There was anyway enough pressure getting an arrangement together of this historic song, it had to be worthy of the amazing Robert Plant. No other concern would've been as significant as that, I guess.

The first thing to do was actually write the fukkin' arrangement. I had an orchestra (21 players), my band (two guitars, drums and bass) and myself. Unless I got some notes down on paper to put in front of everybody there really wasn't going to be much noise. I worked fukkin' hard and after three or four days I'd done it, perfect timing with two days left before the first rehearsal. Planty was pleased to hear that it was ready.

Then, overnight, I had a nasty revelation that what I'd written was a pile of shit with no imagination or originality whatsoever. I only had two days left—I started texting Planty, I was starting again from scratch:

> Do you want some Arabic style in it?
> Do you want Moroccan style?
> How long do you want the middle section?
> Shall I double up the bass line with the 'cellos?
> SHALL I PANIC AND TEXT YOU LOADSA QUESTIONS?

To which Planty replied very succinctly: "It'll all be OK, maybe you should get some sleep, mate."

Rehearsals were great. My improved arrangement was fantastic (worth a couple of sleepless nights) and Planty's radar caught hold of it immediately. His confidence and selflessness lifted everyone, and as you can imagine, working with him was an incomparable high. His perception levels are right up there, enabling him to bounce off what people are doing musically and to create the necessary space. Planty has ears second to none and is a brilliant listener.

Obviously Plant was going to be brilliant. He has a love affair with his fans which is a two way street. The emotion is naturally out there. He is a shaman-ista—energy flows from the ground to his soul and out to us. He is perceptive like fukkk. Another muvvafukka quality he has is trust and, as you know, trust begets trust.

In this performance he told a story from way above. Yes, a story. Not a technical trick, like there so often is in jazz or class music in which the words just might give an obscure clue as to what the story is about, instead of the singer really telling and feeling it. Planty told it from his soul.

What a beautiful night, and it meant something to me that Planty trusted my hands to look after his first 'Kashmir' without Jimmy Page. The icing on the cake was that a mutual friend told me that Page had loved it and had said that my arrangement was the way forward with 'Kashmir'. As a rock n' roll fiddler one can't get a better endorsement from the two Kings of Rock. By Appointment to Their Majesties The Zep.

Transitoire—Musical Prejudice

I'm a muvvafukka who can play anything on the violin. Whatever I hear I can emulate. Bird calls, fire engines, brakes squealing, speech, babies crying, dogs howling, people laughing, crying, talking boringly—and because of that instinctive assimilation that my ears are capable of I can play any type of music (that I want to). Having ears like that isn't particularly encouraged or taught in Class' music—I don't know where I got these fukkin' ears from!

Being able to hear the beauty or greatness in so much music means that I have never been able to understand musical prejudice any more than the prejudice of one human being against another. Of course, as a human being I've been subject to prejudice and as a musician I've been subject to plenty of it—from small minds and closed ears on both 'sides'. Reading the list of musical world leaders I've worked with in every genre of music, however, soon puts the mental midgets[14] in their place. I apologise for nothing, your honour, I am a serial offender of playing good music in every genre.

Meanwhile, the musical prejudices weevil[15] on. Class' music, for instance, while benefiting from government subsidies unheard of in any other type of music, instead of enjoying its comparatively unearned privileges, finds time for plenty of hang-ups about rock music. I'll list their Top 10 in a moment! Jazz is nowadays given less of a rap from the Class' boys because not many jazzos seem to have a good time when playing it—hence it MUST BE SERIOUS!! There's nothing like a good old sanctimonious grimace to show how "serious" you are.

Rock also has a few hang-ups about Class' music and I'll list their Top 10 grouches as well! I should point out that the prejudices I'm about to list emanate not from good musicians but from shit listeners so prone to the same prejudices.

Being rather good at both Rock and Class' music, I have heard these prejudices from both sides....

---

14 Dear sensitive one, please don't cry. In this case midget applies to the size of the mind, not the person.

15 To WEEVIL = to eat away insipidly at the body or a part of it. This verb appeared in the English language five minutes ago.

The Top 10 Class' Music Anti-Rock Music Prejudices	The Top 10 Rock Music Anti-Class' Music Prejudices
(i) Rock is a cheap kind of music for simpletons	(i) Class' music is expensive and is for people who are desperate to look clever
(ii) To be popular is distasteful	(ii) If you don't sell records you're shit
(iii) A melody is lowbrow and doesn't show cleverness	(iii) Class' music fukkers aren't clever enough or talented enough to write a melody
(iv) Electric is way over the mark, absolutely beastly noise from the lower classes	(iv) That acoustic sound is weedy
(v) No rocker can play all our notes, their techniques are non-existent	(v) The Class' fukkers can't choose the right notes
(vi) Dancing to the music is disgusting, standing is too much to stand	(vi) Sitting, or music which makes you sit, is dead people's shit
(vii) Rockers are uneducated and simple like their music	(vii) Class' people are overeducated, can't think for themselves and can't feel anything
(viii) All their music sounds the same	(viii) All their music sounds the same
(ix) Shit attitude (anti-social yobs)	(ix) Shit attitude (toff snobs)
(x) No taste in clothes	(x) No taste in clothes

Ever since I was a kid I thought 'How the fukkk will we get rid of racial prejudice, class prejudice etc., etc., if we are still stupid enough to be prejudiced against little things like genres of music? Either all prejudice goes or none will....'

I think that type of question and conclusion are still just as relevant today. Prejudice in one seemingly unimportant area legitimises and normalises prejudice in other areas and before we know it we've got prejudice all over the place.

There seems to be just as much prejudice now as when Lionel Hampton played with Benny Goodman but just with a slightly different slant. Have things moved on since then? Not if one blames one's misfortune on what one deludedly sees as another so-called type of person. If we haven't achieved, or even tried to achieve a worldwide meritocracy the system is to blame, not the lightness or darkness of someone's skin. In a more ideal world equality of opportunity would start from about year zero and if people really want this, where there's a will there's a way. Where there's an excuse there's no way.

Music suffers the same small-minded prejudices from vitriolic little spuds who are probably very frustrated and very unlikable little people. If they are happy to entertain prejudice in arts and culture they are, while trying to look 'politically correct', probably happy for prejudice to run rampant in areas such as race, class, gender, age, etc., etc.

In an ideal musical world there would be more fukkers interested, I mean really interested, in communicating musically in their own way rather than sticking to their petty little genres, and that finally brings me to THE WHO.

If the useless argument between Class' music and Rock had to be seen as a battle between two sides, there'd have to be a cretin[16] on each side to find two people who didn't appreciate THE WHO for all the different qualities they bring to music in general.

They have an incredibly strong structure to their music equal to that of any Class' music but they have a power and dynamism which could only come from Rock. The WHO invented a new type of music, something which hadn't and hasn't really happened in classical music since the '30s. The truth is sometimes BRUTAL.... OK ok OK ok OK ok OK ... Minimalism, I hear someone squeak. Sorry, come to think of it, Beethoven did that in the early 1800s, but with bollocks.

Despite what egghead propaganda might have us believe, real intelligence doesn't have to make something seem complicated. In fact, the opposite is true—to make something seem simple requires REAL intelligence. Clever bastards also have a propensity to be really, really boring. The WHO have REAL intelligence, they're not boring, their songs have phenomenal clarity and they are ... EXCITING. They also tell stories through their songs about real life and this gives them an unseverable connection with their fans. With their rock opera *Tommy* and also with *Quadrophenia*, The WHO are a band who have brought everything together and have made prejudice look as stupid as it really is.

The Who—Baba O'Riley

Muvvafukka of fukkin' muvvers! Roger Daltrey had invited me to play Baba O'Riley with The Who in the Royal Albert Hall in 2000. This was going to be a KILLA experience and, like always, I was going to give 110 per cent in the true Ron Saunders tradition and learn something along the way. What a way to learn ... on stage with The Who!

---

16 Dear politically sensitive one, I hate to think of you on the verge of tears. No offence is intended against real cretins. I use the term cretin only as a figure of speech. I love, or, at the very least, like cretins depending, of course, on their personality. I also like cretins in my soup...cretins...oops! I mean croutons...

Luckily I didn't have any other gig commitments and was free on the weekend in question for both the rehearsal and the gig. One consideration to make was that I had my four year old kid Sark for the weekend but Agnieszka was kool to look after him while I made the necessary noise with the band. Anyhow, how could it not be good for a kid to hear and experience epic music of that magnitude? Ask Sark now and he probably won't remember a thing about it but anyway, it was all systems go—READY TO RUMBLE!

The rehearsal was at Nomis Studios, Sinclair Road, West London. I arrived with Agnieszka and Sark and we all said hello. Roger Daltrey was charming and enthusiastic, Pete Townshend seemed obsessed with something he had to put right about his guitar sound, the Ox was very at ease in his self-contained way and Zak Starkey was relaxed and waiting to do something.

Daltrey was so considerate that he even gave Sark some earplugs. Treating him like a friend (a four year old friend!) he said: "You probably haven't heard us before, we're pretty loud. You put these earplugs in like this...."

He made sure that Sark got the hang of it and was made a fuss of which made me feel good as well as Sark. To this very day I haven't seen such considerate behaviour from somebody who had every right to be fukkin full of himself. A naturally gallant bloke.

Little did any of us know that John Entwistle wasn't to be long with us on this planet. What luck for me to have played with such a great bass player but so sad he left so early. Never pushing or desperate for a solo, he was a gigantic part of the sound of The Who. He was a bit like the Rock equivalent of another great bass player from the realm of jazz that I've played and recorded with, Ron Carter. You can recognise either of their distinctive sounds immediately from just a couple of notes, and without them the gap in the band would be bigger than the Grand Canyon. Technique at the service of the music, not as is all too common nowadays music at the service of ego and technique.

We started rehearsing and Townshend was fairly off with me from the start. It was NO to this, NO to that, he didn't seem to like anything I did and was seeming to try and coach me. If there are two things which don't work with me they are the word NO and the idea of coaching. (Re: coaching I have been to a couple of decent music schools and I've unlearned 80 per cent of what I was taught as being irrelevant to the music at hand and how my particular personality can serve it). At the same time I was very conscious of Sark being there and that he would probably have preferred to have been with me in the playground or the zoo (or something).

I was perfectly straight with Townshend: "Look, if you don't like the way I play, no problem. You being unhappy, me being unhappy, is no use to anybody. I'd just as soon be taking my kid to the park so I'm right into doing that. I'm happy to stand down and not play in the gig. That way no one need worry about anything and no hard feelings." I got that it was his song but it was my violin and it was going to sound like me no matter what anybody said.

I can't remember what was said after that but Townshend had changed his attitude and we had a really decent rehearsal. Someone later suggested that Townshend was giving me a hard time because I was Daltrey's guest and not his. I don't really subscribe to that. Maybe it's more to do with that after 50 years of playing your own song the way you're 100 per cent sure of it's not always easy to suddenly have a new cat come in doing his thing.

First impressions aren't always correct. My impression at that point was that everyone sounded a bit tired, old and within themselves. First impressions….

The next day was gig day. There's always a buzz about playing in the Royal Albert Hall. I'd probably done it about 15–20 times before but today was going to cap them all, I was playing with The Who. I had a good feeling about the gig, the little rut with Pete Townshend seemed over, and if it re-materialised I was ready to walk and have a quiet evening with Sark. It was a win-win situation, either of those possible outcomes would be fantastic.

Walking into the Albert Hall is pretty kool. From outside, the building looks great and when time allows I like to walk around it once before going in just to get a whiff of the magnitude and history of the building. Once you go in, you go down into the bowels of the building towards the dressing rooms. The dressing rooms are surprisingly moribund for such a venue, even the ☆'s dressing room is just like an extended cupboard. Open the window—what window? But that all adds to the charm of the place. Architecturally there is enough space in each room for a bottle of champagne so bravo to Fowke, Scott and The Royal Engineers.

The soundcheck went well, Townshend was in a decent mood, encouraging instead of discouraging, the Ox was calm and playing as the pillar of strength he always was and Daltrey was already getting ready to enjoy himself, musically probing the empty cavernous space inside this indoor amphitheatre. Not inspirational but a good rehearsal. The only problem was that Sark found out he could run around the whole Albert Hall in the audience walkways. I don't know how many circuits he did but he took some catching up with.

The Who still hadn't been breaking any sound barriers and I left for the afternoon thinking: "The gig will be good, we know what we're doing, but it'll be a shame if that energy The Who have always been known for is still missing."

I got back to the venue in plenty of time to make sure my radio pack was working and talk the required technical shit with my soundman, then there was a fair amount of heel kicking to be done before The Who's set list reached 'Baba O'Riley'. I had an all areas pass so rather than mooking backstage I decided to go and hear The Who from the midst of the audience but close to the front like in a proper Rock gig. I mean, how often do you get to hear an exaltedly great band like that in a proper venue, as opposed to the normal aircraft hangar or stadium? (Let's face it, aircraft hangars are only good for aircraft (Bill Withers will tell you that)[17] and a stadium is only good for football, Jack Grealish will tell you that.

---

17 That's for the music connoisseurs. CLUE: Mr Withers is the only famous musician who could tell you that.

The audience are treated like money sheep in those personality free piles of shit).

And lo and behold—The Who WERE KILLING IT.

TOWNSHEND's guitar playing was like lightning bolts striking at us in the audience, futuristic, earthy, power-controlled but uncontrolled, pure energy with no pretty shit.

DALTREY was radiant, confident, projecting. He was the storyteller creating a three-dimensional narrative, with a delivery worthy of The God School of Acting assisted by Stanislavsky.

ENTWISTLE had his normal fluid structural serenity. Rock solid and stone still he was the stabiliser in that huge circuit of energy.

ZAK STARR was bringing a whole new brand of drumming to the picture. This completed the canvas far more imaginatively than just copying Keith Moon. No explosives were used. Proper great shit!

IT WAS COMPLETELY AMAZING!

The fukkers had been saving it for the gig. I should've known! Even in my experience a phenomenal unsurpassable rehearsal had been the death of many a gig. Once you start trying to play as well as in the rehearsal you know you're fukked. Now I knew I would be playing in a gig to be reckoned with—possibly on a historic level.

The set was progressing and 'Baba O'Riley' was approaching—I returned backstage and waited in the wings. Then it was time to do damage. As you know, the fiddle doesn't start playing until the final section of the song. That meant I had plenty of time to soak up the atmosphere in the hall and admire The Who's stagecraft and relationship with the audience from right in the middle of it.

I started playing and the magic infused and transcended everything. I could see Daltrey getting right into it and Townshend supported me in the build in a way that no other guitarist could. There were a couple of windmills, he gave more and more and my solo went more and more power pagan. I was carried away by the collective power of the band and the solo was a triumph! I even finished exactly together with Townshend—our last flourish completely synchronised.

There you are—a shit beginning turned into a proper muvvafukka and I have a gold album, nicely mounted, framed and displayed that the guys sent me from sales of the video/DVD.

Compliments came in from all types of creatures great and small after that performance, many saying it was the best live version of 'Baba O'Riley' that The Who had done.

ALL MUVVAFUKKAS OF THE WORLD UNITE!

JOB DONE!

EMF / Neil Tennant (Honorary Killjoy And
One of The Best Songwriters I've Never Met)

There are a fair few arguments concerning stature, genre and whatever to suggest that the subject of this story doesn't belong in The Aristocracy of Rock category—but I'm putting it in here as a moment of light relief even though one object in it was definitely medium heavy.

First I would like to say that 'West End Girls' is one of my favourite songs. I can still listen to it today and get just as much pleasure as when I first heard it. I think that constitutes a classic. It's atmospheric and the string synths, by the way, sound far better for the job than any orchestra could—same with Stevie Wonder's 'Songs in the Key of Life', an orchestra would spoil the rhythm and honesty of it … so now to this light medium heavy story.

At an EMI convention somewhere within the borders of mighty Ingulund or Wales I had the good fortune to meet up with EMF and we got on really well. Their single Unbelievable was unbelievable fukkin' killa and is also still one of my favourite songs of all time. The destinies of EMF, a Pet Shop Boy and myself were going to become momentarily intertwined.

EMF and I were hanging in one of our rooms recreating when our eyes settled on the TV. We unanimously decided, what with all the crap on TV, that the only way worth watching it would be to watch it hurtling down from the roof into the outdoor hotel swimming pool. It was a great, honourable and worthwhile venture for all of us. It was going to be worth watching at the same time as accurately representing how quickly TV was going downhill.

We must have made a fine picture crawling around like ants on the slanted tile roof (I can't remember how we got up there), carrying the burden of the television. Not a yuppie-tech flat screen, a proper one with tubes as innards, more like a human.

Our minds were on lobbing the fukker into the middle of the pool.[18] With the steep gradient of the roof, despite the best effort of our collective strength to influence the parabolic curve of the TV's descent into the water, it landed on the lip of the pool, exploding on the concrete edge. This ruined the chance we desired of watching the TV on the bottom of the pool but it did have a high impact effect and it went everywhere. The pool was in the courtyard surrounded by guest rooms so the noise reverberated around the space for quite a few seconds like in an echo chamber. A lot of faces appeared at various windows to see what had happened. The whodunnit factor wasn't exactly huge—we were cackling on the roof like a flock of grounded crows and the scattered components of the TV explained what had happened to any enquiring minds.

To cut to the crux, Neil Tennant had been enjoying a poncing revelry on his

---

18 If you are very impressionable, dear reader, please do _not_ try this at home. Indeed upon indeed, do _not_ try this anywhere. This job is for super heroes only…

terraced area in front of his room which faced onto the pool. Suddenly his idyllic moment had been rather rudely interrupted by the media explosive detonating only a few metres away from him. To him it must have been one of the most explosive television shows he'd ever seen or witnessed. Luckily he wasn't on it and it wasn't on him. Nevertheless, his experience must have been devastating, traumatic, fearsome, loathsome, humiliating, or in other words having his revelry disturbed might not have been very, very nice. One could say that a sitting Tennant became a shitting Tennant.

No harm done, except that people couldn't dip their dainty little toes into the water until the debris was cleared. Some EMI gophers came and broke up the party, which wasn't a very original move but they probably didn't have sufficient imagination to take our good work forward. They also, I suppose, had to protect their jobs of taking 80–90 per cent of every copy sold.

Tennant was obviously not having as much fun as we were (didn't look the type) because, to add insult to injury, he came out with some sanctimonious claptrap to the press to make himself seem venerable and wise. Something along the lines of how immature we were. That's why he gets honorary killjoy status although I hope he's outgrown that problem by now (in which case the award can be passed on to innumerable music business or BBC types of dubious nature).

Look where all that form of posy maturity, which the TV blurbers and the bleeping artists display, has gotten us—fukkin' nowhere!

ALL IMMATURE PEOPLE OF THE WORLD, UNITE!

Jon Lord, Purple, Smoke

I had just started a musical partnership with Jon Lord, he had things to say in symphonic, I had things to say in Rock. We were both fukkin' versatile. We had played together in a couple of gigs and formed an understanding which had absolutely incredible potential, it was the beginning of something monsta great—and then he was gone.

What a tragedy for all those around him that he had to leave when he had so much more to give.

As with all people who have enough about them to have achieved their vision, Jon had no airs and graces. The ones to beware of are the mediocre ones who have to compensate for their lack of quality and ability by attempting to look more important than they are. JON LORD WAS NOT ONE OF THESE LOWER TYPES!

He was humble, a good storyteller but not a gasser and ... WHAT A FUKKIN' HAMMOND PLAYER!! There's a unique British school of keyboard players which includes people like Steve Winwood, Keith Emerson, Tony Banks, Georgie Fame, Alan Price, Rick Wakeman, Chaz Jankel and Jon Lord was right at the forefront. What made him one of the leaders amongst even this select group was his song writing and his soloing and of course his Deep Purple bandmates, none of whom could be called slouches!… and he wrote 'Smoke on the Water', fukkit.

More people on this planet know that riff than that Jesus isn't a Brazilian football player, well, not primarily.

We met up to rehearse in Germany where we were doing two or three gigs. One of the big honours as far as I was concerned was that he was into doing 'Smoke on the Water', something that he was loath to do with anybody normally. It was nice to see that he rated me highly enough to know that I'd add something rather than take it away. Also, because my band had no singer and featured my electric violin as the primary instrument we wouldn't be competing with what Ritchie Blackmore and Ian Gillan had done in the original. If there's no vodka and only whiskey one has whiskey and lo and behold—a new direction. Fuck One Direction unless it's a French tank going backwards.

As well as 'Smoke on the Water' we played a few of my numbers including 'The Hills of Saturn' (everyone inanely goes on about the rings but I presume there's a terrain there too.… Bath University didn't make me a Doctor for nothing) and 'The Invaders' (for one excuse or another people are continually suffering invasions. This song evokes the brutality of the invaders and the dreams of freedom held by the invaded).

I had a good band (NKQ). I learned more from them than they did from me because I'll learn from anything and always want to push it. I would, though, have liked to have seen them learn more from me, it would've been to their benefit. We had a proper level but Jon, in an unobtrusive way, raised it like a muvvafukka.

One thing I noticed was that my keysman was half Jon's age but sat down, Jon was twice his age but STOOD UP. That immediately stated that we now had somebody else proactive in the band apart from myself.

I had got my piano player playing Hammond because the sound is good for a fair few of my songs, the sustain of the Hammond works with the sustain of the electric violin. My guy was doing quite well on it. Then Jon started playing and it was like night and day. Fukkin'ell, we had Rock Aristocracy in our midst. He vibed the show up, man. He turned the energy of the place up to eleven. Jon was standing there, no histrionics or silly faces and the Hammond was zapping it … K'POW! BRRRAM!

And my fiddle reached the stratosphere with him.

We made some proper fukkin' sounds.

I always have a bit of a rumpus after the gig. I noticed Jon had one glass of wine but didn't party. Maybe he was already suffering, one certainly wouldn't have known from his behaviour that anything was wrong.

I was just looking forward to the next time we played together. We were talking about doing some huge fusion big symphonic rock thing.

Might've been. Could've been. Should've been. They're all irrelevant but sometimes I can't help wondering … Anyhow, what a gentleman and creative genius he was/is.

Donovan

Meeting Donovan was a beautiful experience and it took no time at all before we became great friends. I love that he'll get his guitar out and share music absolutely fukkin' anywhere. The pub, the beach, the airport, the Royal Albert Hall. Music is music is music is music to this man. His wife Linda is wonderful as well, wouldn't say bad about anyone and she hangs in the same cosmic cloud as Don. They are pre-destined life partners.

Our paths first crossed because my girlfriend Brixeeeee recorded 'Hurdy Gurdy Man' and she had me come in and play the solos in the middle and end instead of the expected guitar solo. I think it was produced by John Leckie, certainly the trancy grooves would suggest as much. In addition to my electric solo I overdubbed a little psychedelic acoustic orchestra to enhance the vibe.

It was kool for an ex member of The Fall to be doing his song in a more current version and Don appreciated that. When Don said that he loved Brixie's version we were really excited. You can't get a better endorsement than one from the composer themselves, and this was a fukkk of a composer. It was after this that we got together with The Don.

For some reason *The Late Late Show* in Dublin got wind of the single and Brixeeeee, Donovan and I ended up doing it live on TV for the whole of Ireland. Not in this case, but in general, I think singers take up too much space in most songs and that a better song consists of an everlasting, never finishing, humongous, gigantic muvvafukka of all muvvafukkas violin solo! On this occasion my wish came true, well, almost. In a live transmission there's no going back and doing it again so when a camera ran over the mic cords, ripping the mics out of the mic stands, it left Don and Brixeeeee scrappling on the floor for their mics and left me able to slip in a few more notes. Oh, learned one, when you say less is more you could possibly be right. It just wasn't cricket and it wasn't Rock, Jazz-Rock, jazz or any other type of music really! It was fukkup music … We didn't look bad though....

Since those days Don, Linda and I have had proper good times in Ireland, Germany, Morocco, Poland and even Ingulund!… loads of places. He and Linda are free spirits.

It's heart-warming to have a friendship like the one we have. I guess you could say in a natural way we have a lot in common. We both completely changed the genres we were involved in to create new ones, him coming from folk and me coming from jazz and classical with Rock waiting right there in the middle for both of us.

Another thing we have in common is the beautiful uplifting inclusive quality that enables music to bring people together and feel … GOOD! I'm not taking any credit for that—it's just an energy which is already there for anyone of the right disposition to tap into.

Whingeing "Isn't life tough" musicians are nowadays a dime a dozen. Have you noticed that the music of people or peoples who've had a really, really hard time is incredibly uplifting? For instance Klezmer, Romani, Sudanese, Irish, early Blues, Motown, and on and on. It's only the kats with two cars, the latest phone and two computers who seem to have the time to think, "Hmmmm … how can I write as depressing a song as possible? … Oh, I know, it was really tough today … I got out of the wrong side of my super king size bed this morning and I was only able to eat enough bacon for four people…." These depressing bastards swarm out of the woodwork at any opportunity. Look at jazz nowadays. Are they presenting more gloomy shit than the guys[19] from yesteryear? YES. Do they live in worse conditions than the guys from yesteryear? NO—NOT EXACTLY! Are they more intelligent? NO!! In fact, it's far easier and less intelligence is required to do gloomy shit.

There's a great quote from an acting teacher, whose name I can't recall, which applies equally to music and it goes along these lines.…

"If being able to cry was the measure of a great actor then my Aunt Jean would be one of the greatest actors in the world."

I rest my case, your honour. Even outside the arts, in my life I've had the misfortune to have been in close proximity to too many full time professional 'victims' who cling pathologically to their whining blame game.

Donovan has had a fair few heavy challenges in his life, but does he dump them on his friends or listeners? Like all great song writers, in Don's songs there's a romantic radiance underlying the song and you can feel happiness even if it isn't a knees up. One can see that in Zep, Beethoven, Marvin Gaye, Talk Talk, Jay-Z, Fats Waller, Miles, etc., etc. If you listen to the best songs of Don's you know THEY WILL LIFT YOUR SPIRIT. Oy, Don—it's time to catch up. Hope all's kool.

Interlude
Donovan vs Dylan

I don't know which imbeciles in the '70s started this silly game of a beauty contest between a dolphin and a lion, but it definitely happened. Maybe it was because of something so lowbrow as that they were both guitar playing singer songwriters. WOOPIDOO! What a good reason (NOT). Just to humour a few wound up old fogies I've decided to have a go at the game too!

---

19 Sorry, don't cry, you can't catch me there, my corrector. Guy = any gender.

DONOVAN	Vs	DYLAN
Beautifully skilled guitarist and musician		Cutting-edge poet
Open and optimistic		Razor sharp and critical
Always mixed electric and acoustic genres		Criticised, like Miles, for going electric[20]
Cosmic, subconscious, HAPPY		Pushing, searching, edgy
Went to India in the 70s for a long period		Didn't go to India except for 2/3 weeks in early 90s

COULD EXPLAIN A LOT!

Both can enthral you just with their voice and guitar

Jean-Luc Ponty

When I was 14, an au pair boy at The Yehudi Menuhin School saw my interest in jazz and other types of music. The formal listening, and what we were allowed to listen to in our common room, ranged from Bach to Beethoven, so one could say we had a strict listening diet of Bach-hoven.

The above mentioned kat had something that no one else had, in fact two things. Good taste in music and—a record player. Three things! He also had a record collection, a great one. This bloke was a bit anarchic looking and may have felt sorry for all of us hothouse flowers, he probably wanted to corrupt the system and in me he found the right bloke. Courtesy of the kat I started hearing albums of interesting, challenging stuff. Mingus, Zappa, Joni Mitchell, Tangerine Dream, Ornette Coleman, Mahavishnu Orchestra (with Jerry Goodman at that time) and he said if I liked jazz violin I should listen to Jean-Luc Ponty. At that point I only played swing like Stéphane Grappelli or, to be honest, more like Stuff Smith.

I found an album called *Violin Summit*, which for a young fiddler like me was a dream, it had Grappelli, Stuff Smith, Svend Asmussen and the young aforementioned fukker called Ponty all playing together in a live gig. Each of the first three violinists was an absolute world leader but the 24-year-old Ponty just killed it, head and shoulders above the other comrades. There were times during his solos that the audience couldn't restrain themselves, he was kicking

---

20 I know what that feels like! Ow, the vitriol!

up such a storm. His playing was more like a horn and sounded more like bebop or hard bop than swing, which is what most fiddlers were playing at that time. I loved his harmonically adventurous, no bullshit style of music making. When listening to Stuff Smith and Jean-Luc it became clear that the violin didn't have to be a decorative pretty boy icing on the cake thing, it could be a really strong functional part of a band, as important as any other instrument.

Jean-Luc's musical development then saw him take the violin into other realms, using electronic effects such as flange, delays, chorus. He defined what modern violin playing is today, and in the world of jazz he must be the most influential violinist ever, forever.

Like Stéphane, Joe Venuti, B. B. King, Casals and Rubinstein before him he has remained at the height of his powers for more than 50 years. There is no self- satisfied complacency in this man.

Two more things about Jean-Luc Ponty's way in music. In jazz his harmonic sense and mastery are unmatched. His intonation is also musical and perfect. In jazz no one comes near him, he has single-handedly changed the nature of the violin and made it relevant.

I went to New York to become a better musician and violinist, and even though it wasn't part of the Juilliard curriculum, meeting Jean-Luc Ponty when I was 17 certainly opened doors of my perception which hadn't been opened in the corridors of that mercenary career school.

Jean-Luc had also been encouraged by Stéphane Grappelli so when Jean-Luc was rehearsing and playing in NYC with John McLaughlin's Mahavishnu Orchestra (which he had just joined) Steff put me in touch with him.

My first meeting with Jean-Luc was in a downtown rehearsal studio where Mahavishnu were rehearsing and putting material together for a new album which I reckon was *Visions of the Emerald Beyond*. This different music was a world away from all the gypsy jazz stuff I was beginning to feel a bit shackled by. As well as hearing the music, the great thing about the more relaxed circumstance of a rehearsal was that in one of the breaks Jean-Luc had plenty of time to show me his complete electric setup with all the guitar effects etc. This opened a new world and within a month I had got my own second-hand Barcus Berry electric violin and when busking money allowed, I could gradually increase my collection of Boss guitar pedals. The delay pedal was the most significant addition for me. One can build a whole sonic landscape (or soundscape) with it and also develop interesting cross rhythms. Of course, wah wah and distortion are more rock 'n' roll and equally essential. With this panorama of sound there was a quick escape from the normal frilly Hearts and Flowers shit generally expected of the violin.

It was kool of Jean-Luc to make the time for a young muvvafukka like myself. It yielded results in the future, without his inspiration I wouldn't be re-realising Jimi Hendrix and there would be a huge area missing from my own compositions and performing life.

Luckily, we have played gigs together on quite a few occasions. As far as I am concerned, playing with Jean-Luc has been more important to me than playing with Menuhin or any dumbfukktors. The other great violinists I met as a kid all had beautiful and sometimes enlightening things to tell but it was all along expected lines, not that the expected lines were particularly bad, of course! Because of Jean-Luc and Stéphane Grappelli I was able to make giant steps forward in music and they were down to one thing … enjoyment of the journey of unexpected discovery. This had nothing, I verily mean NOTHING to do with curriculum or other people's expectations—two unfortunate afflictions caused by conservatoire institutions of any kind.

Jean-Luc Ponty was my other killa guest in that Royal Albert Hall gig I mentioned earlier in which Robert Plant and I did 'Kashmir' and 'Hey Joe'. Can you imagine what a night that was for me? To get two such inspirational muvvafukkas joining me on one night and make music with them one after the other? Suffice it to say that I had always wanted an involvement in music which could embrace all of that, and that ambition was fulfilled in no uncertain terms. My old friend J. S. Bach also joined me for a bit earlier in the evening.

'Cosmic Messenger', from Jean-Luc's album of the same name, is one of my favourite songs OF ALL TIME so playing that song with him was way out there. Another absolute masterpiece of his that we played was 'To and Fro'. We also played my song 'Solitude', both of us on acoustic. Another great honour—the most killa violinist adding a new dimension to my stuff. Playing with the most influential violinist of two centuries and the mutual respect we have for each other are priceless things.

Jean-Luc's super sophisticated harmonically incisive approach and my, at times emotional and other times get into 'em, fukk 'em up way of doing things, make for a great juxtaposition of styles. We both love our work, work hard, and know what we want, and we enjoy listening to each other's playing. It's a top-level meeting of minds. The musical world would be a right fukkin' boring place for me if Jean-Luc hadn't opened my mind when I was a teenager.

I remember one of the first times I worked with Jean-Luc was in Switzerland in St Prex Festival. I had gotten a small orchestra together as well as members of his and my bands and because he's just that little bit older than me I decided to prepare all the musos so that there would be a good, clear and strong structure for Maestro Ponty to play over when he arrived.

I was preparing the musicians to play Jimmy Hendrix's 'Third Stone from the Sun' which in my version alternates between trance groove and heavy hypno-rock. I'd got everything going and was taking a solo which was cooking hotter than Le Gavroche. Just at the climax of my solo Jean-Luc and his beautiful wife Claudia walked in, momentarily they were like two rabbits in the headlights and then they bolted, reversing quicker than a French tank out of the door. This wasn't the ma non tanto, hypersensitive attitude of the Americans with Robert Plant. Jean-Luc hadn't expected Rock, just jazz and maybe a nice little bit of la-di-da classical loveliness. They crept back in again like after a bomb drop and we started to work. As it happened all went supakool and by the end of the couple of gigs we were playing he was playing louder than me!

Just one last word about Jean-Luc and his family. Claudia and Jean-Luc are both such gracious people, devoted to each other and respectful and encouraging to everyone around them. If that's what marriage is all about then it is a kool institution and I've never seen a better example of it. They also have an incredibly gifted and beautiful daughter, Clara, who I have also worked with. She is a wonderful piano player.

At the time of writing Jean-Luc and I are trying to arrange more gigs, so by the time you are reading this we might have something to talk about.

Come along....

Roy Wood

I met this beautiful fukka a while back in the directors' box at Villa Park after a match. It might have been in the amazing Ron Atkinson era. As far as I can recall he confessed to having been a Bluenose until his daughter made him see sense which helped him evolve over to the correct side. UTV. We can forgive one of the founder members of Brum-pop and ELO pretty much anything.

As with almost all the other Aristocracy of Rock that I've worked with (and become friends with) Woody has achieved amazing things, has absolutely nothing to prove, is down to earth and a proper normal guy. He loves music and is always up to something creative.

We got on great when we met at Villa Park and since meeting Woody I've always wondered what Claret and Blue looks like through red specs but never tried it yet through fear of making our team appear like Aberdeen or Liverpool. Anyhow, our love of Villa, good music and liquid refreshment was bound to bring us together to make music and that's exactly what happened.

Every year Roy does a gig in Symphony Hall, Brum, and he invited me to come and play with him in his show. We played 'Blackberry Way' (from his days in The Move) and all the guests played on 'I Wish It Could Be Christmas Every Day' (from his Wizard days).

The Move was a muvvafukka band, highly underrated, not by musicians, but by how music history is presented to us. In reality who cares? The music is still there proving itself. 'Blackberry Way' is a klassik. Like Elgar or Vaughan Williams, there is something 100 per cent English about Woody's song. Being from a different style harmonically, more influenced by Amerika and Germany, I'm still learning about Roy's way of doing things—so even though everyone thought what I did was OK, I'll do better next time, Woody.

Whatever any selfish pseudo-intellectual might say, everyone would love to have written a monster Christmas hit that gives happiness to everybody year after year. That song of his captures Christmas, not just musically but the whole feel of it. All age ranges love it. I've never written a hit but I can completely appreciate what unique skill that takes.

We've had a great few old times. After one night out in Brum (probably after either one of my or his gigs) we ended up carrying on in my Malvern place. After caning it a little bit I fell asleep in the not so early hours. At some point a few hours later I woke up, went to the kitchen and found Woody asleep on the floor on a beanbag. He was facing upwards like a vampire would in a coffin. I said to him: "Oy, Woody, how's things? Do you want some eggs?"

He opened his eyes and tried to focus straight up at me—it was then that I was struck by one of those surreal moments usually only seen in films by David Lynch. He opened his eyes and tried to focus straight up at me—everything seemed right and normal but there was something wrong. I looked down into his eyes. He'd opened his eyes and tried to focus straight up at me—it was kool, everything was straight, normal and kool, his eyes were red through his famous specs just as normal … but … wait a minute … there were no specs … but the colour was exactly the same. It was the recreation we'd been up to. There's nothing like a good spliff and there's nothing like a good pair of red specs which turn out to be completely unnecessary. I should point out that Woody has never smoked anything in his whole lifetime, not even a cig, which means that I must have smoked enough on that night to make HIS eyes go red! Eventually Woody put the specs back on and it made no difference....

Woody is an inspiration to so many people, he helps younger fukkers enjoy and play music. It's natural to him. He's one of those born multi-instrumentalists who can play anything they pick up. Guitar, bass, 'cello, sitar, saxophones, clarinet, recorder, oboe, bassoon, drums, percussion, bagpipes, French horn, crumhorn, double bass, keyboards … (darts, snooker, tiddlywinks, hide and seek). All those instruments have made a proper good sound in his hands. The more music the better. I'm really hoping to make more sounds with Woody before too long.

Boy George

I met some of Boy George's fans way before I actually met him. Around the time of 'Karma Chameleon' and 'Do You Really Want to Hurt Me' a greedy estate agent tried to sell me a cupboard he called a flat in St John's Wood on a street called Alma something. It was so small that if I'd have played a couple of notes on my fiddle it would have mentally disturbed loads of the nice bourgeoisie St John's Wood residents and possibly ruined the chance of more great songs from Culture Club. George would've had Bach in his ears and that could easily have killed any chance of original brain cell movement. One could tell Boy George was living there because outside the building a few girls were keeping a vigil until their beloved Boy George's return. Do you remember how so many of the girls used to dress up in exactly the same-ish getup as George? The hat, the blouse, the same dreads. The camera just loved Boy George (still does) and he didn't particularly mind the camera. That's why the girls copied him, they loved him as did everybody else.

We first met at Womad. This was before Womad became all corporate and painfully politically correct (i.e. a very long time ago!), and before they used one of my songs for their BBC transmissions without asking or crediting me. (If that had been done to a World musician there would have been an outcry, "Oh my Go-o-o-o-d! Yodel—exploitation, yodel—subjugation, yodel—brain-gyration, yodel—elimination, yodel—not one nation, etc., bleat, etc."

I played a bit of fiddle with him on 'Karma Chameleon'. I haven't mentioned to him that 30,000 of us Villa fans used to sing his song for Gabby Gabby Gabby Gabby Gabby Agbonlahor (our Birmingham born faster than fukk winger). Every home game his song would ring around Villa Park but although I'm not 100 per cent sure this is crucial information for him, 30–40,000 singing your song is better than a slap in the face with a wet fish.

We crossed paths once or twice over a few more years and then I had an amazing idea. I was recording the Nick Drake classic 'Riverman' and I thought "Eureka Johnson! Boy George!" It wasn't just a good thought, Boy George agreed to come in and record it.

For what it's worth, I've always been impressed by George's charismatic, sharp and intelligent sense of humour. He has always been an inspiration for having the courage to be himself. When he came in to record he had been through some of life's ups and downs so now had even more to bring to Nick Drake's musical table.

Even when he came to record for me he had to be back home for an 8 p.m. curfew.

When George started singing it was immediately apparent he was deeply into the song and was going to be brilliant. Compared with his Culture Club days he was somewhere between the old Boy George, Nick Drake and Tom Waits. There was this lived life quality to his voice now.

Sometimes as a producer less is more and this was one of those times. George and his music director John Themis got on with it and I was able to sit back and enjoy beautiful music making. John, incidentally, is a brilliant musician, and had put down some sensitive and sympathetic guitar before George did his vocals. It only took them a couple of hours to finish their revelatory contributions, that was the level of these guys' musicianship.

We got a fantastic version of the song which many people liked better than the original. One can't ask for more than that.

Predictably, EMI chose to completely waste the song. The type of employees they had then are the reason they're called Warners now.

With all the experiences that George has been through or put himself through there's lots more life story to put into his music. If he needs fiddle or strings I am willing and able.

Kate Bush

Kate and I met between 1985 and 1986 because her mum had seen me on *Wogan* (the main TV chat show in Britain at the time) saying that I preferred Kate Bush to Jennifer Rush, who'd just been on. Kate's mum told her that there'd been a lovely fiddler on who liked her music. Within a day or so Kate was in touch, probably through EMI with whom we were both signed at the time.

We became friends and I recorded violin for her on a couple of tracks at various times. It was inspiring and educational to see Kate working in the studio. There were three elements to her. First there was the calm, chilled easy going Kate who made someone like myself feel so at ease when recording for her. This amazing music was coming out of the speakers and there she was, just Kate, humble, kind and no maestra shit whatsoever.

The second element was Kate pushing herself to make the absolute best album ever and to achieve her incredible vision. If it required 200 per cent she'd give 200 per cent. She put herself second behind her art and she wouldn't spare herself when being of service to it. Whatever it took out of herself she'd give it.

Kate quickly became more of a studio creature, I'd always been more of a live gig creature. What we had in common was that absolutely no fukker was going to tell us what to do. The flipside of having had complete autonomy was that there was no boss telling you to work, one had to look after that aspect of motivation oneself. Having that self-motivation is the same quality required by an Olympic athlete or a world-class boxer. No one can instil the desire from outside, it has to come from within—there are no easy office hours to conform to and there's nobody to tell you to "Get on with it, deliver by 11.57 a.m. Friday."

Seeing Kate so committed in an all or nothing kind of way vindicated my approach which was the same. Her direction was studio recording, mine was live performance, but we had that 100 per cent commitment in common. Contrary to the belief instilled into us by rampant consumerism, comfort and convenience aren't everything.

There was also Kate's third element, being able to mix and finish the album, a process far more tiring and demanding than the recording part of it. A large reason why Kate was able to achieve such amazing results within all these elements was her boyfriend, bassist and engineer Del Palmer. He is obviously an amazing musician but also a phenomenal sound engineer. He had a remarkably phlegmatic personality, so whether it was in the studio or in 'real life' he was always there with his feet on the ground. Del always found a practical solution, great miking, great on the desk while Kate was vibing and being hospitable. Finding a functional way in the studio to bring Kate's vision into reality, his sound engineering was second to none. He also understood completely what Kate was aiming at. Lastly, I think it's sufficient to say that those beautifully mixed albums didn't mix themselves.

Another aspect of Kate is how much people owe her, especially female artists, stylistically I don't know what kats like Tori Amos, Alanis Morissette and a host of others would have done without Kate being there first. More important is the debt owed to her by all women in music. The Bush Baby, after Joni Mitchell, was the most important talisman for women to take over their own career and not be told what to do by an unqualified man sitting behind a desk. As a bloke it's always been a muvvafukka challenge to get a record company to see sense but as a woman it was ten times more difficult and unheard of. By taking over one's career I mean writing one's own songs, performing them, producing one's own albums, directing one's own videos, directing one's own shows, all of that and more. Kate was an enormous step forward for women's rights by example, not by bleating on and on.

With most of the musos I've been on about you have been drawn into various aspects of my malarkey and arsing around. Kate guards her privacy more than anyone I know—so there's nothing to talk about in that regard. Seeya, Toodle-pip!

Talk Talk

I was going to deliver a mini rant about the infantile and cheap name change of the Hammersmith Odeon but I won't because Talk Talk are such a deep band that I'll try to stick to the subject. I went there in the late '80s to hear Talk Talk. It was a fukkintastic show and amongst so many exceptional things I remember liking the way Mark Hollis humbly sat on the front corner of the drum riser to deliver many of his emotional, ringing, haunting, intimate but urgent vocals. Talk Talk were one of the few bands that could deliver a show of the same quality as on the album, something not many bands can do any more unless perchance they've made a shit album!

Getting introduced after the show it was clear that there was something going on. The record slumpany were well whingeing upset because the band hadn't played any numbers whatsoever from their current album release. I remember thinking:

"Good on 'em. It's their fukkin show after all and all of us loved it."

One of the band said to me: "It's good to meet you, Nigel, do you want to go for a drink? I know a good place, it's called As Far Away From The Record Company As Possible."

Talk Talk were being heralded by EMI as the next Beatles and there was some inane thinking along the lines that because they had a repeated name they would go down the same commercial lines as Duran Duran! I think the result was no no, maybe not not.

When I got to know them 'Life's What You Make It' was out lifting everybody. It took us on an eco-trip way before Greta Thunberg became the mistake she became. In fact it's the generations of Talk Talk and before which awakened and created the eco-friendly policies of today, we just didn't have silly names for them and we weren't divisive.

The next album they made was, in my opinion, one of the greatest albums of all time in any genre. The album, in fact, transcends all the genres in a deep and spiritual way that we can all understand, it's called *Spirit of Eden*. The record company, of course, adjudged it to be unsuitable and a disappointment. Using the Duran Duran repeat word formula, (I was in the EMI offices at the time when they first heard it), perhaps in a desperate attempt to commercialise the album they were saying "Oh dear, oh dear … the shortest shortest number is six minutes, six minutes long (long) … what can-can we do with Talk Talk?" They walk walked and fukked up their job of releasing one of the greatest albums in history.

It was on *Spirit of Eden* that Talk Talk invited me to play some violin. What I played was completely in the vibe but there's no way I can credit myself whatsoever for the greatness of this album. That was down to Mark Hollis, Tim Friese-Greene, Paul Webb and Lee Harris with some amazing blues harp from Mark Feltham.

Talk Talk's use of studio time was something the like of which I'd never seen before, for two days I just drank with them in the pub ending each evening with "Can you come in tomorrow?" On the third day I actually got 10 to 20 minutes of playing done and that's what they used. I'm very proud to be on that album—and I learned the technique of letting the bow just extremely lightly touch the string like a whisper with the mic an inch from the bridge, getting a sound I'd never heard from a violin before. I later used that technique on my own album *Kafka* and on more recent albums. It was an idea from Tim Friese-Greene and requires a superior bow technique to play consistently lightly at a non-existent volume.

The last time I saw anybody from the band was getting off the ferry with my mate K-Leb on the way to Dingle, County Kerry. On the way off the boat we'd stopped at the exit and were looking at everyone disembarking. A game of lookalike developed between K-Leb and I which involved pointing out someone and shouting "Oy, Curly!" if the kat looked like a Coronation Street character. "Oy, Jaws!" if it was a huge kat who looked like the James Bond character etc., etc. At some point a geezer came walking off the ferry who looked just like Mark Hollis from Talk Talk.

"OY! Talk Talk! Wot's up? How are you doing?"

"Fine thanks Nigel. It's been a while. How are you doing?"

It wasn't a lookalike, it was Mark Hollis for real, talking in his normal quiet understated manner. It turned out that he was going for a biking holiday in South West Ireland. He also said that he'd given up singing and was only playing clarinet. I thought that was interesting but a real shame for us as an audience that we were going to be deprived of hearing his unique amazingly musical and beautiful voice. Another thing he talked about having done was making an album live, the old fashioned way, with a combination of electric and acoustic. To get the balance right the louder the instrument, the further it was positioned from the mics (there was just one cross pair of mics). He gave me a copy. IT'S A MASTERPIECE. His use of silence and space was meditational, personal, humble and spiritual. There's no one like him around now.

Relatively recently he passed away, very sad but there will always be the intimate radiant spirit of his music, it lives on and shows us another world.

I believe the rest of the band are still individually doing original projects—I hope so.

Mark King

I hadn't seen Mark King in years. I had just sacked my bass player for being a miserable 200 per cent kunt and was driving down the M1 when I realised I was playing Hendrix the next day live to thousands and live on TV to millions. It was an "oh dear" situation.

Hendrix with no bass was, well … unfeasible … shit. Then I thought why not replace pretty good with the very best. A phone call from my agent, a phone call between Mark and I and the next day we were playing Hendrix together. Funk, rock, beautiful ballad bass, killer vocals and an attitude of only the best possible is good enough. What a privilege to work and enjoy magic moments with such a sublime musician. Muvvafukka.

ON TOUR WITH NIGEL: MEMORIES FROM ROLF, DAS KOBRA, BUSSALB

First Encounter

At the end of February 1991 I received a call from a promoter looking for guitarist to play some jazz on a live TV show the same evening and come to the studio straight away for some sort of 'audition' and rehearsal. He was not sure what was planned (sudden change of plan by N, originally he was going to do two short classical pieces with a string trio but he changed to one classical and one jazz standard), but he was obviously told to find a guitar player that could play 'jazz'. He said the artist was Nigel Kennedy the new superstar in classical music and it was his first big TV show in Germany. I had never heard the name before, absolutely no clue who he was. I had worked on TV Shows as a sideman for 'Stars', usually playback, live but fake. So here was a classical star wanting to play jazz, I was hoping for the best but actually expecting the worst, big ego little talent syndrome … that sort of thing. When I got there, backstage Alte Oper Frankfurt, I was led to his dressing room, it was steaming hot in there. Someone was leaning over a violin case with a hygrometer in his hand, Nigel (checking the humidity for his 'new' Guarnieri) We got introduced. "Hello I'm Nigel" … handshake … "I'm Rolf" … "have you brought a guitar?" … "Yes, what do want to play?" … He wanted to play 'All Blues' by Miles Davis. There were other musicians as well as they had just rehearsed the classical piece, the classical bass player was there as he could play some walking bass. The two of us kept playing, another Jazz Blues … good, some Who-style chords (I remember calling out modes like 'dorian' or 'mixolydian' to maybe help, thinking he must be well-educated … no need for that … he just played … and very good. I felt relieved … that guy was a real player … I said to him "That's great playing … you're a really good player" and I really meant it. He had a nice balance of leading and bringing in ideas and at the same time reacting to whatever I did. Back then I was an electric guitar player for the most part, but liked playing acoustic very much which was usually played as loud as possible to to match our usual volume level). Nigel was using changes in dynamics in a way that was new to me and I was quick to follow, I loved the effect. Up to this day I believe some of our best playing has happened after hours in hotel rooms, backstage or dressing rooms. We played a bit more ... Django Style ... it sounded good. I had no idea that he knew Stéphane Grappelli and had even played with him! For some odd reason there seemed to be a lot of common ground and it was definitely fun to play with him. We started talking, he asked me what I was doing, I told him I was a 'working' musician, being in a band, gigs, records, studio work etc. It turned out both of us had been to American music schools etc.

Before we left for some food "why not potatoes?"—I have no idea why I remember all this—he asked me what I was doing next week as he was on tour and wanted me to come along. I told him I could not do the first gig in Brussels on Saturday as I was playing at the Frankfurt Music Fair, but he was playing at the Alte Oper in Frankfurt on Sunday, so maybe there?

The TV show started 10 p.m. and Nigel was the last guest to be interviewed. The Classical piece before and the jazz tune after the interview then the host would say his goodbyes and off.

After the interview having played 'All Blues', before the guy said his goodbyes, Nigel started 'Summertime'... but what key? ... what groove? ... we hadn't rehearsed it. I looked at the bass player ... he didn't play ... I have no perfect pitch, Nigel does ... would have been useful now ... for me ... especially as the red light was on ... anyway ... I tried A minor ... think it worked.

After the show he wanted to go to a club, so we went to the Jazzkeller in Frankfurt and Nigel was jamming with the band that was playing ... 'All Blues' again. I remember Bob Degen on Piano and John Schröder on drums. When we left he asked for my contact, I gave him a card ... he stuffed it in his mouth and chewed it (yes)! I gave him another one.

Three days later, while working all day at the music fair, I called my answering machine (landline ... no mobile phones) and there was a message from his tour manager. I played the encores later that night, on the next day I drove to The Hague.

The Hague

Upon having 'joined the Tour' I was given the address of the venue, left home in the morning, drove to The Hague to play the gig in the evening. I arrived just in time, time to relax a bit as he was going to play the Bach D minor Double and the *Four Seasons* before he would bring me on. In the intermission he told me the first tune was going to be 'Sweet Georgia Brown' in D, but he would start with some classical stuff into some solo improvising and then into the tune, I should just listen for the cue. Alright, important information here, good to know the key as we hadn't played it yet and that was the only second gig so I did not know him that well. When it was time for our bit, he started with what he had called some classical stuff. It started real slow but it really building and while I was listening attentively, making sure I didn't miss the cue, I remember feeling that the guy was growing into a giant, the music which was coming out of that fiddle became bigger and bigger and so was the guy. It wasn't esoteric or anything and I had not had any beer yet, but it was funny and amazing at the same time, here was Nigel not so big in size and making a funny face while playing and one couldn't separate the player from the music or the music from the player. Also I remember thinking what a good sound it was and that I, sitting where I was sitting, probably had the best place in the whole venue. Suddenly he started to make weird noises I saw him loosening the strings on his bow and attaching them back on, but now the bow was beneath the violin. Some fiddle tune Irish, Scottish … can't remember. Back to normal he was just playing something that reminded me of 'Purple Haze' (I had no idea he knew or liked Jimi Hendrix), I was thinking I could jam along, but it was still the solo improvisation part, right? There hadn't been any cue yet, or had I missed it?

Eventually he started the melody of 'Sweet Georgia Brown', next we played 'Summertime' (… the 'James Brown version of Summertime' as he called it back then), 'Bag's Groove' … later I asked him what that classical piece was, and he said, pretending not to remember, 'I think it was the chaconne by Bach'. Back home I rushed to the next music shop to get the sheet music.

After the concert, we met in the hotel bar for something to drink and a little jam. I think we played 'Spain' by Chick Corea there for the first time. It was always like. What else can we play? Do you know this song? … or that one? Unfortunately he knew a lot more standards than I did (on another tour we were two guitar players and the other one carried a Real Book in a plastic bag around, just in case;) but 'Spain' both of us happened to know.

Nigel, Phil Bauldry the tour manager, and myself already had a few when the barkeeper announced the last order. Nigel ordered 20 beers … for the three of us … I thought to myself 'That's what you call professional'!

The last concert of that first tour was a secret gig at an RAF base. Some illustrious guests were there, Prince Edward and his wife, and Jasper Carrot. I can't remember what we played but Jasper Carrot joined us for an impromptu jam. After the gig a reception was held for the officers and their families to meet the royals and the stars. After the reception Nigel and Brixie were supposed to fly back with the royals. There was heavy security everywhere as it was shortly after the gulf war. I was talking to Brixie and Nigel was signing autographs when the Prince turned around and said, 'Good night everybody' and walked off, Nigel and Brixie followed. For a moment I thought, "wait a minute, the whole thing is over right now and I haven't had a chance to say goodbye yet?" I wanted to talk to Nigel briefly, but for a second everything switched to slow motion and before I could move my leg, my inner voice said "Freeze!!!" … I don't know how many guns would have been moved up against me. Ok, no "goodbye", but it ain't over till it's over.

Three months later his management tried to track me down, as I was hard to get in contact with at the time. I was on tour with my band and hardly at home, for a week or two they had tried to call me, and eventually sent a letter. So I called the office, and Nigel wanted me to go on a tour with him, Europe, Japan, Australia, optional US. Well, of course I said yes although I had to cancel a lot of my own gigs for almost three months. They sent me lots of papers, Japanese visa, Australia etc. In the end the tour never happened, because of some surgery that did not heal properly it got cancelled. Of course I wasn't happy about it but I didn't blame Nigel that the thing went wrong. They could have let me know about it earlier, but probably played it safe. I remember the tour manager saying, a week before the tour was supposed to start and there was no denying it wouldn't happen... "I really would not want you to loose any money on that"... Well, I did. I think by that time he had already changed to another company. But it ain't over till it's over. The next thing I heard was Dorit Adenauer's voice (EMI Classic representative for Nigel) on the phone, asking if I was available to play at the Bambi Awards.

Bambi Awards Germany 1991

Giorgio Moroder was going to present the award. Lots of famous people were there Audrey Hepburn, Claudia Schiffer, Karl Lagerfeld, Siegfried & Roy etc. In December 1991 the German Bambi Awards ceremony took place. There was a sound-check in the afternoon. Nigel had brought another guitar player from England, Sagat Guirey, (maybe he was not sure if I would show up after having cancelled a tour in the summer, maybe he wanted two guitar players) so there were three of us. I think we played only one tune together 'Purple Haze'. After the sound-check we walked back to the hotel which was just around the corner.

The complete hotel was booked for the event and there was a security check at the entrance ... show your badge etc.... Sagat went through, my girlfriend Susanne, myself, Nigel... not. He got stopped for wearing baggy trousers, Doc Martens with open boot laces, and a hat, a cap rather, that made him look a bit like Andy Capp (at least that's what I thought). His bodyguard had to explain.

When it was time to go back to the venue we took the limousines that were waiting outside, Nigel took the first one, Sagat, Susanne and myself the next one, the guitars went in the trunk. One minute drive—people waiting for the stars to to arrive—the cars stopped, Nigel got out of the car ... applause ... and followed the red carpet up the stairs into the venue ... our car moved on just a bit ... now ... our claim to fame ... we got out of the car, Susanne was waiting while we went to the back of the car to get our guitars out of the trunk, the moment I had pushed the button to open the trunk the car started to move and we were running after the car, screaming, waving hands while at the same time trying to catch our guitars, the driver stopped 20 metres down the way. As we walked back on to the red carpet I was wishing to be invisible having put in such a ridiculous performance.

The show started, we jammed in the dressing room while waiting, I remember we played 'A night in Tunisia' and 'Nuages' for the first time.

There was a Hollywood style stairway and the particular presenter would walk down the stairs with the award in hand to meet the star who had been announced and was waiting in the middle of the stage. We were waiting backstage and while I don't remember the exact order but Siegfried & Roy must have been on just before us since there were rather big cats running around backstage. When Nigel was announced we all went out, he wanted us to sit on stage while he was playing some Bach solo Sonata and then 'Purple Haze' by Jimi Hendrix. Giorgio Moroder was the presenter and he was going to come down the stairs when the music had finished. After 'Purple Haze' had finished, Sagat and me got up and left the stage, Nigel must have felt something was happening behind his back turned around and saw us leaving and since there was no one to hand over the award, followed suit. Meanwhile Giorgio Moroder walked down the stairs, Award in hand, on to an empty stage. Needless to say he wasn't and did not look amused.

Backstage there were still cats running around and lot of people were busy doing their thing, we waited because we knew he was following us, but they didn't. There even was a stage monitor, which showed … an empty stage. When Nigel appeared backstage they freaked "What are you doing here?" … You should be on stage … they pushed him back … it was hilarious … animals … people screaming … Siegfried & Roy … to me it felt like Blake Edward's 'The Party' coming alive … Peter Sellers must have been hiding somewhere.

Nigel received his award, every time I see this thing standing around in his house in London, usually close to the fridge with the drinks in it, I remember this evening … Cheers!

Tour in Germany 1992

For a tour of Germany in 1992 we met in Freiburg. Nigel and the rest of the band had rehearsed in his house in England. The band consisted of a string quartet, two guitarists, bass and percussion.

On the day of the first concert, in the morning a final rehearsal took place. It was my chance to acquaint myself with the music. It was a very eclectic set list ranging from Miles Davis and John Coltrane to three string quartets by Kreisler, Debussy and Ravel, Bartok's 'Romanian Folk Dances', Grace Jones, Jimi Hendrix, some tunes by Nigel and three compositions by the percussion player. A lot. Consequently, the concert could easily last up to three and a half hours … and it did on a few occasions. The three tunes by the percussion player, a friend of Nigel from his time in New York, were written especially for that tour, no one had ever played them before. Two of them had tricky time signature and groove changes.

During the concert when it came to the first of the tunes, Nigel asked his friend what the title was and he announced it. We got the music out, he counted it off, we started to play. 16 bars into the tune while playing my part … listening to what I was playing … I felt a bit uncomfortable … looking at the music I start to wonder where I was … lost … where is one … sh.. I goofed it. Looking around I noticed that the heads of my colleagues, all great musicians and sight readers, were slowly disappearing behind their music stands. Nigel who had heroically soloed up to this point in a desperate attempt to keep it together had to stop it in the middle. It turned out the composer had announced one tune but played another. Obviously his compositions were as new to him as for us. We played it again, with some smiling faces behind the music stands.

Stuttgart

I remember a concert in Stuttgart, during a tour of Germany in 1992; it was a few gigs into the tour. It was in the middle of the concert, and Nigel and the string trio were going to play a string quartet (Nigel being part of the quartet). The players had wireless clip-on-microphones attached to their instruments. Obviously the batteries were running low and they started to make weird noises. (There were monitors on stage and a PA for the audience). Roadies came on stage to change the batteries; it was a complicated procedure and took time. So Nigel decided to play a Bach solo, the 'Chiaconna'. This one is long. After a few minutes Bill Hawkes, the viola player, still waiting for his battery to get changed, got up and whispered, "I have to p…"… off he went, with his viola. One minute later, a calm moment in the 'Chiaconna' a roaring thunder was coming through the monitors and the PA system, for a short moment it was "what the heck is going on here" … then we realised who and what it was! 'Naked gun' live performed by NK & his Ensemble … everyone on stage was cracking. In the newspaper a few days later it said "there were waterfall like sounds from tape". Well, we knew better ☺.

Flying Schnitzel

I remember at least two occasions where the whole band had a late-night dinner in a hotel restaurant, way past midnight. When the actual meal was over it wouldn't take long before someone started to throw some leftover at someone else and soon after there were schnitzel in the air people jumping up and running around the table. I noticed in another corner of the restaurant two people talking, it turned out to be Udo Jürgens (famous singer) and Fritz Rau (German promoter). I found it funny, especially for Fritz Rau, having seen it (and more) with the Rolling Stones, the Who, Led Zeppelin etc., seeking privacy … but here we are. Anyway, a few days later the same happened in another hotel and guess who is sitting in a quiet corner of the restaurant. Udo Jürgens and Fritz Rau, I did not believe my eyes ... the two of them and the flying schnitzels again ... Deja vu? ... I wonder what they were thinking ... Kennedy and his bunch ... again. I think we met one of them again in another hotel.

European Film Awards 1992

In December 1992 the European Film awards took place in Berlin. Nigel and his girlfriend, Jaqui Turner, Mick Hutton the bass player, Peter Pettinger (a great pianist), Jade, a roadie from a former tour this time as 'tour manager', an English sound engineer and myself. We stayed in Berlin, but the actual live show and rehearsals were done in Babelsberg Studios/Potsdam. We arrived on Thursday for rehearsals, the show/live broadcast was scheduled for 20:15 on Saturday. Nigel had accepted to play under the condition that he and Jaqui could watch a football match in England on Saturday afternoon. Nottingham Forest against Aston Villa, (Jaqui's favourite team against his, Aston Villa won, as far as I remember). The production company had agreed and provided a Lear Jet. After the first rehearsal, back in the hotel we met in the restaurant. Being early December there were Christmas decorations on every table. After dinner Nigel started throwing things in our direction, he threw a fir cone at me. My unfortunate attempt to throw it back ended at the next table where a couple was eating, the gentleman I had hit wasn't amused and even worse, as it turned out was related to the hotel manager, to whom he obviously complained. That event led to a half-page-long article about Nigel with the headline "Punk violinist throws ashtray at hotel guest".

On Friday after another rehearsal Nigel, Jaqui and someone from the production company (to ensure they came back), left for England, the rest stayed in Berlin. They were expected to be back in Babelsberg while the show was already 'on Air'. Everything worked out as it was planned, we played our set, hung backstage with the ladies from 'Zap Mama'. After the official show the whole event changed to an organised 'after show' party. Nigel didn't approve and wanted to party in his suite. I remember hearing German actor Otto Sander trying to convince Wim Wenders ... this could be interesting ... to join us, probably hoping for some action, I guess Wim Wenders had other plans. We went back to the hotel and met in his suite, we were listening to music, there was food, talk ... party routine. I remember Mick Hutton in front of a mini bar for a peculiarly long time. When he finally turned around, he had all bottles out of that mini bar in his crossed arms. While shouting "All mine" he leaned back and poured all of it over himself trying to catch as much as possible. That seemed to be the signal for heavy air traffic ... vases, bottles, glasses, phones, food, vegetables ... champagne shower ... or any liquid ... on the carpet ... against the wall ... the British rock heritage. I remember sitting in a chair, motionless, watching the mayhem, when somebody said "Rolf, you're not wet" and started to squeeze an orange right above my head.

When there was nothing else to throw, room service was ordered and kicked over upon arrival ... Later the whole party tried to go for a swim, there was a private elevator that led directly to the pool. Luckily the door to the pool was locked, thinking of Brian Jones there could have been even more British rock heritage, mortal fame included. When that did not work, the scene moved to lobby of the hotel at 4 a.m. It was like a big hall, with big concierge desks, two bars, a grand piano in the middle, not many people at that time and not many staff. Everything in here sounded like being in an empty church. Nigel played on the piano, the staff did not like it, when they came he tried to order champagne they replied that everything was closed. When they refused to serve him he decided to help himself and tried to snag a bottle from the bar. All of a sudden two security guys were chasing Nigel commuting from one bar to the other. Mick Hutton was playing the piano and the staff did not like that either, so one guy tried to close the lid while Mick was playing, Nigel noticed that and started to shout "You're breaking the hands of my bass player" and tried to push him away from the piano. Meanwhile a blonde, Marilyn Monroe look-alike and her company had appeared and was thrilled to meet Nigel Kennedy and quite happy to find so many people not willing to go to bed and that so much was going on at that time (... so much happening ... so late at night). She probably felt she had come to the right place. It was absolutely bizarre. The next morning most of us left around 11. During check-out we called Nigel, not really expecting someone to pick up the phone. But to our surprise Nigel answered, we told him were about to leave and within three minutes he was downstairs ... that had never happened before.

Half-dressed, the violin in one hand, Jaqui on the other. In hindsight the better choice as 12 months later it still wasn't clear who would pay for the suite.

As said before there was a big article and headline about the whole thing in one of Germany's biggest-not-best newspapers. From "throwing ashtrays to wrecking a hotel suite and of course condoms all over the place!" I haven't seen any and I was there the whole time.

Nyon

Nigel had a double bill concert with Jean-Luc Ponty. The programme consisted of one set for each band and at the end both bands playing together. Travels on Monday, rehearsals from Tuesday to Friday, concerts on the weekend. That was going to be special, Jean-Luc Ponty is part of my musical upbringing, the second concert I ever went to, Zappa's 'Over-Nite Sensation' and 'Visions of the Emerald Beyond' by the Mahavishnu Orchestra being two of my favourite records from the '70's. Also I could hear traces of him in Nigel's improvising, maybe something that sounded familiar to me right from the very first time we played together.

Jean-Luc's band arrived and they turned out to be nice guys, very French, and fantastic players. Jean-Luc, already in his mid-seventies was in great shape, flawless technique, and absolutely to the point, very clear ideas, I was impressed. We rehearsed in a little church, a stage set up, two drummers, two bass players, two violin players, one guitar, one keyboard player plus a four-piece string section and a oboe player. Lizzie Ball was brought in to lead the string section. Some tunes had open solo sections, great for taking turns or battles, whichever way you want to look at it. It was interesting to hear and see, there was respect on both sides for the person as well as the player, at the same time no one would step back. There was lot of energy and it was f….. loud. Heavy Heaven for electric fiddlers so to speak, whenever one raised the level the other did the same. Nigel with more of a rock approach, shooting from the hip and Jean-Luc very articulate, with great phrasing, serious musical statements there … from both of them. The idea for the concerts was Jean-Luc and his band in the first half, Nigel and band in the second half and a finale with both bands. The first night went well and back in the hotel the band and crew met for a 'little' party which ended in Nigel's room … I left at 6. The promoter, a very nice Swiss lady, had invited both bands to her house for a 'reception', some drinks and talk, Nigel didn't come, but Jean-Luc and his wife, the other musicians some crew members. We came back to the hotel at 4, when I got out of the car I heard Nigel's voice, coming from a corner where we had breakfast in the morning. I thought maybe he recently got up and was having a late breakfast. When I got there he was with two girls from the string section and they obviously hadn't slept at all, instead one could see they had been at it since the party had started … he looked at me … like a schoolboy in disgrace. I went to my room to play a bit, the concert started at 9 and the band had to leave at 6. Steve Cox, the tour manager left at 5, I saw him shaking Nigel while shouting at him, I didn't hear what he told him but I can imagine what it was.

Nigel had his own driver, he came late but in time. I asked him: "How is it?" he replied … "Aw, man … horrible." The sound of his voice was telling the truth. When it was our set he started with Bach, a slow movement. I have never heard him play that shaky, I'm not sure if the audience could tell but I could. I think there was a danger that he would trip. It was fragile but he got through and it was not bad, rather interesting. On to the next tune, but what he played was not what we had rehearsed, it was from another project we had played before. The next three tunes were not on the set list, but from programmes we had played in the past. We tried to tell him … no … wrong piece … as we didn't have the music on stage, sometimes only one of us was playing with him, whoever was able to play the tune from memory. But the more he was playing the more he was getting into it. By the time Jean-Luc came on stage he was ready to jam and the two hit it off like the night before, it was amazing.

On the way back to the hotel, at a crossway we found a traffic light lying on the street, it had fallen off the lamppost … in Switzerland! Nigel wanted to take it home, it took three man to stuff it in the back of the van. These things are big and heavy … it probably ended in his storage place somewhere in Poland.

Back at the hotel … party again. Unbelievable … he was at it again. At 4 a.m. I was standing on the balcony smoking a cigarette, looking at the calm Lac Leman when I noticed a police car passing by. I thought maybe someone had complained about the noise. There were still some people inside, smoking and listening to music so we told them to turn it down. Next thing I saw was a giant 'New York style' fire brigade silently coming down that small street, it looked completely out of proportion, it stopped in front of the hotel. It was an unreal scene, the lake, the moon, the fire brigade … silent movie, I didn't believe my eyes. A fireman got out in full uniform, helmet, axe everything, then a second fire brigade just as big, this time with a huge ladder arrived. Knowing there was no fire, but us probably being the reason for the alarm, I thought … jail (to quote tour manager Steve Cox). For the next five minutes nothing happened, but I could see they were still there. Then a knock on the door, Nigel got up. "Let me handle it" … he opened the door and there was this huge fireman. Nigel babbled something, the guy looked at him pushed him out of the way and walked into the room, looked left and right, turned around and walked off. That was it, a few minutes later the fire brigades left as silently as they had come. I left at 6 … again, hard to believe but Nigel was still at it.

Amsterdam

The day before the concert in Amsterdam Nigel had a promo appearance in a talk show, no artistic endeavours allowed, straight talk only as made clear by the director more than once. Nigel insisted on bringing me with him and that we hold our instruments, needless to say there was a little jam in the middle of it, no way to cut it out;) In the meantime Brixie, his new girlfriend had arrived at the airport and was taken to the studio. After the talk show we went to a café, had some drinks and a little jam then all of us squeezed in to a Limousine. While stopping at a crosswalk in the middle of crowded Amsterdam, when Brixie who obviously hadn't gotten the attention she expected, screamed "talk to Rolf, he is your new lover", opened the door and off she went. Nigel looked a bit puzzled for a second then jumped out of the car leaving his violin with us. Gratuitously the tour manger explained or maybe complained that you should never bring your lady on tour. A few hours later a happy couple arrived at the hotel. Brixie appeared to be a very nice lady but that first encounter I never forget.

Miscellaneous

… While helping some elderly person (probably twice his age), showing him the way by saying "This way my monster" … hilarious.

In an interview Nigel was given keywords, when the interviewer said: … Richard Claydermann, Nigel replied: "I'd shoot him". ☺

THE BBC

Where does one begin when talking about our BBC? I suppose the fact that it is OURS is a relevant starting point. We licence payers pay over 75 per cent of the BBC's revenue and the government (our hard-earned tax) pays the rest. This means that we, the public, own this organisation and that the people working for it are our employees. Considering this fact, which is rather inconvenient for the BBC, rather too many of their/our employees go about their business in a rather autocratic way, as if suggesting they are just a bit above us but really more like a badly trained dog which bites the hand which feeds it.

It is surely a good thing for us to have and own a broadcasting service which isn't dictated to by commercial forces but these employees are wasting our chance of having this in the future.

The Bleeb hasn't always been a teeth gnashing, pitiful and desperately wannabe politically correct institution but unfortunately it is now. Public reaction to this self-indulgence is already taking the shape of even more apathy and resentment which will inevitably lead to refusal to pay the licence fee and the discarding of TV in general in favour of the Internet. Then what will we be left with? Yet another broadcaster completely influenced by commercial forces. Save The Planet—BUY A BIG MAC, IT'S GOOD FOR YOU! It's a shame to see the demise of what was once such a great British institution. The combination of positive discrimination, complete lack of meritocracy and namby-pamby editorial will be the end of this broadcaster that we have sunk such incredible amounts of money into.

My Relationship with The BBC—The Beginning

I've had a long sometimes fruitful, now completely fruitless, relationship with the Bleeb.

My relationship with our state broadcasting company started when I got chosen as the most obnoxiously and wilfully talented little bastard that the Yehudi

Menuhin School had to offer and went to play on a flagship performing arts show of the BBC's called *Gala Performance*. I believe they had called the Yehudi Menuhin School because they needed a last minute replacement for Rudolf Nureyev who was ill. Being rather a lot younger I was Ready To Rumble! I played the second movement of Bruch's main violin concerto (G minor) with The New Philharmonia Orchestra and it went great. I've always had a special route into that particular music and, in fact, most slow melodic music. This is one of my more special qualities. Most classical or jazz musos find it easy to play 1,000 notes but are completely at a loss when faced by a melody of four or five beautiful notes. It's a deeper feeling thing and being around one of the master channellers like Menuhin can't have hurt me in that direction, but primarily it's something you're born with. You either have it or you never will.

This Gala Performance thing was a multi-stellar line up in which I was the only non-stellar entity, nevertheless the BBC were providing a car for me to get back to the Yehudi Menuhin School.

Patricia Foy, the producer of the show, checked with me about the correct address of the school etc.

"I understand that your car is meant to take you to the Yehudi Menuhin School near Cobham in Surrey, is that correct?"

"Well, in fact it would be preferable if the driver could take me to Ronnie Scott's, Frith Street. Dizzy Gillespie is starting his first set pretty soon."

"Have you arranged tickets?"

"No, I'll just try to get in."

"It might be sold out, and anyway you're not really old enough to be going around London on your own."

"I'm 14—I can walk from here. I don't need the car even though it's really nice of you to offer it." I sensed I might be packed off back to school.

Paddy Foy had somehow been looking inscrutable but quite amused and the conversation, from my point of view, took an unexpected turn.

She said:

"You played beautifully this evening, some people are saying your performance was their favourite part of the concert. I tell you what, I'm going to call up Ronnie Scott's, arrange you a table and get them to look after you. The driver will wait and take you back to the school afterwards."

Wow! Plus that was going to save me the two months pocket money that I'd been saving for a special occasion.

"Can I stay for both sets?"

"I'm not going to be there, I can't exactly stop you."

"Wow, that's amazing, not that you're not going to be there. I'm not sure how to say thank you adequately."

"Don't say thank you at all. In fact, the BBC can't be seen to be encouraging truant and suchlike, so if anyone asks, you should say you asked the driver to go to Ronnie's yourself and that we didn't know anything about it."

"I understand. Anyhow, if I'm a bit late getting back I'll still have learned more in one night at Ronnie's than in a year at the school. A secret not big enough thank you." (This was well before all the blind eyes the BBC allegedly turned towards paedophilia within their domain, otherwise it might've seemed a bit strange sending a young kid off to Soho on his own—this was also well before Soho was turned into a yuppie coffee shop area.)

Of course, the night was fukkin' kool and Paddy Foy had obviously arranged everything. Ronnie's looked after me, gave me a table which I shared with a nice couple who shared their champagne with me. On the way onto the stage Dizzy came up, shook my hand, pointed at me and said:

"I hear you're sumthin' else, man."

Paddy had sorted a phenomenal night for a young 14-year-old fiddler. I sneaked back into the Yehudi Menuhin School at around 4:30 a.m. and all my room mates were awake wanting to know where I'd been and how it all went. Apparently, some of the teachers had been 'missing' me. We didn't sleep because it wasn't long until musical dictation at 7 a.m.

Going to Ronnie's wasn't the only good turn of events that came from that evening on Gala Performance. It's true that I might've been seen as a bit of a hot prospect having got 100 per cent marks at my ARCM exam at the age of 14 but Paddy Foy had seen something else in me. I wasn't capable of the boredom factor achieved so efficiently by most classical prodigies and suchlike—they wouldn't have been hot footing it to Ronnie Scott's when they should've been going back to school. She'd also heard me play and knew I had something. To cut a long story not quite so long, it turned out that she and the BBC wanted to film me for five years and see where I ended up. The result is a two-part documentary called *Coming Along Nicely*. When I was 16 and ready to go to Juilliard School, the BBC started filming the documentary on me and it eventually culminated in my London debut concerto. Luckily, there was no pressure from the cameras. It was just an interesting experiment. As Paddy Foy said: "You don't need to feel any pressure. It'll be an interesting film whatever happens. It doesn't matter if you end up busking on the street or playing in the Royal Festival Hall."

It turns out I did both and in 1977, the film finished with my performance of Mendelssohn Violin Concerto in the above mentioned RFH.

What makes me quite proud is that the film didn't come about because of some smooth spiel from a damager or something (I obviously didn't have a manager at 14 years old). The film came about because I had a bit of talent and wasn't boring. All substance and NO STYLE. Got to lose a bit of weight, nothing's changed, too much substance.

Not Exactly Overpaid

They have to keep us artists starving in a garret somehow. I remember playing a recital at Broadcasting House when I was 17 or 18 live on the BBC. It took about five weeks to learn and put together the repertoire for this gig and I got paid the princely sum of £50. I remember thinking at the time that something was a bit wrong. I could go busking on Fifth Avenue, have a lot more fun, no preparation, and walk away with $250 within a matter of two to three hours. I gave my pianist £25 so in fact made £25 myself.

It was a great compliment to be chosen to play but one doesn't do very well physically on a diet of honour alone. Ey-ooo, classical is a rich person's game, aey wott, Jeeves Fortescu?

The Proms (The Henry Wood Promenade Concerts)

I've had a fair few good nights at the Proms. (I've experienced a mixed feeling or two about the toffs waving Union Jacks. First of all I found myself a bit averse to all of that jingoism but now that everyone in the media is so anti-white British my feelings towards these white fools has become a bit more tolerant. And once the Scottish finally have to leave our UK, we won't see the Union Jack anymore and it's a killa looking flag.)

Walton Viola Concerto with Previn (absolutely the best Walton conductor of his time), solo Bach juxtaposed with the equally great keyboard players/composers Fats Waller and Dave Brubeck, Elgar Concerto, my NKQ playing my own compositions (with Jeff Beck making a muvvafukka guest appearance on my 'Hills of Saturn'—he just plugged straight into the amp without any effects pedals and sounded like a superb version of … Jeff Beck). All of those gigs left a deep impression on me and, I hope, my audience. There are, however, two gigs which stand out even more than these, not only because of the intensity on stage but also because of the brand of malarkey/bullshit which went on around them.

Myself, The Palestine Strings—
Vivaldi Including The IV Seasons

It was obviously a disgrace, but no Palestinian group had ever played in the Proms before this night.

The BBC had asked me to play a night of Vivaldi. When I suggested The Palestine Strings to play with me the Bleeb must have been in a good mood (maybe the licence fee money had just come in) because there was no objection.

I had worked with these wonderful young people/musicians in Palestine on two previous occasions and in spite of the daily adversity they have to face in their own country my time with them and my experience of Palestinian hospitality was one I will never forget. Of course those visits will not be the last.

It is one of my great career achievements to have facilitated this historic first night for these beautiful friends of mine.[21]

We rehearsed in BBC Maida Vale and the rehearsals were a great adventure. There was one moment when, at my request, Gandhi Saad sung from the back of the second violins and he brought me to tears. Man, the beauty when that guy sings—it wells up from the ground, through his feet and body and astrally projects out of him. It's an act of God.

His brother Mostafa is an incredibly talented violinist and communicator who also has the intelligence and charisma to be a great representative of his people.

The Palestinians, the Irish, black Americans, have all had to fight but they are not terrorists, they are sophisticated, cultured, educated people who have faced invasive colonial adversity of the most merciless kind.

During a break in rehearsals someone needed a picture for the newspapers of the orchestra and myself to publicise the gig. I proposed to the orchestra that we go and do the picture in front of the Houses of Parliament. This would be a visual question about what the evasive smooth talking politicians were really doing about the apartheid being faced by all the members of the orchestra and every Palestinian in their own country. The Thatcherite government dragged its feet at a tortoise pace about addressing apartheid in South Africa, so right wing self-interest had already shown itself to be totally opposed to respecting human rights. There's a lot of Parliamentary lip service given to human rights issues but in an area of the world so close to home it is incomprehensible that basic rights which we all take for granted (freedom of movement, electricity and water seven days a week, and the right to own one's own land) are being withheld from people in their own country.[22]

The shit hit the fan when people who thought they could exert their will over us tried to stop my plan. I made sure that the threats of withdrawal of sponsorship, cancellation of the gig and various other suggested forms of retribution went unnoticed by my Palestinian brethren and all the Gormenghastian deviousness only motivated me even more to get a straight result.

All of The Palestinian Strings were overjoyed, firstly, to have been invited by me to make beautiful music on such an important platform and were also very grateful that their problems at home might be given momentary attention by people at large. WE DID THE PHOTO which appeared in newspapers with all of us playing our instruments in front of Parliament.

---

21 Dear whingers, having friends from Palestine doesn't make me anti-Semitic. In fact, many of my Jewish friends were born in Palestine.

22 Being very, very white and against apartheid in South Africa didn't make me anti-white. Being part Jewish and against apartheid in Palestine/Israel doesn't make me anti-Semitic. Semites, by the way, include many people and of course include people of Jewish origin.

The gig itself? Well, it was an unforgettable memory for all of us on stage. Palestinian flags were flying proudly all around the Royal Albert Hall—you could cut the atmosphere with a knife. The electricity was evident on stage and the free flow of my flexible but strong structural views of those Baroque masterpieces were realised with intelligence, inspiration and tenacity by my Palestinian colleagues.

No one would have realised that our rehearsals had been severely compromised by the Israeli authorities initial last minute refusal to let many of my friends out of their country, meaning the loss of valuable preparation time. This ploy backfired because it added an extra intensity to our performance. The solo contributions from Mostafa Saad were charismatic and finely crafted, and all the other solo contributions I engendered from various individuals in the orchestra were deep and radiant.

You can see this performance on YouTube. It is a special offering both culturally and socially.

There was one sinister aspect of censoring applied by The Masters of Bleeb which involved cutting out 30 seconds of words I said which were relevant to the situation and to The Palestine Strings. Before the gig when I was, as usual, vibing up and helping my comrades feel at ease, many of my colleagues were asking: "Are you going to say anything?"

"What are you going to say?"

At some point in the show, while realising that we were primarily there to make music and make our point that way, while the audience were there primarily or exclusively to hear music and enjoy the incredible level of culture displayed by my Palestinian colleagues, I just dropped a 20–30 second comment. I always talk to my audience and they like and appreciate that I get rid of barriers rather than put them up. Briefly I mentioned how lucky we were not to live under a brutal APARTHEID regime like the one experienced daily by my friends on stage, but that nothing can defeat human spirit and culture. Very brief and to the point, forgive me if in true journalistic tradition I haven't quoted myself word for word. That was the gist of it.

BBC Censorship

These completely harmless and truthful words of mine brought on a mini hurricane of mock indignation and, of course, the old chestnut … false accusations of anti-Semitism started being directed my way. A former governor of the BBC called Baroness Screech or some such name, who didn't believe in Palestinian human rights, abused her position of privilege by using her contacts to get my few little words censored from subsequent repeat transmissions of the concert. Funnily enough, this Screech character had earlier that year spoken out strongly against support for the establishment of an independent self-governing Palestinian state … and strangely enough, there are no former governors of the BBC of Palestinian descent, get my drift? 'Impartiality' and all that. The Screech's manipulation and control of BBC editorial caused far more focus and longevity regarding my comments, to the extent that I'm even writing about them today, eight years later! The decision to censor my words for being too political was far more political than the words themselves. In my opinion people like this baroness lower the Jewish cause into disrepute and are an unwitting contributing cause of some of the disgusting anti-Semitism we see today.

The word apartheid wasn't used regularly in connection with the Palestinian people before my little speech, now it is. So I must have done something right.

To speak out against organised subjugation, displacement and brutalisation is the opposite of prejudice, although some insidious political game players would have us believe otherwise.

The last Answer & Question I have is for the Bleeb Bleeb C:

A. In football it seems desirable that you constantly show players taking the knee in what has been decreed a politically free sport by the authorities (to the extent of not even being allowed to wear poppies on Remembrance Day), but it was equally desirable to censor my remark regarding the brutalisation of my Palestinian brethren as being too 'political'. From this one can only surmise that the BBC reckons that Black Lives Matter (2,000 horribly lost in the US to violence from authorities in the last 20 years) more than Palestinian Lives Matter (7,000).

Q. Aren't we all meant to be equal?
Q. Or does equality come second behind fashionable politics?

The net result is that we did a fantastic gig which showed the beautiful culture of Palestinian people, in this case demonstrated through music, the eternal proof of human values.

The Farce Night of The Poms

It was really a nice, nice thing to be invited to play on what is known as *The Last Night of The Proms*. Quite a lot of people watch it on TV and it's a bit of a party atmosphere. After some discussion the BBC and I agreed that I play Vaughan Williams' 'The Lark Ascending' in the first half of the gig and Monti's (the one hit wonder) 'Czardas' in the second.

It wasn't long before it became clear that *The Last Night* was quickly becoming *The Farce Blight*, as far as highlighting any artistic aspirations of the show were concerned. The BBC, perhaps unwittingly, were finding themselves in the laughable position of being responsible for presenting yet another pseudo politically correct fiasco.

On this most British of British nights, the BBC had decided to homogenise the evening culturally by casting two Americans as the other main protagonists. If one wanted to avoid thrills and spills at all costs their A&R choice was perfect. The conductor was quite conservative in her approach to music, unadventurous in her interpretations but proficient and professional enough not to cause problems. The other cat was a singer, equally as efficient as the conductor, nothing unpredictable or inspiring but a good level.

Rehearsals were about to commence and it was then that *The Farce Blight* started. The singer and her PR representatives in their wisdom, or lack of it, decided that it would be beneficial for her to bleat out obsequiously that she was dedicating her performance to transgender people around the world. WOT D FUKK?? WHY? WHAT FOR? That type of irrelevant superficial claptrap was too much to take and had nothing to do with the music she was to perform, unless she thought that her music couldn't stand up for itself. Mind you, whoever her smarmy PR was maybe deserves a fair share of the blame. It certainly made sure that a musician such as myself wouldn't touch such an embarrassing PR company with a barge pole.

HOW CAN THE BLEEBLEEB C SANCTION OR BE ASSOCIATED WITH THAT TYPE OF GOBBLEDYGOOK? To think that we pay a licence fee to hear that kind of spouting.

With that in mind I went in for my first rehearsal with the orchestra. Once in front of the players, I quipped in a similar bleating manner as the singer: "I would like to dedicate my part of the performance to all the forgotten and displaced heteros reyownd dee weeruld."

At the finish of my sentence my eyes rested on the front of the viola section. I saw two very unamused women glowering at me as if heterosexuals shouldn't be allowed to be recognised or celebrate anything. The conductor also seemed rather unsupportive.

I know some people suffer from a chronic sense of humour shortage or a lack of cognitive appraisal of our equality as human beings and I truthfully, sincerely wish them a speedy recovery. We're just who we are, all of us, it's not such a huge, huge deal, surely.[23]

What with all the bullshit flying around I decided to keep my head down and do what no one else was talking about doing, concentrate on breathing fresh air into the music instead of stale air out of my mouth. The music, as I said before, was 'The Lark Ascending' and 'Czardas'. 'The Lark' is natural for me because the English pastoral style is so close to my heart whether it's Nick Drake or Vaughan Williams. Living in Malvern for a long time means I have experienced that picture in real life. 'Czardas' is also right up my street partially because of my numerous real life sessions with Romani musicians in Romania, Hungary and Serbia. Real Life Matters! 'Czardas' can also be … fun! And it can be spelled Csárdás.…

---

23 Dear potential whinger, please let me help you draw the line between preference and prejudice. I really get bored by people who go on and on and on and on about their own or other people's sexuality. Whatever gender you are, I love you, until you go on and on and on and on about…

I saw it as my job to introduce a little bit of musical feel and *joie de vivre* to the evening. Something stratospheric, something inspirational, something improvisational and something … fukkin OK. Mission Possible—mission accomplished. The orchestra and I had a great time playing the music and the audience, as ever wherever I go, were a large, large part of it.

Did I get any thanks from the Bleeb for rescuing their *Farce Night* from being a boring politically correct debacle? I guess that would've meant having to admit presiding over a farce but I bet there were a few sighs of relief from our employees working for OUR BBC.

Some people might wonder why I play less and less classical music, the above pseudo-trash might be a clue. The music itself is like a diamond deep in a giant cesspit. In the end all that shit can put you off the jewellery. Having said that, once the music starts I feel like the luckiest man in the world. All that positive energy—once the music starts real life starts and there's that magic irreplaceable moment called NOW.

N.B. Because of my Irish heritage I hate Blight.

A Life in The Shit of A BBC Radio 3 Controller Circa 1990

Chapter 1

I love it here in this bog. It is my perfect habitat. If I hadn't found this lovely bog, a swamp or even a ditch might have done. I love it here because it's a place where people called listeners don't exist. This is exactly how Radio 3 should be, no people and none of that inconvenient classical music drowning out my cumbersome mating call. PAAARP! … CRAAARP! … My mating call seems to be producing absolutely nothing and no prospective partner has been in sight anywhere at all for more than 400 years … KRARAAAAP! … EUREEKARAAAP! That's it! That's what I need! This idea will extend my habitat and simultaneously help me find a Frogeena. I'll turn Radio 3 into something perfect for my self-procreation. The best thing to do will be to get rid of all the human listeners by culturally cleansing the station of any reasonably pleasant classical music and replacing all of that claptrap with music composed by turgid, boring bastards who can replicate my mating call on air on Radio PAAAARP! I mean Radio 3. None of the licence fee paying proletariat will notice the difference, and of course I will hardly notice the difference myself, but I might enhance my chances of finding a mate by doing this great coup de culture. It's the only way … KREEEYAAARP! I can turn Radio 3 into one gigantic bog just for me where only my species of frog can communicate to survive, other species will fail to prevail and will perish. Mind you, I don't want any of them to fall by the wayside because there might easily be a nearby ditch which could very likely become my second licence fee paid home … PRZKRAAP! We don't want any of those dirty lowly listeners soiling my environment. This purge of decent classical music must commence … now.

Chapter 2

What?? Only 250 people listening on a Saturday 10 p.m. around the whole of the United Kingdom and British Isles? My strategy is working. No one will tell me to HOP IT now. The bog is mine! My precious!

My BBC Remit

So this was the environment I was confronted by when I started rescuing classical music from the Radio 3's controller and his like in the early nineties. It was completely true. At times he/it had managed to reduce the Radio 3 audience to 250 people, in close to peak hours, in the whole of the UK. This meant that around 59,999,750 people on these islands from licence paying households found it more beneficial not to listen to his choice of 'music' and presentation.

I, on the other hand, was shifting two million recorded copies of a work which had previously, at best, done about 40,000. I was also communicating classical music at the highest level to audiences of millions through my concerts and TV appearances. Many from these audiences were hearing classical music, and liking it, for the first time in their lives.

It was an unheard-of situation. The BBC remit was to bring high level culture to as many people as possible. With my new way of doing things, I was single-handedly doing that while 'The Controller' was turning Radio 3 into an unattainable exclusive club unfit for normal human beings. There might have been one entity who enjoyed the farmyard noises they were broadcasting ... a BULL****frog?

One problem about the unheard-of success of my career was that it showed up the complacency in the classical music world and made the people who weren't doing their job (or at least weren't doing it properly) look like the wallies they probably were. Radio 3's abject failure with The Controller was a case in point. My success was embarrassing those in Bleeb Radio 3 who were enjoying their cushy licence fee paid jobs without doing anything much to earn their salaries.

Chapter 3

PAAARP! ... Oh no, and I thought this bog of mine was nice and peaceful, a beautiful melody free environment in which I could doze away, every now and then emitting a futile mating call ... but what is that sound? ... PEEEUKRAPAAAARP! ... it sounds like horrible melodic, rhythmic music on a violin with orchestra ... it's ruining my lazy complacent slumber ... in fact, good God, if this is allowed to carry on it will threaten my whole wallowing existence ... in order to survive in my work free oblivion, even though it's against my nature, I might have to do something ... I know, I'll turn the whole animal kingdom against him … kill him! Then I won't have my revelries interrupted by real music on Radio BOG! … Ooops! I mean Radio 3 … KRAAAARAP!

Attempted Character Assassination

The life of 'The Controller' would've been much easier if I hadn't been around, working hard to bring classical music to as many people as possible. He was in between a rock and a hard place when comparisons between his and my listening figures started to be made.

A character assassination might've had a chance of making him look a bit better by comparison if he had had any sound basis for it. The whole thing was like some kind of weird chapter from *The Name of the Rose*—I was Sean Connery and he was one of the other wankers. He (the other wanker) started in on my clothes and the way I was presenting music. He then abused his position of power for his own personal advancement by using his Bleeb Bleeb C media contacts as a vehicle for his sanctimonious whingeing voice. Poor little wanker, you was messin' with the wrong bloke, matey!

It just so happened that I had a gig in a jammed packed Royal Albert Hall a few days later during which I was able to bury the little twerp. My manager, John Stanley, got Rick Parfitt (Status Quo) to lend me a special tailcoat perfect for the occasion. John had got reporters and camera crews into the RAH so the coverage was BIGtime. This was the perfect way to put the little overreaching 'Controller' back in the soggy bog where he would be more ideologically comfortable.

I went on stage all ponced up in the tail suit, bowed extravagantly and announced to the RAH (which was packed to the rafters) and to the TV cameras at the front of the stage: "Ladies and gentlemen, this is what Bach sounds like in this fopping getup."

I played some pretty nice Bach for around 15–20 seconds.

"And this, ladies and gentlemen, is what the same music sounds like without the waiter's uniform …"

With that, I ripped the velcro at the front of the tail suit, tore it off, then threw it in a ball to the ground and emerged, like a fukked up butterfly out of a chrysalis, in my normal clothes which some people have described as punk.

The same phrase of Bach, believe it or not, sounded just as fukkin' lovely. The simple message being listen to the music and enjoy—only the unfortunate illiterate have to judge a book by its cover.

The audience were amused and the scenario appeared all over the news the next day.

EASY! KENNEDY 1, CUNT ROLLER 0.

Chapter 4

Eeeeyoooo deeeare, that didn't work despite all my posh education ... KRAAARP! ... now
they are talking about changing Bleeb Radio 3 from my perfect pip-squeak bog standard
into a station of decent classical music. The Houses of Parliament has even passed a motion
proposed by those Labour scoundrels that what Kennedy is doing is good for classical
music! What'll happen to my job of just croaking a bit when I'm on heat? PAAA-ARP!
What's making things worse is my justifiable paranoia of fruit bats. AAAAARK!
Those blasted spiffing bats eat creatures like me for breakfast, if one came to my NECK
of the woods I wouldn't stand a chance ... SLAAARP ... they love the taste of a putrid
body like mine. The BAT would be FAT, next day I'd be SHAT. I'm frightened. Laarst
nayit when I was watching televeeezhyun that Kennedy punker bastard DAAAstardly
scoundrel momentarily wore some clothes of the type I would recommend ... and he
looked just like a giant ... oh my Gawd...FRUIT BAT! It gave me the willies ... I've
never had a willy before! LIEEYAAAARP! The least he'll do is bite the blood out of my
neck ... like Bela Lugosi on blasted amphetamines. Eyoooh neooo ... this is just beastly
... ghastly ... BLOODy awful! And he's playing Berg Concerto next week and I have
to go ... Eayooo ... drat!

Attempted Defamation

I was scheduled to play the Alban Berg concerto at the Royal Festival Hall. This
violin concerto is entitled 'To the Memory of an Angel'. The angel in question
was Manon Gropius, Alma Mahler's daughter who died of polio at the age of
18. Berg was one of the closest friends of her family and the concerto culminates
in Manon's soul leaving her body after the ravages of the disease and death.

I was at a peak of my violin powers (one has many peaks in a musical career)
so was as confident as one can ever be of doing proper justice to the music in a
great performance. In order to represent the picture described in the concerto I
visually represented death with a black cloak and some ghostly make up. My
violin was more than capable of representing Manon's spirit.

This concerto is a symphonic work in which the violin is just a slightly more
featured component of the orchestra, so rather than the orchestra following the
soloist it is often the other way round. We were celebrating a fantastic team job
after the performance when The Cunt Roller came into my dressing room and
was polite to the point of obsequiousness. He left (hopped out) with both his
faces, we carried on partying.

Within a week he had gone on another attack, or should I say PRATtack? Or
even Shakatak?

This time his paranoia of me being a gigantic fruit bat in disguise had really
got the better of him. He accused me of belittling the music by dressing up as
Dracula, even citing the violin mark on my neck as being vampirical make-up.

Hundreds of violinists must have suffered from this mark of our trade when under his employ as 'Controller' of Radio 3. Maybe he was squatting in his bog standard instead of going to work, thereby not noticing the obvious.

This out of Controller was either completely ignorant of the story behind Berg's concerto or was attempting and committing defamation. Or he was succumbing to his ever increasing paranoia of me being a nightmarish gigantic fruit bat in disguise.

This case of ignorance, lying or paranoiac mistaken identity didn't even need an answer.

EASY! KENNEDY 2, CUNT ROLLER 0.

The Kuntroller was the most futile over-educated toff I have ever had to deal with but plenty of other Classico admin types were also angry and humiliated about being shown up. They hated their private little club having its closed doors blown open, and hated us lowly proletariat obliterating their sordid activities.

I quite often am asked why I don't play so much classical music any more. I see all of music as being a most positive form of shared energy, but the problem with classical music is the predominance of unqualified people like this kunt roller who are so above themselves, I can't afford to let too much of my life be subject to these pillocks.

Dratted moment of dratted moments ... ZAAARP! My poncing frog tactics have completely failed ... K-A-A-AARP! The giant fruit bat ... ermm ... I mean Kennedy, is going to change Radio Bog Standard ... ermm ... I mean Radio 3 into a decent station with decent classical music on it. And I don't look very cleverererer. If I was a ... dog ... I could have a nice kennel without a hint of listenable classical music in it ... WOOF! ... PAAARP! ... WOOF! Yes, to look more intelligent my name will now be Cat Roller The Dog ... Grrrrr! Yayyeelp!

THE END

N.B. The Kuntroller was out of his job in less than a year. Snide muvvafukkas. Mess with me at your peril! I hope this truthful reminiscence demonstrates what can happen if you have a better vision of how to do things and refuse to toe the line. One expects illegal shit every now and then but not at the expense of the honest taxpayer. Onwards and upwards!

The Best of Suppressed

The Bleeb Bleeb C won't make any shows with me anymore. Jimmy Savile was OK but apparently I'm not. At the time of writing, The Head of BBC Music Commissioning won't even respond in any type of way to my representation, so I'm told. All very strange!

If you are also a British citizen like me, and have a TV licence, it's us who own the BBC. You own it! These kats like The Head of Commissioning are our employees because our licence fees and tax pay their salaries. So do me a favour, if you'd like to see a show of mine on your Bleeb please communicate this to: The Head of BBC Music Commissioning; or www.bbc.co.uk.

Maybe you might even get a response from your employee. If a show of mine gets made it will be your show too—and it'll be far less boring than what we've seen on the Proms and suchlike last year!

At one point the Bleeb and I discussed a very good idea they had about J. S. Bach. I was to introduce an orchestra of young kats to the inspirational music of this genius. The facts that improvisation was a big thing in Bach's day, I have the linear championship for Bach through Menuhin, the linear championship for improvisation through Grappelli and Ponty and that I have been an inspiration to loads of kids to play violin meant that I was perfectly placed to do the show. There was one ominous moment when racial quotas were suggested (which are a horrible hindrance to the meritocracy which would bring true equality to absolutely everybody) but no orchestra that I would think of would fail to be multiracial. I was just surprised that the subject even needed to be mentioned, maybe it was one of those politically correct bees so often found in the Bleeb's bonnet. So there we go, no problem, nice idea and … NOTHING … just phone and email disappearing acts. Maybe the Bleeb were 'too busy' thinking of new job definitions or something. For instance Chief Controller could be changed to Controller in Chief, really useful …

Head of BBC Music Commissioning
BBC Broadcasting House
London W1A 1AA
www.bbc.co.uk
Main switchboard: 0208 743 8000

Gordon The Gopher, Rip Off D Sofa

The Bleeb Bleeb C have an ever so cutie cute story about how the hand puppet Gordon the Gopher was attacked by a sweetie sweet little puppy. I don't want to disappoint you (believe that if you want) but that inane little Gopher was attacked by a human first … live on air … and it was ME! "Sorry I done it, Ossifer" (not really because it just had to be done).

A geezer called Philip Schofield was presenting. At the time he was a smooth type of presenter who professionally works their way up by being smoothly professional. I could see in his eyes that he thought me a bit too unpredictable and that he wished I wasn't there because I might fuck up the smoothness which was his ambition to achieve. I thought that the least I could do was to let him trust his instincts.

The gopher used to skit about on the back of the sofa in a pseudo-endearing type of way. I was having to sit on the sofa with the pesky rodent scuttling around behind me gesturing in an infantile manner. At some point Schofield was being far too professional and ingratiating with the annoying little hand puppet so I ripped it off the operating hand and lobbed it to the kids. I thought the kids might want to take the deflated little rodent home as a kind of trophy or souvenir but no, they were tired from all the fake energy of the show and tried to evade the trajectory of the furball as if it was a dead flying rat. It's never a good idea to forget about what happened within those Bleeb Bleeb C walls and in those days a suddenly exposed hand with no clothes on should've been right up their street.

Vivaldi IV Seasons

Someone within the ranks of the Bleeb came up with a fukkin' great idea for me. It must have taken an extraordinary amount of brain power. What was their line of thinking? Looking into the Fela Kuti legacy? A musical life party with my Palestinian friends in Ramallah and Jericho? Duke Pearson? Bach? Krzysztof Komeda? Zappa? The Buzzcocks? Desmond Dekker? Baxter Dury? ... no! ... erm ... Vivaldi IV Seasons, surely not! Yes! Vivaldi IV Seasons. Oh my Gawd, humongous, what a giant step for the Kennedy-kind.

While having to admit that I wasn't exactly slaughtered by the enterprise and originality of the idea there were good aspects to it:

1. It was going to be broadcast in the Christmas holidays so I could give Viv to a whole lot of fukkers who might like it.
2. It was going to be shot in Venice.
3. The Bleeb agreed that I could find kats playing contemporary popular Venetian melodies to compare with the popular melodic styles Viv used in his day.

I had already won a Rose d'Or for my first IV Seasons film so if I was to make a second film concerning the same repertoire it had to have some consequence, reach and be a muvvafukka otherwise there was no incentive for me to go near it.

Everything was agreed and then the contract came in for me to sign. Like the well trained monkey I am (no, I trained myself, fukkas) I read the contract and prepared to sign it. Well, the days when monkeys had to dance on the Bleeb barrel organ are well gone. So when I saw that numbers 1. and 3. from above were missing but all the things they wanted were in it I sent a polite reminder that a contract between two parties can't cover the interests of only one. Just for the record a lot of my working relationships are not contracted and I'm happy like that. If there had to be a contract, despite my Irish heritage, I wasn't putting up with that type of Bleeb autocratic malarkey. There was no point to all the BBC Bleeb politically correct equality of opportunity outcome if they were going to treat artists in an imperialist manner as if they were slaves from a far-flung outpost.[24]

I waited for their reply, and waited, and waited … and waited … and … NOTHING! Not even a polite fuck off, we own you—BOY!

Tinariwen

There is a band from Mali that I like very much called Tinariwen and when I found out they had done a version of one of my favourites by Nusrat Fateh Ali Khan, Mustt Mustt, I had to check it. Their version was great and went quite a long way to being as uplifting as Nusrat's. After the song had finished the nice little algorithm bastard chose another song.

"WOT D'FUKK'S DAT?" I thought. "THAT'S ME."

Unusual because I don't listen to my own shit.

I went to the poota to see why the fukk it was playing my stuff and then it went into Tinariwen's gig at Womad in 2004.

The BBC in conjunction with Womad had used my song with Tomasz Kukurba's Kroke Band as their 30 second long title track.

Like the Bleeb, some of the festivals like Womad get above themselves and forget that they are a vehicle for the artists, the artists are not a vehicle for them. No noise = no BBC Music, no festival = SIMPLE, nice and quiet.

NICE: More than 5.25 million had watched it.

NOT NICE: No one had thought to ask if it was OK to use my music.

NOT NICE: There were no credits for my music at the beginning or end of the show.

NOT NICE for Tinariwen or myself that people might have thought my music was theirs.

NOT NICE that these two organisations have such a propensity to view artists as subjects of their autocracy.

My view of it all:	NOT NICE
And probably	NOT LEGAL
And:	THEY'RE NASTY…(!)

---

24 Exactly, dear friend. There were slaves of all colours including white.

Suppressed, Censored, Defamed And Ignored

In the meanwhile, I have many ideas for great shows which would be interesting and which absolutely no one else could do. These ideas come from having instinctively and technically mastered rock, jazz, swing, jazz fusion, Klezmer, Celtic, folk, soul, Gypsy Romani, Balkan, dub, as well as the expected classical—and what makes me good for TV is that (particularly compared with the other Classicos we've seen on the Bleeb this year) I have fun and am not over earnest and boring. I'm not one of those Classicos who mistake solemn for serious. In truth, the ones who ACT serious are the ones who have the least to offer.

MY UNIQUE GIFT IS MY KILLA EARS—whatever I hear I can play. Plus I interact with people very naturally, unlike some of the over/under prepared automaton kats shown at present who are completely instinct free.

IF YOU'D LIKE TO SEE YOURS TRULY ON THE BLEEB (the company
you are paying for) DOING SOMETHING KILLA PLEASE BOTHER
THEM AS MUCH AS YOU CAN ON MY BEHALF.

Try the HEAD OF BBC MUSIC COMMISSIONING
BBC BROADCASTING HOUSE
LONDON W1A 1AA
www.bbc.co.uk
Main switchboard: 0208 743 8000

SEEING THE SEASONS CHANGE

Pausa—Family Time

During the mid-nineties, I stopped playing classical music for about five years. A few years after the success of the IV Seasons, I became really bored and disappointed with the whole situation. The guys at EMI were like: "There's our formula, we don't have to do nothing else", and they started wanting me to do Vivaldi: 8 seasons, and Vivaldi: 12 seasons. After doing a couple of classical albums, I'd been wanting to write my shit, but everyone was saying: "Look, you can write it very soon. Just one more classical album." It went on for a few years, until I thought "Well, fuck that, I'll leave it." And that's what happened.

Contrary to what you might think, stopping playing classical music was really a great thing for me, because that was the beginning of me gaining confidence as a composer, as opposed to being someone who plays other people's stuff.

To have some space to write music helped me understand all of the music I played before. It helped me understand new types of music. It gave me a new incentive and energy for being involved in concert work or in rehearsal work or recording work. It gave me a whole new mojo. I came back with recharged batteries.

During that period of time, me and my girlfriend Eve had started a family. My son was born in 1996, in the second year of my absence from the classical music. I think with the classical stuff, if I would have been touring all the time, I wouldn't have had enough time to make Sark. So, I'm glad I stopped for a bit. Eve already had a kid with a partner of her's, Kyran, who's four years older than Sark. I have known him since he was knee-high to a grasshopper, so now, I still see them as being kids. But obviously they are a lot more independent now—being 25 and 29. Kyran is doing journalism and Sark is doing quite a lot of renovation of houses. He is more into the building thing than into music, which is probably a much better living than what a musician can aspire to. I think I will be going to him for a loan before he will know what happened.

Anyway, what could have been a one or two-year sabbatical turned into something rather long because it was great to be around when Sark was born and to be able to see him growing up, making his first steps. To have been there when he started walking, started talking and all of that was fantastic. Becoming a father also changed me in a way, because you can love other people, but it's not unconditional unless it is your own kid, that is when it becomes an automatic thing. Whatever the fuck they do, you are going to love them, even if they annoy the shit out of you.

If you've got a girlfriend, you can just say: "Look, let's call it a day, it's not working." But if you've got a kid, that's for life. I was used to having a structure, but you can't just not make breakfast before they go to school or that type of stuff, so you got to give them a structure, too. And I think he was glad of that. But he does behave much more maturely than I do, probably always did.

It's funny: I bought the Malvern house because Brixie didn't want to be in Birmingham, but I stayed there because of Sark, and he's living in Birmingham now, actually in the area where Brixie wouldn't let me live. Malvern is a great place with good schools for kids and good environment, fresh air and sporting possibilities and shit like that. It's a good place for bringing up a child. I wouldn't have stayed in Malvern so long if it hadn't been for my kid. Every now and then we go to a Villa game together, but with COVID and the Brex-shit, I've been kind of stuck in Poland. The Malvern house has gone a long while ago, and although I have another one in the south of England in a similar area, I'm hardly ever there so there's no fucking point in it, now that I live in Poland.

I gradually came back from my sabbatical, first with an album called *Kafka*, which consists of original songs that I wrote in 1995, and later with my Jimi Hendrix record published in 1999. However, it took a while until I was open to classical music again. A friend of mine, Cora Lunny, who's a great Irish fiddle player, started doing classical as a kind of rebellion against the Irish music. One time, she was talking about it, saying: "Well, you know, the people in classical music are just dreadful and it makes you really not like it. But unfortunately, the music's so good." And that's when I realised that's the way I felt about it, too. After having played quite a lot of music, with bands and stuff, where you're doing sound checks which go on forever, and it's electric, I was quite hungry just to play some shit where you didn't have to worry about all your equipment. With the classical, you're just playing acoustic, there's no worry about all this equipment, you either play well, or you play like a pig. You can't blame it on the equipment, or say that someone had set it up wrong. So, I just wanted return to that simple situation, and it was quite refreshing to get back to that. Some of that music is just amazing music, it started to become hard to think about the rest of my life that I wouldn't play it. Quite a lot of other people were playing classical music like shit, and I didn't think that's fair. Let me give people a decent version of it. So I came back and done some.

What I was careful to do was not overload my classical schedule. Maybe 30, 40 per cent of what I do is classical music, and then I'm playing with my band a certain amount, or I'm playing jazz projects with other people, or writing and playing that. So, there's a much healthier balance now compared to what I used to have. I don't feel I've got to give up one type of music anymore. If it's good music around, you might as well play it.

Germany—Mein Deutcheland

Germany is a wonderful country and I have a deep love for its people, culture, varying landscapes and the phenomenal audiences who come to my concerts and gigs. The people I meet are intelligent, respectful and generous.

Bach, Beethoven, Brahms, the absolute greatest Central European masters, the way that I first experienced Germany was by doing gigs, more often than not playing music by those guys. However, whatever type of music I was playing, what I encountered was an audience with every quality that a musician could want. Not desperate to pigeonhole everything, understanding every type of music I play. In quiet moments the audience's concentration is like a séance, something absolutely unique to Germany. Of course, more extrovert moods are appreciated as well but it's the chance to communicate on a deep level of inner meaning which means so much to us artists. Every time I visit Germany I think to myself "Wow, great! Now I have people I can really play to…"

Another reason why Germany is a bit of a dream is the quality of its musicians. Whether it's rock, jazz, techno or classical there are fantastic musos. I've spent so much time in Germany that it's like a second home and it's been an experience close to my heart to have worked with so many wonderful people—and that extends beyond the musicians to the promoters, soundmen, backline and all the people who work so hard to make a concert happen and who do it so well.

Another thing I've seen is that whether one's a hippie or someone with a more orthodox approach to life, the living standards one can expect are higher than in any other country in the world. Germany offers great work opportunities and from what I've seen has an incomparable record in regard to the protection of human rights.

Cities of which I have particularly fond memories are Berlin (Philharmonic and great nights at the A-Trane whether playing or listening), Hamburg (Musikhalle, Große Freiheit, St Pauli), the coal pit area (Köln, Düsseldorf and Essen are all killa audiences), Leipzig and Halle (people really cultured but with their feet on the ground), Dresden is a beautiful city and then there is the cultivated opulence of München with all its beautiful surrounding areas of Bavaria. And I almost forgot Frankfurt! I'm not sure about American influences but certainly American musical influences did Frankfurt no harm at all in the old days. In other words there are so many great places and an unbelievable amount of contrast for one country—a huge one in the centre of Europe.

The Berliner Philharmoniker deserve special mention since they are the best in the world bar none.

By the late nineties, when I returned to classical music, we formed a special relationship doing a lot of concerts and quite a few recordings. The reason we started our collaboration was quite funny: EMI had a contract with the Berlin Philharmoniker, and they had an A&R in EMI who hated Vanessa-Mae so bad, he wouldn't talk to Vanessa-Mae, but he wanted me to do well. She was famous for playing electric violin and he hated that type of music. I mean, electric violin, when you kind of got a wet t-shirt on, it's not very safe really ... So that's how come I think the thing happened with Berliner Philharmoniker and myself in the first place.

We always worked with a smaller orchestra, so I think the projects I brought into them were a refreshing break from the large orchestra stuff they normally play. I also think the more spontaneous approach I bring to the moment within a strong structure was something they weren't averse to.

I, for my part, was very refreshed to be working on Baroque music with such amazing musicians, because they can do anything and they have a beautiful sound and great appreciation of music in every type of way. It was interesting from all of our points of view, to be able to work with an orchestra as equals instead of having to lead excessively. When I was the musical director for our Bach and Vivaldi recordings, what I would do was bring my interpretation in and then they'd relate to it. But there were always very good suggestions coming from the orchestra as well, about how to turn a corner in the music or whatever. Some orchestras are a little bit like "Wouldn't it be better to be in the pub now?", but these guys love working and they like to rehearse.

Our work was fruitful and led to three great recordings plus multiple tour gigs in Germany, Japan, the UK and Austria.

We had some very good parties although in one knees up I'd made some great, great chocolates which looked as if they'd come from a posh shop. One of the geezers came up to me and said:

"Hey, Nigel, these are lovely chocolates. Where did you get them?"

"How many have you had, mate?"

"Oh, between eight and ten, maybe nine." ... *vorsprung durch technik* ...

"Oh, dear."

We got him home where he went into a foetal position for a while to get over it. He hadn't realised what I'd put in them.

Another amusement was when our Japanese promoter took some of us to the poshest private restaurant in Japan. There was a bit of a hubbub developing on my right hand side so I checked over the other side of the table. It was Albrecht Mayer going red in the face from demanding ketchup for so long. The place was too sophisticated for the ketchup. A flustered geisha type eventually had to run out and across the street to get some. Albrecht got his ketchup and was able to fuck up his meal with no barriers. I thought he might ask for pommes a bit later.

A different development between the Berliner Philharmoniker and I was when in 2003 we played some of my Hendrix arrangements in Potsdamer Platz. I can honestly say that even in this field I'd never heard my arrangements played better.

Other short memories I've got are playing a killa outdoor gig in Leipzig with Bobby McFerrin to a really large audience. A while later people started bringing commercial DVDs of that gig backstage for me to sign. I was surprised because no one had told me, let alone paid me for the fact, that it was going to be released that way. Still got to look into that!

I remember playing a five-to-six-hour gig in Große Freiheit, Hamburg—last one standing! It was with my band doing Hendrix and it was fantastic, following all of those amazing bands who've been in there, in such a great part of Hamburg and near St Pauli FC. We were just jamming, I think the gig was meant to last about one and a half or two hours. But now six hours later, we were still doing it. The promoter was like: Oh fuck, when can we get out of here? How are we going to get dinner? He was really fucked off about it. But the audience was sticking there, so it was very nice. I always want to give the audience value for money but maybe six hours is overdoing it. For the other poor fukkers.

I remember playing or listening to many great nights in the A-Trane, Berlin. The bands which Ernst Bier puts together are just superb and he is such a devoted and exploratory drummer.

I remember getting my first St Pauli shirt.

I remember getting my latest St Pauli shirt.

I remember checking the quality of German beer. First place = ROTHAUS. Alternatives = BERLINER, PAULANER and RADEBERGER. KÖLSCH beer is beautifully light, but what is it with those tiny glasses? Weissbier of any type is just appalling—why make that shit?

As you can tell, I love Germany and consider it a second home. What you might not have guessed is that I am going to try and make it my first home. That will all depend on whether the authorities will let a dyslexic violin virtuoso become a citizen.

I pride myself on always having given more to whichever community I've lived in than what I've taken out of it. I would enjoy doing the same in Germany. I can imagine being very productive for the society around me, particularly when I already have so many friends to help me find the necessary infrastructure to make a valid contribution.

I am a European citizen and I don't believe that a selfish meMEme vote should be allowed to take that away from me especially when there was hardly a majority. Brexshit wasn't conceived by positive generous people but whoever wanted it has now got it. Cameron, Sham-eron. Please let in a dyslexic fiddler, mein Deutcheland. I'd be quite proud to be fucking living here.

MEIN FREUNDEN, BITTE LASS MICH EINTRETEN!

Ireland

One of the biggest regrets in my life is that nowadays I hardly ever get to Ireland. There's no green like the green of Ireland, the Emerald Isle, and there's nowhere where the Guinness tastes as good.

My ancestors are from County Kerry and Kennedy is not an unusual name in Ireland. On the street you can pass by Kennedy's Butchers, Kennedy's Hardware, Kennedy's Gardening Centre, Kennedy's Pub and to finish it all Kennedy's Undertakers.

Maybe it's in my Irish blood but for sure I have the same attitude as a lot of other Irish musicians. You play because you love it, not because you're being paid or because someone told you to do it. In decent Irish towns there's a session every night full of amazing musicians playing for the love of it. In fact, many of these phenomenal musicians have a 'real' job in the daytime.

Gary Moore, Donal Lunny, Sharon Shannon, Mary Black, Rory Gallagher, Matt Molloy, Kevin Burke, Phil Lynott, The Pogues, Sinead O'Connor, The Waterboys, Cora Lunny and the list goes on. I've been lucky enough to either have these kats coming out of my speakers or play with them for real, or should I say reel.

Sharon Shannon's smile, for instance, doesn't just light up a room, it lights up a whole country. And Cora Lunny is one of the most talented violinists I know. She came as my guest second soloist all over the world when I invited her. Japan, China, Taiwan, New Zealand, Germany.

Lastly, there's a unique charm to Ireland ... One time my mentor Yehudi Menuhin was playing a concert and after the gig the promoter took him to a pub to hear some of the local music. People saw his expensive clothes and his violin case and after a lot of clamouring he got the fiddle out and played some Bach. The next day a couple of cats were talking in the same pub: "That bloke on the violin was pretty good last night, wasn't he?"

"He wasn't that bad, what was he called again?"

"Oh, he's a famous classical man, he's Yehudi McMenemy...."

Japan

What a unique and amazing place! The juxtaposition between tradition and modernity is really very beautiful.

I have been a fair few times to Japan, with the Berliner Philharmoniker, my own Polish chamber orchestra, and with my own band NKQ to play in the beautiful Tokyo Blue Note Club. All of the trips were a revelation and a learning experience I will keep with me for life.

I have since become even more immersed in Japanese culture. In music the names of Ryuichi Sakamoto and Stomu Yamashta come to mind immediately and even Kyu Sakamoto from older days. Deeper into history I'm still getting into

Shomyo and Gagaku but I already relate to space, time and placement. These are aspects I work very hard to achieve in whatever types of music I play so I relate to the use of the Shakuhachi, Biwa and sparse percussion. In my own style I wrote a song called '15 Stones' which was about a garden I saw in Kyoto in which there were 15 stones. Whichever vantage point you chose to assume in the garden only 14 were visible. I guess the point was that when you see something it's not really possible to quantify the whole story.

Despite my life being musicMUSICmusic my big breakthrough moment with Japanese culture was through literature. Haruki Murakami and Kazuo Ishiguro were great, very great obvious ways in and I have read every book each of them has written, maybe! Then, at the top of the tree of influence I read everything of Yukio Mishima, all following Japanese literature seems to be influenced by his radiant writing in some way or other. Then Kafka-esque Kobo Abe and books by Ryu Murakami, Osamu Dazai, Takashi Hiraide, Junichiro Tanizaki, Genki Kawamura, Banana Yoshimoto, Toshikazu Kawaguchi, Yasunari Kawabata and probably more. I love Japanese literature for its clarity and pictures of individual personal worlds so unique to Japanese people. Mishima is the artistic father of all these kats. All the above mentioned artists just go to show what an imaginative and cultured country Japan is.

I love playing in Japan and unfortunately haven't been back since my last promoter attacked me. He didn't like me keeping the ball up backstage and there I was thinking J-League football was pretty good!

I would love to come back to Japan and send my love to all my beautiful fans who were kind enough to give me such valued presents or even to come to my gigs.

I am imminently starting to arrange some Sakamoto for my chamber orchestra, so I am sure there will be (East) winds of change—TONG POO!

Australia

How can I not mention Oz? I have three, soon to be four, sisters there, nieces and nephews, cousins, the whole caboodle from both sides of the family not to mention all my dad's side, the classical aristocracy! They are mentioned elsewhere in this book.

Of course there are all the cute one and only creatures that we see on the post-cards and on Twitter or whatever anyone is stupid enough to do on the poota. But on landing in Oz it really is startling, it's like seeing colour for the very first time. Another less remarked upon revelation is that unlike the world of European people's hidden agendas Aussies are straight up—no bullshit façades.

OK, the politicians have been remorselessly turning this country of free spirit into a place where you're not allowed to do anything but it would take another whole book to go into that. Suffice it to say that the prohibitive fear culture of the last 10–15 years has been brutal against the live music club scene. Enforced Stepford Wife licensing hours have put down many a club.

On a more formal level the culture is now on a level with any other country bar none. Aussie artists and musos are sharing muvvafukka stuff with the rest of the world. In the '40s and '50s last century this might not have been seen to be the case.

One of my most exciting projects in the near future is co-writing a double concerto for didge and violin with Will Barton, the world number one didge player. We had a fantastic meeting and jam in Brisbane last time round and it's led to us doing this exciting project. We'll be playing the concerto all over the fukkin' shop including Australia.

One of my best appearances was on court at the Australian Open, no, I wasn't competing for the women's title. I played my composition 'Face Off' before Federererer beat Nadal in the final. Seeing those guys play from a couple of yards away … WOW! My performance flushed out and riled a couple of fogies, mission accomplished. I've been known as the Nick Kyrgios of the violin for the last 40 years or so…? …!

Back to the creatures of Australia. There's a big PR thing about all the dangerous muvvafukka species in Oz. Sharks, spiders, snakes, jellyfish etc., etc., bla-blah … but last time I was over a rather humiliating statistic came out. In one year domestic horses were responsible for four times as many casualties/fatalities as all the rest of those creatures put together. My kingdom for a—NO—BEWARE OF THE HORSE! Nay, Sir, N-a-a-a-a-aiy.…

I can't wait to get back to Oz, see everybody, and make some killa horses, sorry, I mean killa SOUNDS.…

Poland

I first fell in love with Poland in the late nineties, when I got invited to play Elgar, believe it or not. I was really struck with the kind of heart of the musicians who I was playing with and their intellect, whether it was that Elgar thing or after the concert, the jamming that we had in various clubs was just excellent from both sides of it. The classical fuckers had great heart and like real attitude towards work. They weren't looking at the watch, the rehearsals just went on until we got it as good as we wanted to have it, that was great. With jazz, it was the same type of attitude, music for music, not for fucking other reasons.

But then I went back to Malvern and I met Agnieszka there, who is my wife now. (Malvern is quite responsible for quite a lot!) I'd played in Warsaw before and she said, "Look, if you like jazz and that, I'll show you Krakow." So, she took me to Krakow and we became kind of what you call "in a relationship", and we kind of fell in love with Krakow. Because it wasn't the tourist thing. It was just Polish people and quite a lot of jazz clubs. There was a whole future that we thought Krakow might have because it's within that triangle of cities, Prague, Budapest, Vienna. We thought it was going to be another of those. We didn't realise that it was going to be completely inundated with tourists and that in the end we'd have to move away because I'm not going to fucking live surrounded by fucking tourists, it's horrible, it's meat market all over the fucking streets. So, a couple of years ago we moved out into this mountain area near the Slovakian border, which is very beautiful. The village has only 60, 70 houses and a jazz club. People are coming from Germany and from America to hear the gigs there, it's some of the best of kind of Polish indie rock and Polish jazz. We kind of fell on our feet there, and we've built this wooden house. Obviously, we've got glass in the windows, but the whole house is made of either wood or straw, even the tiles are made of wood. The drains are made of wood. Everything's made of wood, and it's a beautiful feeling being surrounded by this warm substance. So, there's no kind of fake bullshit in it.

It's sheep territory there. We've got a lot of sheep—or rather the local shepherd, who's a friend of ours, does. We let him use the land and he'll help us in the winter when there's snow everywhere. We help each other and he gives us free sheep's cheese and whatever. So, it's all pretty nice. We're growing all of our vegetables; we're doing beekeeping. It was Agnieszka's idea to start the beekeeping and it was a brilliant reaction to all of the fucking negativity going around, to think, "well, fuck it, at least let's get something growing out of the ground." The amount of honey which comes out from these little bastards, it's phenomenal. The fields which we have all around us, they provide so many different types of flowers and pollen that they can fucking collect—it's rewarding! We only just got the beehives in last spring, because that's when you need to do it, when something is out there for the bees to go and collect, and now, our swarms have divided because they're doing too well. They've got so much fucking food that they fill the hives with fucking honey and think: Oh, let's go and populate somewhere else.

It's funny, I'm allergic to a lot of stuff, to more stuff than Agnieszka is, but she's really much more allergic to these bee stings. I'm not very frightened of them. I think they can smell fear and if you are frightened, then they are going to fuck with you worse. We've got the hats, where you walk around looking like Miss Saigon, it's cool, we got all the shit, but if you just want to quickly go and do something and you don't want to put all the gear on, put on long trousers. It's important to wear long trousers! Also, we've had a bit of help from a local guy, a real person telling us stuff (not the internet or something), because I don't want to do American beekeeping, fucking them all up. They'd probably say: put a mobile phone in there and see what happens. I'm also not a big fan of computers. I've never opened an email in my fucking life. it makes people fucked up, I think, that virtual so-called communication.

Being in that beautiful mountainous area, I also do a lot of hiking. I love hiking, man! All the views you can gain to see and the wildlife, it's unbelievable. There's wolves and bears up there. They'd kill a dog immediately, but they're frightened of human beings. So, there's not really any danger for a person, they'd just fucking run off. The wolves, they kind of come and polish of a couple of sheep every now and then, that's the main concern. But all of the flocks of sheep in Poland have a guy, a kind of under shepherd, with them. They've got dogs, obviously to protect them, but they also stay with the sheep and so they can scare wolves away or just keep the flock guarded. I've seen a wolf once, I haven't seen the bears yet, but there's only about 10 of them. It's funny, because since we're on the Slovakians' border, there's quite a lot of discussions, the Slovakians think it's the Slovakians' bears and the Polish think that they're Polish ("It's our bear"—"no, it's ours, we saw it first"—"no, we saw it yesterday.")

In terms of neighbourhood, we get on very good with the locals. I did a concert to raise money for the bridge which goes to the club, because their wooden bridge was collapsing and getting all the amplifiers into the club and shit was becoming very difficult for the musicians. It has my name on it. The Kennedy bridge.

There's just one horrible neighbour, who's been the worst neighbour I've ever had. She'd bring in fukking concrete mixers on our land and dumping all kinds of bullshit. The police have had to be called not just by us, but by many people on many occasions with this woman. There's quite a lot of strange politics in Poland and I think she's a representation of it. But everyone else, we all get on good because we all help each other. Right now, there was a huge fire in the village near us. I'm going to play for them guys because they weren't insured. You know, a lot of the older people in farther Eastern parts of Europe, they don't have insurance. When they're left with no farming gear, their barns all burned down, it's just fucked up. That's the problem with the wooden houses, they can go down rather quick. So yes, we'll do stuff for each other. It's a good, tight little community.

Agnieszka lives almost permanently in the village because we've got this old dog that we look after called Huxley, a Weimaraner, and he can't really move. He can't really walk, we're stuck there, looking after him. We can't take him to fucking England, we couldn't even bring him to Berlin because how would he have his shit and piss when he can't really walk? It's great for him that we're surrounded by fields and hills, but for me? I've got to have some fucking interaction with people in a cultural town, I started missing it quite a lot.

The Barbarossa, Her Lebensraum Policy, The Wooden Tub, And The Burial Mound

DOCTOR: *Good to see you, Mr Kennedy. What seems to be the problem?*

I have a doctorate so maybe addressing me as Mr is a little inappropriate … I don't do poota games idiocy but in at least one aspect of life we didn't need the game or the poota because we well and truly got the Neighbours From Hell.

DOCTOR: *Carry on....*

I will … *Carry On Doctor!* We started building our house in one of the most beautiful villages in Poland about 15 years ago. Being in a mountainous area we were particularly considerate not just in building any old wooden highlander style house but in creating something which was even in the architectural style of our specific small and beautiful area.

DOCTOR: *Yawn.…*

Eventually we moved in and during the elapsed time I have played more than 50 gigs for no fee in the local music club Muzyczna Owczarnia. Gigs appear before the audience as if they have fallen like an apple onto Isaac Newton's head but contrary to the laws of gravity a lot of work is involved in order to make them happen. Booking each member of the band, organising rehearsals, organising travel, organising food for everyone involved in the show—Agnieszka did all of that never ending list. I wrote and arranged the music and of course rehearsed the band and … played the performances!... Neither Agnieszka or I want to be a leech so we prefer to give more to the society we live in than that which we take out of it.

DOCTOR: *You are nice.*

During the time we have lived here we have found the local people to be honest and kind. The customs around here are traditional and important. There is a local form of highlander music that I have become involved in and am trying to get to grips with. What with my shitter than shit dyslexic Polish, music is a great way to communicate.

DOCTOR: *You are nice.*

We also let the local shepherd use our land to graze his sheep. Sheep are an integral part of the traditional agriculture here in this area. From the local shepherds there are sheepskins, sheepskin slippers, and various delicious sheep milk products including oscypek, bundz, bryndza and other sheep-originated cheeses. The presenceof the sheep and their products are also a huge asset around here to attract the godforsaken tourists who generate essential revenue for many local people who rent out rooms.

DOCTOR: *Very, very nice-ish … yawn …*

After a while a remorseless development of the village started, not by people who want to live here but by people who live elsewhere while wanting to cash in by renting more and more rooms. These kats, as well as making the amazingly clean air much more interesting because of the constant pollution from their building projects, put the icing on the cake with their garish light displays used to advertise and call attention to their rentals. The clean air and the night sky gone in one very foul swoop. Also, if you don't like quietness, the endless noise of bulldozers and industrial vehicles is fantastic.

DOCTOR: *Are you feeling all right?…*

"Excuse me, we don't want to be rude, but do you realise you are walking on someone else's land?"

"Oh, it's OK. We have permission from the owner."

"We are the owners…"

We can't count how many times this happened and they were always guests who were renting rooms from The Barbarossa. She advertises having accommodation for 30 people in what was given planning permission for two houses, each consisting of one family dwelling.

DOCTOR: *Are families very large in Poland?*

Very droll, Doctor. It turned out that the calm before the storm was well and truly over before guests were being directed illegally onto our land. The Barbarossa was here.

DOCTOR: *Good God. You mean the attempted German invasion of Russia?*

Not exactly but something very similar in mentality. For want of a better word or name that's what we call her and is how I will refer to her here.

We first became aware of The Barbarossa when she started developing and building on her plot which is in close proximity to our home and land (the end result unfortunately looks like a wooden tub on a burial mound). Concrete mixers and other heavy works' vehicles started coming up our private driveway to gain easier access to her building plot instead of using her legal access below it. She lied to us, telling us that she had permission from the local council to do this. We found out that the council had flatly refused her any permission whatsoever.

DOCTOR: *My professional character evaluation is that she's a LIAR. No one likes liars.*

Of course not, Doctor, and those were our exact sentiments. She then continued these illegal trespasses by her workforce despite us letting her and them know that they were not allowed on our land.

We then had an IDEA. We put up a gate with a NO ENTRY sign and got the council to remind The Barbarossa that she had no permission to go on their land or ours.

DOCTOR: *Was that all sorted then?*

NO! Her workmen/builders vandalised our gate five times and continued to trespass our private driveway for convenient and illegal access to The Barbarossa's building site. Our patience was by then worn thin enough to call the police and we then finally got a bit of respite.

DOCTOR: *What a sodding bitch—oops! Sorry—I mean, was that the end of the matter?*

NO! Doctor. We also have a bit of land. The Barbarossa's husband started to shout raucously on it like a right bonehead—sometimes at 7 a.m., right next to an inner fence which has been erected close to our house. He/it also continued driving his car over our land despite being told that we would not permit this. We and some friends who own neighbouring land decided that the only way to deal with this persistent antisocial and illegal trespass was to jointly fence our repeatedly abused land off and thereby fence The Barbarossa in. Hopefully she would then get the message that she wasn't able to comprehend verbally or in writing.

DOCTOR: *Inspired idea, Mr Kennedy—sorry, Dr. Kennedy.*

Thank you, Doctor.

DOCTOR: *That's fine, Doctor. Was that the end of the matter?*

OF COURSE NOT—don't be silly, Doctor, I mean not so clever Doctor. She didn't like the fence. A few days went by and it was then that the attempted intimidation commenced. At 1 a.m. between five and eight no hopers started driving their silly little jet skis as noisily as possible on our land, damaging it as much as possible. On one of these occasions the little halfwits attempted to assault Agnieszka by trying to run her over. They thought they were afforded anonymity by their little tin pot helmets covering their smaller wooden tops, but their collective intelligence had left tracks in the snow which we followed the next day. At the end of the tracks we found the same jet skis parked next to a bloke who we knew hung out with The Barbarossa. A little bit of enquiry and we had the identities and addresses of all the assailants.

DOCTOR: *Very Sherlockian, Mr Dr. Kennedy. What did you do?*

Well, Doctor, it was all we could do to prevent ex-military friends of ours from going round to the little pillocks' homes and giving the cowards a lesson they'd never forget. After it became clear that we knew who the petty criminals were The Barbarossa's husband coincidently stopped leaving their tub (I mean house) on his jet ski at the same time that the other boneheads were out disturbing the village on theirs. Simultaneously and coincidentally (ha! ha!) our fences were repeatedly destroyed and vandalised.

DOCTOR: *Oh dear, couldn't you try landmines? They're effective.*

Not very humane or practical, Doctor. That type of advice is NOT what I'm paying for … after the failure of those guys' intimidation tactics the third and fourth prong of The Barbarossa Operation were 3: to try and whip up a frenzy of indignation about our fence amongst others in our village. This even included trying to turn other people against us in the club in which I've given more than 50 gigs for free … Her conniving efforts fell on deaf ears (unusual for a music club!)

DOCTOR: *Very droll, Mr Doctor Kennedy. Ach, mein gott. Vot nixt, I mean what next?*

Well, we weren't the first people in the world to fence off our land, won't be the last, and we had more reason than most having a disgustingly overreaching neighbour like The Barbarossa who thinks she's above needing to consider other people and what belongs to them—And guess what we saw her laying a concrete base for in the middle of her anti-Kennedy's fence propaganda campaign?

DOCTOR: *Ach, vasss, vot, what?*

A fence!!…

DOCTOR: *She is a hypnokit—I mean hypocrite.*

Verily and amusingly so, Doctor. The fourth prong of The Operation Barbarossa was in fact lucky for us. She started using and trying to appropriate the land of two other people without their permission. The first was by digging up her immediate neighbour's land and creating a huge land shelf for the use of her paying guests to sunbathe or barbecue on. These neighbours were taken completely by surprise and also had to call the police in order to get The Barbarossa to reverse the ugly damage she had caused.

Some other friends of ours had their gates repeatedly opened and their garden reversed into with a tree being taken out in the process. In the same garden of theirs their gardener was bitten by The Barbarossa's dog.

DOCTOR: *this is typical of an Operation Barbarossa process. It is a Lebensraum Policy. Oh deary me. Well, I have heard that these friends of yours are considering moving out because they can't bear living next to such a revolting neighbour. Try to persuade them not to move....*

Of course, we need as many decent people around as possible to counteract these petty criminal types. It's also not good for the village as a whole to get a reputation for this type of repellent criminal activity. In 15 years before the arrival of The Barbarossa we never had trouble with anyone but now I can hardly recommend the village as a safe place to come for a holiday. As it is, all of the village supports us now that they have seen the Barbarossa's true nature.

DOCTOR: *What this lesson should have taught you Herr Mr Dr. Kennedy is wherever you are, don't let lowlife fikkeners spoil everything for everybody. Fight them all the way and don't give an inchen. Mr Dr. Kennedy, it seems that there's nothing wrong with you, but send this Barbarossa thing to see me. Maybe I can cure it.*

Maybe—if you have handcuffs. Anyway, anyhow, this session was really cathartic for me and far better value than all those psychoanalysts who work near where I live in Belsize Park. Thank you, reader, I mean Doctor.

DOCTOR: *And was that the end of the matter?*

Well, if so I will no longer have to pay for any more appointments with you, my lovely matey....

N.B. Dear Reader, many thanks for bearing with me on this. It was therapeutic, so you've done me a favour. It's possible that only a couple of hundred people in Jaworki will find this interesting or amusing but who knows, this book might sell even less than that. That'll have been up to you and other people. You might be one of quite a few people who have had to experience a Neighbour From Hell so I thought I'd share this experience with you. If you've never had a Neighbour From Hell, beware, one might move into your vicinity at any moment! Looking back on it, I think we ponced around trying to be reasonable for far too long. If we'd have called in the police earlier we might have nipped a load of shit in the bud. That's my advice anyway. Boneheads don't turn into Gandhi or Einstein overnight.

(Contrary to possible perception the above narrative is 100 per cent true apart from the Doctor, who I put in to lighten things up a bit).

Enforced Inactivity

In this period of enforced inactivity, it's been good to realise that the planet is still carrying on, potatoes still grow in the soil, carrots grow, fucking turnips grow, the bees are still fucking working, and whatever Boris Johnson wants to do, he can't stop all of that kind of stuff.

I only mention this fucking disease on Mondays and Thursdays. So, if you read this on any other day, just skip the part. I don't want to spend all week moaning and whingeing. I'm not sorry for myself, I was really lucky compared with a lot of people, look at all them pubs and fucking clubs, which are having it incredibly difficult. Things are starting to get a bit ridiculous now that the shit is more or less over: When the restrictions had been like lifted, what do people want to do? Do they want to rebuild a fair society? All the things they're moaning about not having, do they want to rebuild them? No, they "need a holiday" and everyone's got to get on a fucking airplane. I think, two days a week, that's long enough to manage this stupid moaning.

On a financial level, last year was kind of weird, although Poland is not so expensive to live in. But being in one place for the whole year, it's actually been amazing, seeing the seasons change when normally I'd have been travelling around. I have played the IV seasons so many times, but I've never seen them all happen. I'd always be going somewhere. It's been great, otherwise I would have never seen these beautiful changes that happen in fucking nature. Actually, it was quite a fruitful time and I did some stuff which I would never have had the chance to do. I wrote quite a lot of this book and I wrote a concerto, too, because with touring you're in and out of cars and hotels, it's too schizophrenic. After all, the best shit happens is when it's completely quiet and this countryside area is perfect for writing. So, in many ways, the pandemic gave me a chance to do stuff.

I'm Not Retired Or Anything

I'm not retired or anything, only in the metaphorical way that I retired from artistic slavery. I divorced myself from the typical jazz scene or the typical classical world, because I don't want to be in such a boring case scenario where people are just doing everything by the book. I'm only doing the shit that I love doing. I'm keeping the amateur spirit. People use amateur in a disparaging way, but in fact, it's the real business about what art or musical sports could really be.

So, as one of my dreams, I want to see Aston Villa win the FA cup! I also want to go to a game of St Pauli, I've been in the stadium, but I've never seen a game. I really want to go and see Union, too, particularly with the stadium being built by the fans, that is just such a beautiful story. It must be a special feeling, coming from just standing in there. On the musical side of things, I've got a dream of getting an album on inclusivity done. Because I think everyone's starting to worry now about themselves. LGBT is now divided up into about a hundred different sexual categories where everybody only worries about themselves. People worry about antisemitism, others worry about racism, but we need to all join together and be inclusive, not worry about each separate individual. I don't want any prejudice. There's a lot of divide and conquer shit going on, and whoever's doing the dividing, they're doing a great job at it because we've all been divided up into these little compartments. It's just so sad that everyone's kind of feeling so marginalised thinking they're the only one in that situation. So, me and the singer Cleveland Watkiss, we're making an album of inclusive music. I would like to get out a message to a few people: "Look, let's deal with things together. Rather than unfortunate minorities, let's be a fortunate majority with everyone in it." This ambition is probably a more concrete, tangible one, more tangible than Aston Villa winning the FA cup. I don't think that's going to happen in my lifetime.

One of the other dreams, I suppose, is perhaps to move to Berlin. I like living in the Polish countryside, but I want to live also in a fucking city where there's some stimulating cultural shit going on and if this city fucking fits the bill, man, it's very good. So if any of you readers are renting out a great flat in Berlin, don't be shy and write me a letter or something.

When it comes to young violinists—or young folk in general, I'd like to pass on a few things, but in a way which is not teaching, because teachers or professors, they do it in a way which is convenient for them. And they end up with all their picket fences, all that people playing the same shit in the same way. That's exactly not the way to do it. There's this school in Birmingham next to Villa, which I want to start doing some stuff in and it's got every racial denomination that I know about. I want to bring these young kids together, even if it's just playing hand drums at first … music is a great collaboration, it's possibly even better than football because you can have like 30 fuckers all playing together and benefiting from collaborating with each other. So, I'm interested in trying to get music across to these people and—in conjunction with Aston Villa, trying to get these kids playing for the Villa because … out of the Indian and Pakistani community, not one person has made it into the first team of the Villa although it's surrounded by this incredible wealth of culture. There's so many young kids, obviously there's an untold amount of talent either for football or for music. I'm just starting to talk with the Villa about it. It'd be great to help people getting into football, getting into music, expressing themselves. I dread to think how long it is I've been going to the Villa, probably 50 … more, 55 years. It'd be nice to put something back into that, you know, so that's an idea I've got. I want to include a lot of cultures and lots of different financial backgrounds and when it's not only for rich people, then one has to find a more homogenous heterogeneous? approach to it. Not that you've got practise your violin for fucking four hours a day. I see sport and music both as being forms of self-expression with collaboration, two beautiful things that people can benefit from. I want to continue breaking the barriers.

As for the rest, I think I'll carry on playing because what else is there better to do? You know, I love playing the fucking music.

MY POLICE LEAGUE TABLE

During my travels and even at home I have had the interesting experience of meeting various representatives of our tax payer funded police forces around the world. On some occasions this has been a more dubious privilege than on others.

I have found it interesting to compare my police experiences and make a league table (considering that Aston Villa invented the whole concept of league tables I appreciate a bit of order!) with number one being the best and last place being the shittest of the shit.

Here are the results of my personal investigations. Those results don't include the rather obvious phone tapping I was subject to in London (because of having the Irish name Kennedy) at the times of the troubles involving the IRA and the English.

Joint 1st The London Metropolitan Police and The Berlin Police

THE LONDON METROPOLITAN POLICE
(A Southern Version Of A Geordie Band?)

While working with Paul McCartney during the mid-eighties I had made friends with the guitarist Keith Airey and had arranged a jam session in my place with musos including Mark Price (drummer from All About Eve), Phil Gould (my mate from Level 42), and amongst others a brilliant group of Egyptian musicians I'd met when doing a charity gig. A lot of friends were in attendance including Donovan (who was having a very intelligent conversation with a lampshade), Dave Gilmour (who I think had introduced the lampshade to Donovan) and a lot of other nice fukkers. Nick Laird-Clowes was taking notes on the aforementioned conversations. Knowing his originality it is probably in one of his songs somewhere. There was plenty of alcohol and other stuff flowing, enhancing the vibe.

In the meanwhile the jam was steaming. My electric violin was wailing over heavy rock beats and the ney, oud and qanun (all amplified) were producing a pulsing vibrancy which was permeating and lifting the whole room. Torrential notes and primal rhythms were visually changing the colour of the air along with a good bit of healthy recreational smoking. The music was of course killa loud and the whole atmosphere was like that of a club which without much imagination could have been called The Rock—East Den Of Iniquity. Then in the middle of a psychedelic build Nick Laird-Clowes started approaching me and I thought to myself "Interesting, he wants to free form a vocal". But in fact the reality was something different. He wanted to tell me something.

At first Nick's attempts to communicate with me looked like a speech by Marcel Marceau so I stepped away from the band and drew him aside in order to hear him.

NICK: (*looking nervous*) The Police are here.

ME: (I had become friendly with Andy Summers through playing with him and John Etheridge in Birmingham Ronnie Scott's and had also had one or two conversations with Sting) That's great man. I've got another guitar kicking around if Andy wants to play. Let them in!

NICK: No mate, you don't understand. It's the law enforcing police.

ME: What?...

NICK: law enforcement men, man!

I go to the front door of my place and find myself staring at two members of The Old Bill.

ME: Ummm. Hello Ossifers. Nice to see you. Is there anything I can do for you?

OFFICER No 1: Yes Sir. I'm afraid we have received a complaint so we need to ask you to turn your stereo down.

ME: I'm sorry ossifer but there's a problem with that. Come in and I'll show you what I mean.

OFFICER No 2: The music sounds fine Sir but we need you to turn it down.

ME: Come in and you'll see what I mean... please.

I lead the officers through a little vestibule past my small glass doored bathroom within which some of the kats are satisfying their habitual needs with their beaks. Luckily the officers completely disregard their folly and follow me into my one and only main room.

ME: (*pointing to the band who are still blasting it out*) See what I mean guys? There isn't really a knob I can turn to lessen the volume of this kind of stuff. (I scan the room with a quick glance at all the joints and the resultant haze but it's too late now) Would you like to stay and have a drink?

OFFICER 1: I'm sorry but we we're on duty so that is impossible. The music's not bad. (In England that is regarded as a compliment)

OFFICER 2: To tell you the truth the complainant has wasted our time before. He's uptight but that's his problem. We have another call so please make sure it doesn't get any louder here and we'll leave it at that. We've done our job by informing you of the complaint.

OFFICER 1: This was less boring than most of the callouts we get.
At that point they start leaving and I show them out past the beak bathroom.
I then go back and rejoin the astral jam.
NICK: Wow—groovy!
DONOVAN: Who were those dressed up guys? You're a lovely lampshade.
The session went on until 2 p.m. the next day.

LONDON METROPOLITAN POLICE: SCORE = 10/10, 1st PLACE
Remarks: Worth the tax payers' money. Like politicians who are also our employees and representatives, the more above themselves employees get the less they are worth. These guys were cheerful, they dealt with the situation and didn't escalate the problem when there wasn't one. Some of the guys would do well to learn from the example shown by these officers and to remember that it's us taxpayers who put the food on their tables.

THE BERLIN POLICE

Berlin is one of my favourite cities because of the people. Whether playing in The Philharmonie or The A Trane I find Berliners who understand and love their music. Berliners have also had a long history of being accustomed to people of strong individuality so my Knut loving friends never find me any trouble at all.

Pre-concert I spend all day in my hotel suite. I don't see anyone. I just do all the little things necessary to be as prepared as possible for the gig. A bit of violin practice time and a wee bit of space to think seem as if they should be automatic and simple to get but if you don't consciously protect your time and space you never get them. If you are dedicated to music then concentrating on doing a better gig than yesterday and honouring your audience with beautiful music are the name of the game. Talking inanely over a midday cup of coffee doesn't come into the picture. A new chord sequence or dynamic contrast for Body and Soul, or a new tempo for the last movement of Beethoven's violin concerto, or writing a new song or composition—all of these are far more interesting. Coffee is anyway a gateway drug to cocaine, neither of which I like. Both are the domain of the chattering classes and they often lead to people becoming jumped up about themselves on the crest of a fake wave of energy.

In short, I want every gig I do to be as well prepared and spontaneous as possible. Oddly enough, in music one aspect doesn't survive well without the other. On the other hand we shouldn't be burdening our friends in the audience with too much of a diligent appearance when they've turned up to relax and get carried away. After all, one smile from a cretin is worth more than a hundred ever so serious haughty frowns from a classical musician. As performers it is our duty to take our audiences on an enlightened and emotional journey, not to reveal how hard it is to flick our fingers in the right order or get to the depth of a Beethoven Fugue. A chef's perspiration should stay in the kitchen, not end up on the plate!

Anyhow, having said all of that, my social time starts at the beginning of the gig with my colleagues and audiences, and doesn't normally finish until well into the next morning. I'm not one of these artists who turn off the musical tap at the end of the gig once they've got the $$$. It's music all the time for me. That's what has kept me pretty young. This love of music frequently results in a late late jam session or musical hang after leaving the venue, either in a small club or in my hotel suite. Having asked the hotel to accommodate my travelling party above, below and around my suite there should be no danger of disturbing any other innocent guests even with my involvement in music day and night.

On this occasion we finished partying at The Philharmonie and proceeded to The A—Trane where courtesy of my friend and great drummer Ernst Bier there are often amazing jam sessions. After a killa session there we went onto my suite to carry on killing it. I love Berlin and have a fair few friends there who I always enjoy hanging with so we had to be thorough!

Things had calmed down to the extent that we were alternating between listening to a bit of music and jamming on piano, guitar and bass with one or two others joining in with whatever instruments they had. Nice and calm—no rumpus! A bit of spliff, wine, beer and vodka like normal. Each one to their own but together so to speak.

It was at this point that we had a polite visit from two of the Berliner Landespolizei. One was BIG and the other SMALL. I invited them in so that they could hear the lack of loudness of my music and also see the activity or lack of it in my suite. Admittedly we were pretty wasted and not at all energetic.

ME: Hello officers, do you speak English?

OFFICER BIG: Yes Sir, not very well but I try.

ME: Well, thanks. That's a lot better than my German.

OFFICER SMALL is looking through the gandja cloud at everyone uselessly trying to hide their joints behind themselves or under tables etc. ... Curtis Mayfield's Pusherman synchronistically floats towards us from the stereo.

ME: How can I help you? Is anything the matter?

BIG: We are here because of a complaint from another hotel guest.

ME: OK, but we've got and are occupying all the rooms around here so I don't think it's too loud ... and I'm not paying for this suite here in order to be Howard Hughes ... anyway, the geezer should pay for the privilege of hearing our music. He's probably been lurking in the corridor which is the only place he could hear us from. He obviously suffers from penis and music envy.

BIG: You are having a good time.

ME: Yeah. Look at all these nice people....

Both officers regard my friends who are sitting around two low tables. They all look up with inane grins on their faces. After patrolling the room SMALL returns to the side of BIG.

BIG: To me the sound is not too loud. The person who complained is not a good person. Please don't make things louder and perhaps keep the door closed.
SMALL: Gute Nacht, Sir.
ME: Guten Morgen and thank you. We love the Berlin Police!
I close the door behind BIG and SMALL, take a long toke, a long sip of beer and say "Long Live The Berlin Police!"

BERLIN LANDESPOLIZEI: SCORE 10/10, 1ˢᵗ PLACE
Remarks: Like the London Met the Berliner Landespolizei are not an abuse of the tax we pay for their services. They realise that a complainant can be a negative busybody arschloch causing more trouble and wastage of police time than the people they complain about. We and the police in all countries should take a leaf out of the Berliners' book and remember that they are here for us, not vice versa.

Joint 3ʳᵈ Policja Warszawa and The London Metropolitan Police (When My Kid Sark Was About 5 or 6 Years Old)

POLICJA WARSZAWA

A while back I was invited to play at the Singer's Jewish Festival in Warsaw. After not having heard anything of the festival in the prior years I was pleasantly surprised that they were still a going concern. The promotion of Jewish culture is important.

I had finished my composition 'The Magician Of Lublin' inspired by the book of the same name written by Isaac Bashevis Singer whose chronicles of Jewish life in Poland and America are some of the most inspiring ever written. At the time I was also playing a well-established programme of works by George Gershwin (most of which I had learned when playing as a kid with Stéphane Grappelli who was an inspired master of these songs). I decided that combining these two projects would give our cultural Warsaw audience an original, stimulating and varied perspective of Jewish culture. Because of my long love of Klezmer, Jewish jazz musicians (such as Artie Shaw, Benny Goodman, Dave Brubeck[25] etc.), Jewish culture in general being part of my life as far back as I can remember and after receiving beseeching claims of poverty from the Singer Festival I agreed to go up to Warsaw for a vastly reduced fee which was tantamount to performing on a charity basis.

You can imagine my surprise when the majority of Gołda Tencer's employees met my team and myself with an un-trained arrogance, unchecked hostility and an ignorant obstructive attitude. Despite being faced with parochialism of the level I had never before experienced in a concert environment my band and I

---

25 For the pernickety small minders, Brubeck identified as Jewish.

managed to play and give our audience something special and of the moment. It was, of course, our job to make sure that our audience were totally unaware of the boorish behaviour the Singer Festival staff were subjecting us to. Amongst some magic moments were a beautiful bass solo from Piotr Kułakowski and some wonderful 'cello playing from Peter Adams. Neither of them Petered Out …. sorry!

The audience demanded a fair few encores after which we went back to our dressing room to celebrate having delivered for our beloved Warsaw audience. Our audience in this historic capital has very high intelligence and a huge heart. I've always loved them because of that.

When reaching backstage did I receive any thanks for delivering such a successful gig for next to nothing? NOT EXACTLY! The pig-like behaviour continued with various friends being refused entry or turned away despite having completely correct accreditations. These included the legendary jazz violinist/saxophonist/composer Michal Urbaniak, the wonderful healer Zbigniew Nowak and important high status ambassadorial people from the Middle East. Judging from their staff's behaviour the last thing The Singer Festival considers necessary or desirable for the Middle East is peace!

Then, only a short time after the end of our concert and in a totalitarian style attempt all too reminiscent of recent history the "Festival" called the police to try and turf us out of our dressing room. We were on the verge of leaving anyway but we decided to stay a little longer just to show who was BOSS! Prior to leaving I thought I'd go and have a word with the police. From our easy-going conversation it was clear that they were embarrassed to be having their time wasted by being called so unnecessarily and could see that my people were kool. There really should be far greater penalties for wasting police time. These first three league positions have all been examples of self-indulgent people trying (and failing) to use or abuse police time for fabricated and selfish reasons.

As far as the Singer Festival are concerned, in a career travelling all over the world spending well over forty years playing between 50 and 120 gigs each year, they are the worst promoters I have ever worked with. That is unfortunately the only reason they merit a mention in this book! I hope what could be a nice little festival survives but it won't do very well if it continues to be run by such a ghastly mix of old style informer types and inane nouveau bourgeoisie airheads.

POLICJA WARSZAWA: SCORE 7/10, 3rd PLACE
Remarks: called for self-indulgent reasons which wasted police time Policja Warszawa did a good job preserving law and order regarding the promoters and did well to see the real picture. They weren't fooled into being used as a tool for someone else's vindictive purposes.

THE LONDON METROPOLITAN POLICE
(WHEN MY KID SARK WAS ABOUT 5 OR 6 YEARS OLD)

ME: Sod it, Sark, let's drive back to London and think of what to do for our holiday.

SARK: OK Dad, that should be fun.

This particular episode involving the London police happened in 2001. We were surrounded by water which should have augured well for our canal boat holiday. However, ironically enough, there was no access to our canal boat because of flooding! It was quite a laugh looking at the new lake languishing where the River Severn and the confluent canal should have been. We were near Upton where there's a riverside pub which has a new naïve landlord every year because each incipient never takes into account the yearly flooding caused by the river breaking its banks. This time we were one of the victims. I had never imagined a situation of a boat being useless because of too much water.

ME: Yeah, the car is full of provisions so at least we can cook and use the food at home.... and there's plenty to do in London.

SARK: Daaad …. (*trying to be as sweet as possible*) can we stop at McDonald's on the way?

ME: No.

SARK: (*for the one hundredth time thinking the conversation might have another outcome*) Why not, Dad?

ME: The packaging looks nice and bright on the outside but you know what dark shit they put in the inside.

SARK: But I like it and Mom lets me have it (*in all likelihood this is a little fib*).

ME: You've seen my nice postcards (*my absolute favourite French art that I bought in Paris—pictures of Lenin addressing an old microphone labelled PRAVDA with the McDonald's logo behind him truthfully altered to McShit*) I'm not spending any money that I worked so hard for on that trash food which makes people sicker than its contents.

SARK: Aw Dad. You don't understand. It's really good.

ME: It's only really good for the people making loads of money out of it.... (*I feel myself becoming really boring but one can't let a 5-6 year old kill his health by eating shit food marketed primarily by silly bright colours*).

On the way we get a service station meal and I of course steer Sark away from the silly McColours McRipp-off and get a couple of lamb shanks which are easier to trace back to once having been an animal. It's really hard to fuck up a lamb however McImaginative you are. (One of the best things I've done for Sark and Kyran [his elder brother] is helping them not to become veggies, but that was definitely not in order for them to ruin their health by eating shit fast food). After the meal and some more driving we eventually arrive home. I can immediately tell that something is wrong. We enter my little courtyard and I detect movement within the house. I tell Sark to stand outside the gate while I investigate and also call the police. It's impossible to tell who is in there—if they are armed with a knife or whatever it could be a terrible scene for a kid. There's still movement in the house and I see someone in a crouched position wearing a dark hoody running from one side in the house to the other.

Luckily the police have been having a pizza a few metres down the street (I often see them there if I'm getting a pizza for the kid) so their response to my call is utopian. They arrive within a minute! Within about five or ten minutes there is also a police helicopter flying overhead. The result of their response is that they found my driver of the time, who had the same initials as Venereal Disease, but whose name rhymes with Shit-tor Boiley, in my back garden which only has access from the house. He has sustained an injury probably from trying to climb down the drain pipe and he has a substantial amount of Polish złoty in his pocket.

After the police leave Sark and I get ensconced, get some… ummm … pizza delivered and watch *The Lavender Hill Mob*.

ME: Nice eventful day….

SARK: Yeah Dad … kind of….

So … that's how it turned out on the day. The police followed up by looking for fingerprints etc. and found the balcony door which had been repeatedly crowbarred up to gain entry and then closed by the burglar behind them. Despite the fact that in these days not many people had Polish currency because, unlike myself, they didn't frequently visit Poland with their Polish wives, the police weren't able to make any charges stick. This failure was in the face of the fact that my driver was the only person to know my movements accurately enough to be aware exactly when I would or wouldn't be in my home. According to English law he was just coincidentally in my garden, the guy I saw in the hoody could have been someone else and all the stuff which had repeatedly gone missing (to the tune of around £30,000 in value) was just disappearing into thin air by magic. Needless to say, because of the "circumstantial evidence" I changed drivers and my stuff stopped going missing (by more magic?).

LONDON METROPOLITAN POLICE SCORE: 7/10, 3ʳᵈ PLACE

Remarks: Amazingly quick response but in obvious circumstances were completely unable to apply the law. Plus point—they have good enough taste to know a good pizza when they see one.

5ᵗʰ The NYPD (New York Police Department)

At the time that I first went to New York to study at The Juilliard School of technical excellence and musical mediocrity, the New York Police were famous for their surly bad manners—their grumpiness was part of the charm of a city which was totally out of their control. Unlike our nice Western European police, they wouldn't give directions (apart from telling you to get a map) and if asked would seem to be on the verge of getting their silly little gun out. There is the old and well-known anecdote (I won't call it a joke) about a lost violinist in Manhattan which sums it up nicely:

LOST VIOLINIST: How do I get to Carnegie Hall?

NEW YORK POLICE BOLLOCK: Practise…

Obviously, it's important with the aid of logic to take this case scenario one stage further:

LOST VIOLA "PLAYER": Off-f-fic -s—s—er, how do I get to Carnegie Hall?

NEW YORK POLICE BOLLOCK: Turn back immediately. You have no chance.…

After living on Staten Island for a while (which involved a fantastic ferry ride each day passing The Statue of Gliberty and approaching an ever-growing Manhattan skyline on the way into Whitehall Terminal) it became apparent that I was spending far too much time just getting to and from Juilliard every day. The commuting including walking to Staten Island Ferry terminal, the ferry trip, the subway trip and the walk to Juilliard and this was wasting at least three hours there and back every day.

My violin professor was Dorothy DeLay (aptly named because she was always VERY late for our lessons with her—she was truly a significant DeLay) and she suggested that I could better maximise maximise the use of the day for practising, meeting other students and cultural activity in the most cultural city in the world if I wasn't wasting all that time commuting. It was then that I met my violinist friend Andy Schaw—Hi Andy, fukkin' long time no see and now you're in my book! I hear your selling fiddles as well as playing. Can you help me out?

Andy was already renting a bedroom in the flat of a psychotic old woman called … Nathorf. There was another room going so I rented that. This arrangement was short lived however. For some reason she had left some of her pans in the oven. Where I come from people don't use frying pans and saucepans in the oven but on the hob on top in order to fry and boil things. The result was that when preheating the oven to the heat my Stouffers TV dinner would need I went back to my room to practise a bit of repertoire which would most likely prove completely useless for my future career, probably something loathsome like Mozart or Paganini. After around twenty minutes of shit finger flicking a horrible acrid smell started enveloping the flat and soon appeared as black smoke. With Sherlock-esque deductive powers I tracked down the cause to the kitchen. It seemed that without informing me that it was where she kept them Nathorf had jammed a couple of pans in the oven in the most slovenly manner. It was their burning molten handles which were responsible for the foul pollution. My Stouffer's TV dinner just became a remote memory of an idea when being faced with such a salvage job.

Nathorf's reaction wasn't good. Something along the lines of:

NATHORF: Dub Eingleeeshy schweinpeeeg. Ich haf nezzzer leeiked der EEeengleeish.

ME: I love you too. What about my TV dinner?

Anyhow, the lovely meeting I had with the NYPD was as follows:

Mrs (who married her?) Nathorf grew to hate me because of the pan fiasco. She wanted me out, the feeling was mutual. She did however pursue achieving her aims unilaterally in a very interesting and unstable way. Some of her jewellery suddenly "went missing". She called the police and I was her prime suspect. The pigs arrived and after having a quick look at my longish hair and hearing my foreign accent they took me up to the 20th Precinct station for questioning. Apart from a few fun fingerprints the session was completely unproductive. I wasn't suddenly flush with cash and I hadn't stuffed Nathorf's crown jewels up my arse!

My freedom restored Andy and I immediately set to finding another place. It soon transpired that our favourite landlady "found" her jewellery again in her safe where she had put it. Nathorf—Bathorf—Shathorf—Spathorf—Prathorf—Fukkorf.

Andy and I soon found a new apartment to live in. (By the way, don't worry about my scholarship budget being too much, all dingy little places in New York are called apartments.) This new place was also not devoid of incident and when it came to "helping" two students the NYPD were far less eager to act. I remember there were four attempted burglaries in quick succession by some mental retard(s?) who most likely wanted our violins (having heard us practising) but didn't have the noodle to realise that if we were out so, invariably, were the fiddles. Each burglary became a tiny bit more desperate, a tiny bit more futile and a lot more invasive.

BURGLARY 1: The little widget(s) had simply picked the lock, found no fiddles and made off with our small TV. What a sacrifice for us living without American TV—how did we manage to enjoy life without all those lovely commercials? We upped it and put two locks on the door. N.B. the widgets had courteously left the door open to make our entering more convenient.

BURGLARY 2: The gidgets broke the two locks again and left the door open in a very welcoming manner. We put three locks on the door, one of them being a bastard bolt lock.

BURGLARY 3: The gidgets got in again! This time we got three new locks plus a big metal contraption making the door look like a Trojan horse. It was a right big unassailable fukka.

BURGLARY 4: In those wonderful days before compoota garbage-for-mation overload I used to get the huge *The New York Times* Sunday edition in order to find the microdot half inch long football score comprising of Aston Villa's Division Two result of Saturday's game (Saturday at 3 p.m. by the way—no selfish TV companies ruining it for the real fans by changing kick-off time). The NYT was the only way of finding out how we'd done. Phone calls were too expensive in those days.

I beetled up the stairs to get to the apartment as quickly as possible and read the result. This time I was confronted by something completely different. Having been defeated by The Trojan Horse Lock the little wankers had drilled and hacked a huge hole in the wall next to the door big enough for a man to walk through. Thinking "fair play to them" I availed myself of this facility and walked straight through it to the armchair. I needed to see our result. Having sat down comfortably I leafed through the sports section. The news was not good. We'd lost 1–0 at QPR. That season we eventually finished 3rd missing promotion to Division One by one place. The hole, meanwhile, was quite good. I could easily see whoever was walking up and down the stairs past the apartment door.

Incidentally the wankers could have easily got my fiddle with no trouble a couple of weeks later if they'd been bright/brave enough to follow me to D'Agostino's. I'd been back for a few hours when Andy said "Hey Nige (Yanks use "Hey" as a greeting quite frequently as in "Hey, Hey We're The Monkees") do you want to read through some Bartók duos?"

"Sure man" I said. (Yanks use the word Man a lot in order to clear up gender confusion. In the last 30 years my use of the words Baby or Man randomly to either gender with BBC-esque political correctness hasn't helped clear up this type of confusion at all)

"Oh shit man, where's my fiddle? Bollocks, I must have left it in the milk section. I definitely had it in D'Agostino's…"

The violin was a little cold but still sitting there in the cold storage surrounded by milk. It was obviously so shit that during the three hours it had been sitting there no-one could be bothered to take it—or maybe no-one wanted any milk.

NYPD SCORE: 4/10, 5th PLACE
Remarks: I'm sure that it's not for the first time and I'm sure the NYPD have done many worse things but arresting someone because of accusations by a psycho or for being a foreign student is not quite up to the required standard. There was no apology for wrongful arrest afterwards. AND … where were they for our four real, I repeat—REAL burglaries?

6th Frankfurt Airport Police

(*Special Award For Naffness)

In the old days when touring with my rather straight classical stuff (or should I say the world surrounding classical is a bit straight? One can't pin that on Beethoven or other emotional geniuses) I used to get my great friend K-Leb Clark to come along and help me loosen it up a bit. K-Leb is a fantastic singer song writer and one of the best rhythm guitar players in his own music that I've been lucky enough to play with. The mix of his Jamaican heritage with acoustic rock allied to his wonderful voice, charisma and song delivery is completely unique. I love his songs and we used to play spontaneously everywhere: Pubs, bars, hotel lobbies waiting to check in, streets, my after gig parties, backstage during autograph signing, airport transit buses, airport baggage collection areas etc., etc. It was great to hang with a good friend prizing that very moment which could happen any time playing very different music to that which I was playing in my gigs. We always had a good time (as did the people around us) and got up to some quality malarkey. Another plus is that K-Leb is a Villa fan so no fukkin' problems.

As it happened we were in Frankfurt Airport surrounded by glum business automatons more concerned with their phones than their lives. Or were their phones their lives? Our live renditions had already cheered them up in the transit bus from the plane so we decided to keep the vibe up at the baggage belt. We got the fiddle and guitar out and were having a great time. So were the suited fraternity, they were getting unexpectedly good music for free and a dead boring part of all their journeys had been brightened up a bit.

It was then that the little piglets turned up and informed us that busking was not allowed.

ME: Show me the money. Where is it? Without money changing hands this is not busking. Why not expand your mind and be nice?

PIGLETS: (*in a squeaky chorus*) NEIN!

NEVER BEING ONES TO CAUSE ANY TROUBLE (!) we packed our instruments immediately. Unlike the boisterous applause we had been getting earlier the little piglets were met with a chorus of boos and hisses and hurriedly left with their little pink faces. Whether this skin colour was momentary or hereditary I'll never know. Anyway, we had another good song in the band bus on the way to the hotel. Having been moved on by the police wasn't exactly a new experience....

FRANKFURT AIRPORT POLICE SCORE: 3/10, 6th Place
Remarks: no offence caused but low marks for being totally insignificant and completely naff. At least move us on with a bit of charm or menace. Where's the fukkin' attitude to match the nice toy uniform?

7th Madrid Police

Got to admit I have a soft spot for Atletico largely because of their proud and vain neighbours. Any team calling themselves "Los Galacticos" have to be a bunch of tossers and there is a huge emperor and his new clothes factor about them. They need a kick in the arse and that's why when watching them what I see is Los Turdos. The game we went to involved two real football clubs: Atletico Madrid vs Aston Villa, 3rd March 1998.

This is a short chapter so a few other self-entitled media teams which leave proper football fans underwhelmed are Bayern München, Man Ewe, sorry, United, Wisła Krakow, anything with Red Bullshit in it and Hamburg SV.

Following your team away in Europe or away anywhere is always a special experience. The hard-core and exuberant fans are the ones around you—no fair weather librarians like one sees at home sometimes. I made the trip with Pieter Daniel, the absolutely exceptional German—South African violinist (white). We are great friends and have been since being flatmates in New York in the 70s. What with football being so romantic we went with our girlfriends Foxie and Brixie.

The night before we'd had a bit of a night of it with a number of Villa brethren so were feeling a bit rough on the inside. Things got a bit rough on the outside on the way to the ground when the Atletico fans started to kick off with us. The claret and blue face paint we were wearing looked good and the Atletico were probably jealous of our good looks. Luckily for us it was before every five year old kid did those horribly naff Cats impersonations. What with having two girls with us and my lack of boxing skills mentioned elsewhere in this book we could have been in a vulnerable situation but that wouldn't have taken the Villa brethren into account. With the Villa it's one for all and all for one. Also, as a more effective weapon and in order to protect my sweet delicate violin playing hands I had developed a decent head-butt which had been successful pre and après match in England. The secret weapon remained unused on this occasion because the Villa brothers easily warded off the Manuels and we went on to watch a tight match. We lost 1–0 and won the second leg 2–1 thereby losing on the inane away goal rule which was only invented to satisfy TV scheduling, not us fans.

The Madrid Police deserve special mention for what they didn't do to prevent any trouble. They actually contributed to the trouble by administering a bit of truncheon to us from the safety of being behind their own fans and on the backs of their more intelligent horses.

MADRID POLICE SCORE: 2/10, 7ᵗʰ PLACE
Remarks: a waste of tax payers' money and their hospitality was reminiscent of the special dictatorship that employed them a few years earlier. (To be perfectly Franco, that's what I think) Plus point: nice to their own fans.

8ᵗʰ The West Midlands Police

Where the fuck am I? What am I doing here?.... and why is it so dark? Where's all the noise from the ground? (n.b. not stadium—that's a pseudo-name for a shit modern ground built in a shit industrial area thereby displacing a football club from its real community in order to enhance the bank account of a slimy property developer and more often than not line the pockets of the treacherous chairman. Why don't the Tories stop this happening again and again? Stupid question. This is just the type of capitalism that these Old Etonians and their sycophants love to see in action. If we're not careful next they'll decimate the NHS for personal gain... oops! They already have.) Where are my mates? It's really quiet ... and muddy ... my head hurts bad, man ... bollocks, there's fuck all happening ... it's all a bit ghostly around here. The match is over—there's no-one here—I've missed it all—what's the score? Where's my mates? Well ... I'll walk back into town and get the no. 34 bus back home. What a match ... NOT!

Gradually the pieces came back together. I'd been running to get to the back of the queue before it became even longer when one of the mounted West Midlands Pigs whacked me on the bonce with his truncheon. This happened near the Holte End turnstiles on Trinity Road. I must have made it to a kind of muddy ditch border of a hedgerow a few metres away in the Aston Hall Park which is where I came back to consciousness a few hours later. I was going to meet some friends on The Holte End below the half-time scoreboard on the left-hand side (facing the pitch) but when I didn't show up they thought I'd joined some other mates on the upper right hand side. (In those days 1: We weren't all mobile phone zombies because they didn't exist. 2: Fans were allowed to stand at games affordably because the Tory Justice Taylor Report trying to destroy football hadn't happened yet. 3: Police brutality on fans was normal and considered to be totally OK).

With both possees thinking I was with the other I was left to have a nice undisturbed sleep in the park—but really all my thanks for the insomnia cure should go to The West Midlands Police. My match ticket cost around £3. Oy little piglets! Can I have my money back?

WEST MIDLANDS POLICE SCORE: 1/10, 8ᵗʰ PLACE
Remarks: The one undeserved point is for accuracy with the truncheon. I should mention that all my other encounters with the police in Birmingham have been friendly and civil. It was just the type who were detailed to football matches who seemed to be prize boneheads.

9ᵗʰ The Hungarian Border Police

Sometimes the initial response of the police is correct! The next anecdote by and large is one of those cases even though the ensuing follow-up procedure was not quite so exemplary.

Just as John and I were breaking down walls in the music world, there was another, very real wall coming down. It didn't, unfortunately, affect the walls around a small Hungarian police station by the Romanian border. It was December 1989. A while back before every Tom, Dick, Harry or Teacher's Pet had been told to affect an interest in world music or jazz by their record company or manager in order to monetise their career I received a request to make a programme for Melvyn Bragg's South Bank Show. I had long had an interest in the music of Béla Bartók which was at least partially inherited from my former professor/mentor Yehudi Menuhin. He had known Bartók personally and had commissioned his sonata for solo violin which is the only work of its kind to attain a spiritual, technical and compositional level comparable to those by Bach. Incidentally Yehudi gave Bartók this commission a year before his death as an elegant way to lift him out of the atrocious poverty he was suffering from in New York as an anti-fascist

Hungarian exile. Even from Bartók Yehudi couldn't have quite guessed what an extraordinary landmark in the solo violin repertoire he was going to receive.

The idea I had for the show was threefold: 1: Bartók used the folk melodies of Hungary and Romania as spiritual and intellectual inspiration—find living guys still playing these original melodies. 2: To learn and play these folk melodies with those guys. 3: With my friend and colleague the great guitarist John "Ethel" Etheridge evolve a few new versions inspired by the same melodies as Bartók used but taking them our own way.

This idea involved flying to Budapest and then driving across the Romanian border to the Transylvania part of Crişana. There we would meet a very old Romani guy who knew some of those melodies in the original form we were searching for and which Bartók found so inspirational. This old fiddler was called "The Devil" because he only had two fingers on his left hand but could still play like a muvvafukka.

We landed in Budapest and then picked up a hire car. There were four of us: John Etheridge, the camera guy semi-director who I will now call Eyes, the soundman who I will now call Ears, and myself. The weather was horrible. Raining heavily with low clouds and fog with a visibility of maybe twenty or thirty metres. It was the kind of weather that we (who were brought up under capitalism) were led to believe was perpetual in any communist country.

Eyes was driving very unattractively like a rollercoaster going at 5 miles an hour. As well as the weather it seemed that driving on the right hand side of the road was another far too overwhelming challenge for him. I knew that taking over the car would probably save our lives plus there was the added advantage of no longer having to share my seating arrangement with Ethel's obnoxiously long legs.

Once in the driver's seat things went a lot better what with my experience of driving on the right hand side of the road (most of the time) when I was in America as well as in Europe. Eyes's snail like driving had slowed us up a lot so while driving safely I was trying to make up for lost time. There was a bit of a spoke in the wheel when we reached the Romania–Hungary border. The checkpoint was already closed and unattended. The next nearest border crossing was a whole fifty kilometres detour north and would have added almost 100 extra kilometres to our trip and all in the shit weather—plus it was getting dark.

I had an inspiration and thought "What the heck, let's give it a go." And with that I tried to drive the car under the red and white barrier post boom bar thing. The car was quite low to the ground and the barrier quite high but not low and high enough. There was an unpleasant grinding noise as the roof got caught under the barrier just above Ethel's long neck which made him duck—an unpleasant sight for me in the rear view mirror. I reversed out from under the barrier with more ominous scraping noises which sounded pretty bad for both the paintwork and the shape of the roof but at least we weren't stuck. Having done all of that I was ready for action.

ME: Right….before we head up to the other checkpoint let's at least walk over no man's land and have a piss in Romania to say we've already been there.

EYES: I don't think we better do that.

ME: What about you mate?

EARS: (*very originally*) No thanks, we better not.

ME: Ethel, are you a coward like those two?

ETHEL: (*calculatingly and bravely*) Well, old man. I don't need a piss right now old man and I think I'll guard my guitar old man. (*I was about 40 and he was a 48 years 'old man'*)

ME: Alright you wusses. I'm off to Romania. You lot can enjoy guarding the car.

I trudged off through the rain, under the barrier, through some muddy no man's land and under the Romanian barrier. I was now in Romania and it looked remarkably like the Hungarian wasteland I'd just been on. Better though for the absence of the lame wusses. It was also a relief to relieve myself. I turned round and trudged through the rain and mud back to the car. The wusses and myself were all back in the car and I engaged gears to Sputnik it up north.

EYES: (*using the visual skills finely honed by his job*) Hmmm… It's still raining hard and quite foggy. It's getting darker.

ME: Yes Sherlock.

EARS: (*using his soundman's audio skills finely honed by his job*) The rain is still heavy and making a lot of noise on the roof and windscreen.

ME: Your ears of a bat will help us greatly in Transylvania.

ETHEL: Oh-oh, old man.

The car was suddenly surrounded by Hungarian police who seemed to have appeared out of nowhere. There were three armed officers (better than the regular two provided by the cheap profit-making capitalist world!). One was fat-ish, one was skinny and tall and one was squat like a brick. I opened the driver side window.

FAT-ISH: Szekely bartokian puszkas árpád mokiks magyarország….

ME and EYES: (*together like a chorus line*) What? Sorry?

SKINNY: Orszáy mäné.

ETHEL: Mmm, errrr, old man.

SQUAT: árpád gíga dohnanyi béla hunyadi.

Etheridge studied the officers in a scholarly manner.

ETHEL: I don't think they speak English old man. Are they Hungarian?

ME: We're in Hungary so they might be.

I try to think of a way to appear as an endearing learned foreigner.

ME: (*to Fat-ish, Skinny and Squat in an all embracing manner*) I like Béla Bártok, we all like Puszkas, do you?

SKINNY: (*remorselessly*) Útlevál.

FAT-SIH: Paszzzzz…..portok.

EARS: (*showing remarkable linguistic skills*) I think they want our passports.

We got out our passports and passed them through the window. Bearing in mind Ethel's height I wondered why his passport was only the same size as the rest of ours. Officer Fat-ish passed all of the passports to Officer Skinny. Skinny looked at Etheridge with dislike, possibly because of his part Indian heritage (?) and gave him back his passport. Eyes and Ears got theirs too. Skinny was however far more fascinated with mine. Was it because of the ever so handsome picture lying within? Skinny gave a knowing look to Fat-ish who exchanged a glance with Squat who was doing a fantastic impersonation of a big white Hungarian turd.

SQUAT TURD: Te rendörörszoba (*signs me to the large police car parked behind our car blocking us in*)

ME: Looks like I've got to go off with this lot (*to Ears*) here's the keys.

EYES: We'll come and see what happens. This might make a better film.

ME: Wanker.

In the local police station I was assigned a cell all to myself probably because there were no other guests. The cell had all the mod cons like a dirty piece of foam rubber on the floor for a bed and a light bulb which worked hanging from the ceiling. The 'Commie' countries were obviously not as poor as we'd been led to believe by the British media what with having electricity and everything. There was an armed guard permanently stationed behind my locked door so if I needed some intimidation it was conveniently to hand.

ME: (*after an hour appreciating the decor I summon the guard in my best Hungarian*) Toilétkely puszkásál pleasély.

GUARD: (*showing me down the corridor and pointing towards the door of the toilet*) Elybáskádakselyáy....

ME: Köszönöm (*I enter and smiling at me is one of these old Eastern European kazis in which there's a kind of porcelain shelf at the back and a pipe at the front down which your creation plus all the toilet paper gets flushed after the act. The creation sits there literally like a pile of shit until being flushed*) IDEAL! (*to myself*) I'll leave this here without flushing it. This Christmas present will show them what a lovely guest they can enjoy hosting here.

I exited the toilet and left my compost behind. The guard showed me back to my cell. It was two hours before they took me to the interrogation room which made it around 10 p.m.:

LIEUTENANT PISZT: (*Silly name, reeking of alcohol and exuding a Stasi -like attitude. Looked like Herr Flick from 'Allo 'Allo*) Well Mr Kennedynyi, why is there a page missing from your passzportók? And why did you enter Hungary illegally from Romania?

ME: (*sitting the other side of the desk from him — two armed guards stand behind him*) I think my kid tore it out.

PISZT: You are lying.

ME: No I'm not.

PISZT: Yes you are.

ME: No I'm not.

PISZT: I know you are lying. How old is your child?

ME: Three years old when I last checked on him.

PISZT: You are lying about the missing page from your passzportók. This reverse imprint of your US visa on the facing page the other side of where the missing page should be is dated from before your son was born. Where is the missing page? Why is it missingnyst?

ME: Nice work officer—it seems to have gone. (*I remembered that I had in reality ripped it out in Houston airport four years earlier to give my phone number to a lovely girl.*)

PISZT: Your passzportók is fake. You are a Romanian gypsy illegally entering Hungaryok.

ME: (*they had probably seen me walking back across no man's land and thought I was one of the gypsies they love to hate*) If you think I've come from Romania why don't you put me back there? That's where I'm trying to get to and from my experience in your hotel Romania seems like a far preferable place....

A couple of days in the cell ensued. I quite liked it. I'd made friends with the guard who took me across the street to a little shop where I was able to buy myself some lemonade, oranges and bread so I didn't go hungry. On the first morning Etheridge turned up.

ME: (*to myself*) Great, I bet he's brought me something good to eat, he loves food. These oranges and lemonade are getting on my tits.

The guard showed John to the other side of the visitor's area.

ME: Oy Ethel—good hotel? Mine's shit.

ETHEL: Hello old man, yes, good hotel, lovely breakfast, old man. I've brought you something.

ME: (*expectantly and with premature gratitude*) Oh, wow, that's great. What have you got? (*a picture of a giant croissant dominates my headspace, maybe with some jam, honey and/or nice cold cuts but hopefully not pork*).

ETHEL: Well, I thought you'd be pretty bored in here old man, so I brought you a copy of *The Guardian* which I had on the plane trip. I've finished it now so you can have it. (*He'd eaten all the food and hadn't brought me any*).

ME: You boring greedy wanker. What do you think this is? A five-star hotel? Did you bring any food?

ETHEL: I'd have thought they might have given you a bit of goulash, old man. Better get going man.

I looked through the bars at him leaving and got shown back to my cell.

To tell you the truth I didn't mind it in the cell for the few days I was in. Capitalists bang on about freedom (mainly the freedom to exploit the lives of others with no freedom living in a country far away from sight and mind or at least benefit from their suffering and toil) but in that very short captivity I enjoyed the freedom from the success of my career which involved endless phone calls answering questions about my future plans and intentions. After my internment the next few days were a pleasant chance to think without demands being made of me. However, Christmas was coming up. I would've been quite interested to see what the celebrations in the cell might've been like but very urgent was the fact that Villa were playing Man Utd on Boxing Day. I had to get back.

In the end in my one phone call I asked my damager to get the British Embassy and their crowd to threaten to make an "international incident" out of it and to publicise it. Something like International Violinist Misses Xmas And Villa Game Imprisoned In Parochial Brutal Hungarian Jail type of thing. My hosts then saw the beauty of letting me check out of their hotel. One comparatively luxurious night in The Hilton Hotel Budapest with room service and everything and then I was on a plane back to London.

The match was a great day for all of us, especially Paul McGrath, with Villa beating The Red Scum 3–0. I think it was the game where Graeme Souness famously summed up United with the comment "You don't win anything with kids". The kids in this instance included some unknown guys called Beckham and two Neville brothers etc. HOME SWEET HOME.

THE HUNGARIAN BORDER POLICE SCORE: 0/10, 9ᵗʰ PLACE
Remarks: The lieutenant had alcohol on his breath and appeared drunk on duty. I have named him differently for legal reasons but I have noticed that he appears to have been promoted to a much higher position in the force. It's sad that all of these years later the official attitude in Hungary doesn't seem to have changed towards less fortunate outsiders. Crashing the border wasn't Mensa level but it was educational to receive the prejudice normally reserved for the Romani community. My sympathy goes out to anyone dealing with the Hungarian Police who doesn't have the same violin strings to pull as I did.

10ᵗʰ The Bavarian Police of Bad Wörishofen

(*Special Award for Racism)

Admittedly the Hungarian Border Police's attitude was prejudiced against me because they thought I might be a Romanian gypsy but as far as real overt racism is concerned the Bavarian police who visited my after gig party in Bad Wörishofen (uninvited) were on another level, practised experts of the real thing.

In those days I was doing a concert programme which brought together two beautiful Bach concertos with early poetic and exuberant works by Duke Ellington (pre Strayhorn) arranged for orchestra by that nice punk violinist. On this occasion the Bad Wörishofen Festival der Nationen had delivered me a Czech orchestra to work with and we'd been rehearsing with them for a couple of days. For the Ellington works I also had a rhythm section which included the great composer, vibraphonist, percussionist and producer Orphy Robinson plus acoustic guitar, bass and drums. With my experience in classical music and jazz improvisation one of the aspects I enjoy and am very good at in rehearsals such as this is bringing the musicians from different genres together, helping them understand each other's musical core while enhancing their joy of the moment.

Despite my incurable scruffiness and the Bad Wörishofen audiences' elegance they were immediately 100 per cent with me. Attentive, empathic and great fun to play for. I have since established an exceptional relationship with this lovely town and their audience. The gig went brilliantly. My new Czech colleagues completely understood my musical directions and my band, as always, played beautifully. Ellington would, I hope, have been proud; particularly with his middle name being Kennedy.

As I have elaborated elsewhere in this book, after a Kennedy gig the music doesn't finish. We chill and party backstage until the venue have had enough and then we take it on to my hotel suite or wherever else we can have a good time without infringing on any one else or they on us. The Czech orchestra players joined my band and I in my suite and room service kindly delivered fifty beers (in exchange for a rather a lot of my hard earned lolly).

Some of the Czech kats new original traditional folk music from their own country's heritage and it was fascinating and wonderful to hear them singing and playing with such passion. Cora Lunny (who had played the Bach concerto for two violins with me) and I were dropping a few Irish songs along the way as well.

Then in mid song someone passed me the hotel phone:

ME: (*with startling originality*) Ullo.

FRONT DESK GEEZA: (*with equal originality*) Hello, Sir.

ME: Ullo.

FRONT DESK GEEZA: Hello Sir. You have to stop your party because of a complaint. Ein gentlemenne hast complained.

ME: Alright-ish. We'll stop the music, finish our beer and call it a day.

F. D. GEEZA: Nein Sir. Dub hast to stop now Sir and everyone hast to leave.

ME: You've sold me all this beer. We'll come down and drink it in the bar.

F. D. GEEZA: Nein. Die Bar ist geschlossen.

ME: Oy wait mate. Any hotel pretending to be five-star must have a place for people—guests to drink what they've already paid for. Give us somewhere to drink where we won't disturb the guy who might call himself a gentleman though he and us all know what he is.

F. D. GEEZA: Nein. Alles sie gehen—dub must go.

ME: Nein mate. Not until we finish the beer you sold us und took the money for. Either that or YOU have to drink ALL of das.

F. D.GEEZA: Nein, Sir.

ME: Nein mate. Danke.

End of call.

ME: All right kats. I think we may be better off if we finish with the music. Let's drink up our beer and call it a day. Fukkin' good gig peeps.

CZECH ORK GUY: Céská republika smetana bohemia bilý potok smĕzka Reichsprotektor.

ME: Ummmmm—yeah....

ORPHY: Nice version of Cottontail tonight mate.

ME: You cheeky bugger....

Knock, KNOCK RAPP KNOCK! I open the door to my suite and there are three of Der Schweinehunden, sorry, I mean The Bad Wörishofen Bavarian Police with a nice big healthy German Shepherd dog in attendance.

SCHWEINEHUNDE 1: Dub hast drugs. Given me the drugs.

ME: Come on officer or whatever. Can't you just be satisfied with a drink? What are you doing here?

SCHWEINEHUNDE 2: Gizz me der drugs.

ME: Sorry, you'll have to make do with alcohol. If you're used to something heavier you'll need to do it back at the station.

Schweinehunde 3 just stands silently with the dog.

SCHWEINEHUNDE 1: Vee surch you.

ME: Look, if you need a condom just ask for it.

After forcing their way into the suite Der Schweinehunden had set up an interrogation and search room in the 2nd bedroom. Maybe they really did need condoms.

ME: Alright. I'll go first.

Schweinehunde 3 tended the dog. It was me and the Schweinehunde 1 and the Schweinehunde 2 in the spare bedroom. Woooopydooo!

ME: I don't have anything.

SCHWEINEHUNDE 2: Give us zeeee drugsen. Vots innen deine pocketen?

ME: (*turning my pockets inside out*) See what I mean? The best you'll get from me is a single vodka or a beer but that offer is now off the table because of your shit manners. You guys are a bit of a joke aren't you?

After that Schweinehunden 1 and 2 continued to use the spare bedroom as an interrogation and search booth like in an airport, searching each guest individually before ordering them out of my suite. Each guest was made to turn out their pockets like naughty schoolchildren hiding sweets.

In the midst of this process Schweinehunde 3 brought the German Shepherd dog into my living room in order to try and do a drug search. Unfortunately for him the dog calmly sat down to watch the TV, transfixed by it. *Police Academy* was on (with German dubbing!) and what with his colleagues bungling all around him it must have seemed like a familiar and favourite documentary.

ME: (*to Schweinehunde 3*) Oy, get the dog out of here. He's very nice and obviously likes me much better than you but my bulldog is in my main bedroom the other side of that door. He doesn't like uninvited guests so he might not like Brutus here and he certainly won't like you and your silly uniform. Get that dog out of here because it'll be you who are responsible for what happens next. I'm letting my dog out, it's time for his walk and there will be blood. (*Cora Lunny translates for me, she is half German as well as a killa violinist*).

(Cora: Vorsprung durch teknik....)

The dog gets taken by Schweinehunde 3 and reluctantly exits in the middle of his favourite show. The way is clear and I bring Bully out to enjoy the action. He had actually been sleeping throughout the whole proceedings probably enjoying dreams of room service breakfasts.

In the meantime the 'search' had continued with each guest having to turn their pockets out. I went back to my second bedroom/'search' room—I was getting angry that der schweinhunden had broken into (or forced entry into) my room without my permission and in a way that I considered illegal by international law. It was opportune that I went in at that moment because what I saw was unbelievable apart from that it was unfortunately happening.

ME: Get out you fukkin' racist pigs. You're not going to get away with this without people finding out. (*After looking in everyone's pockets these mental midget schweinehunden have got Orphy stripped down to his underpants. Because he's the only black guy they have assumed he is a dealer; none of us whites have been subject to this treatment*) You ignorant bastards, do you really think that people won't learn of this? (*Well, now they are! I put myself in front of them so they will have to use physical violence if they want to remove me. This also gives Orphy the chance to get dressed.*) You ignorant fuckers—get out. You're making Bavaria look shit with your stupidity. It's not fair on Bavarians to be made to look so backward by having police representation by people as shit as you.

Eventually the pig dogs left but that wasn't the end of the matter. I'm not reticent about the fact that I appreciate a good smoke. It has helped me become the improviser, composer and classical interpreter that I am today. It just happened that on that particular night when they chose to barge into my hotel suite there was nothing to be found.

To my knowledge it is only possible for police to prosecute if a crime has been truly committed or when they have discovered proper evidence. I also believe and hope it is against the law for any police action to be informed by racism. These particular schweinhunden need to learn a lesson from their counterparts in Berlin or elsewhere on how to treat people equally and on how to avoid the temptation of fabricating evidence (a glass pipe had been 'found'). Also they should give their dogs a more challenging job than watching TV.

BAVARIAN POLICE: SCORE: -10/10, 10ˢᵗ (LAST) PLACE
Remarks: racist and made false insinuations regarding heavy drugs. If boredom constitutes cruelty to animals they are guilty of cruelty to Brutus.

N.B. I see that the Bavarian Police have an orchestra. I would be happy to play a charity concert for no fee with them to try and help them teach their one or two renegade members a lesson in peace, tolerance and racial understanding. I know that what happened that night wasn't representative of the whole force—but I'm also well aware that it shouldn't have happened at all. So I would love to do something which would help prevent further victimisation of innocent people. Friendship is what I and my music are all about.

POLICE LEAGUE TABLE STANDINGS

Standing	Police Force	Points
1	BERLIN POLICE	10
(1)	LONDON MET	10
3	WARSZAWA POLICJA	7
(3)	LONDON MET RESERVES	7
5	NYPD	4
6	FRANKFURT AIRPORT POLICE	3
7	MADRID POLICE	2
8	WEST MIDLANDS POLICE	1
9	HUNGARIAN BORDER POLICE	0
10	BAVARIAN POLICE OF BAD WÖRISHOFEN	-10*

*10 point penalty for racism.

A Police Extra

I had been driving four hours and was half a kilometre from home. When I saw the hitchhiker I thought "not today mate, I'm almost home and no detours". Then he, for he was indeed a bloke, stepped in the middle of the road and I tried to swerve around him. The next moment his body was rolling off my windscreen onto the road. "Oh no, I've killed someone". I got out of the car to try to save him. I had my phone in my hand to call the ambulance. The body got up and he was a policeman. He brushed himself down and then looked me in the face. "You're that violin player aren't you? IV Seasons? It's a big offence to run over a police officer. I like your music so just go on home and never run over a police officer again".

I went on home and never ran over a police officer again.

FRIENDS AND INFLUENCES: ASTON VILLA

And it's ASTON VILLA, ASTON VILLA FC.
(We're By Far The Greatest Team, The World Has Ever Seen)

Introduction

"Hello, Miss Moneypenny, I hope life is keeping well for you today. I'm back from holiday and ready for duty. I hear that I have a trip to Moscow planned. Might just have a blini, it'll make my hair quite sheeny."

"I'm very well thank you, James. I'm glad you enjoyed your pigeon manoeuvres over Scunthorpe … M wants to speak to you immediately and has instructed that you go straight into his office."

"OK. Thank you Miss Moneypenny."

20 seconds later…

"I am reporting for duty, Sir. When do I depart from Moscow?"

"Hello, good to see you 007. There has been a change of plan. As you know, as well as foreign interests we do have to look after the interests of our own people here at home. Even though, from the information we get from the BBC, *The Guardian*, *The Times* and suchlike one would never believe it, there are rumours of the existence of a huge industrial town in the middle of England called Birmingham."

"Burrminghumm?"

"Yes, 007. Birmingham. Now, if this huge city actually exists it is being subject to a cultural cleansing the size of which has never been seen before in the whole world. There are supposedly six million people living in this city and the London–Lancashire vegetarian media want to wipe them off the face of the Earth. In the years when Warwickshire might have excelled at cricket, what do we remember? Lancashire and Middlesex. There is a team rumoured to exist in Birmingham called Aston Villa...."

"Aston Vanilla?"

"No, 007. AS-TON VI-LLA. They are supposed to have won the League and the European Cup in the early '80s but what do we remember? That Manchester United weren't very good and that Tottenham reserve team won a couple of games."

"So, M. What you're saying is that this city Brumminghamm actually exists but has been subject to a huge cover-up by The Vegetarian Globalised Media of London and Lancashire."

"Yes, Bond. We'll call them the VGMLL to save space on the page. We have started to collect evidence of Birmingham's existence and therefore of the dastardly plotting of VGMLL. Another example of the London Lancashire Bias Plot, which we will from now on referred to as LLBP, is this list of music which, formerly assumed to be from London or Lancashire, is actually from this secret city: Black Sabbath, Judas Priest, Dexys Midnight Runners, ELO, Roy Wood, Wizard, The Move, UB40, The Beat, The Moody Blues, Duran Duran, Steel Pulse, Traffic, Steve Winwood, Musical Youth, Napalm Death, Bachdenkel, Bhujhangy Group, The Punjabi Villans, Bentley Rhythm Ace and the list goes on. In fact, judging by the name, The Beatles might very well be a long-winded version of The Beat.

"At the moment we are not sure if this cultural cleansing programme is being operated from centres of political correctness in Manchester and London owned by the BBC and The Guardian, or whether the operations are being run from further afield. Russia, for instance, or the Isle of Man Yoga and Vegetarian Institute of Moral Dictatorship."

"Good God, Sir, not them!"

"But that's the least of it, 007. These Masonic correctors are coming up with something altogether more dangerous. They are threatening to undermine the relevance of truth by undermining the relevance of football as a whole. The so-called 'lovely, lovely beautiful game' is under threat of being turned into the 'lovely, lovely big brother surveillance game'. If the propaganda merchants carry on in the same vein they will soon come up with some fabrication of a TV series called something like The English Game, pretending that football developed in Eton and Lancashire. Birmingham, if it exists, could possibly get no mention at all. The whole situation could be on a par with the Chinese Cultural Revolution, with Brummies from the decent side of Birmingham having to secretly bury their Villa shirts in their gardens."

"How can you bury a whole villa in the garden?"

"You don't understand, 007. Villa, Aston Villa, are a football team from Birmingham, kept secret, obviously, by VGMLL and the LLBP. They are not a house. They are a football team who invented football as we know it today. They are the best and most important team in the world but have been kept secret like the rest of their city by these dastardly organisations."

"This is despicable, M. Do you want me to try and find this Birmingham? Having only read *The Guardian* and watched the BBC I didn't know this town might exist in reality. What is a Brummie? Is Birmingham South or North of anywhere?"

...y with his own memoir *To Be or Not to Bop* published in 1979. *Wikimedia Commons, courtesy Bernard Gotfryd*

Of course, the night was fukkin' kool and Paddy Foy had obviously arranged everything. Ronnie's ...ed after me, gave me a table which I shared with a nice couple who shared their champagne with ... On the way onto the stage Dizzy came up, shook my hand, pointed at me and said: "I hear you're ...thin' else, man."

Signing my first recording contract with Peter Jamieson and David Hughes.

At an early concert, 1985. *Shutterstock*

Doug Ellis making me the proud owner of an honorary share in Aston Villa.

With Graham Taylor when he was manager of Villa.

With Vernon Handley after winning the *Gramophone* Record of the Year 1985 for the Elgar.

I've just received the BPI Classical Record of the Year from Sir Georg Solti while Noel Edmonds, show presenter, watches. Brit Awards, Grosvenor House Hotel, 10 February 1986.

With Kate Bush at the Brit Awards, Grosvenor House Hotel in London, 9 February 1987. *Photo by Duncan Raban/ Popperfoto via Getty Images*

My Walton Violin and Viola Concertos CD front panel. André Previn was one of the most talented musicians around. He was right up there with his mastery of jazz and of twentieth century classical music.

With Paul and Linda McCartney on the U.S. Top of the Pops, 18 December 1987. These are very grainy stills from a domestic video recording but worth including to remind me of the evening.

That I'd played a lot with Grappelli and had musical abilities beyond the boxes somehow had brought me to the attention of Paul, hence him asking me to come and play on 'Once Upon A Long Ago'.

The Cathedrale Stradivarius which shared my world during four important years.

I was renting a small one-room building in the garden of a much larger house at 11 Rosslyn Hill. That evening I had become acquainted with a girl I met on the street dressed as a clown who was getting a bit on my nerves because she was talking rubbish far too much. BRRRRINNNG!! ... I go and answer the door and, fuck me, it's Sean Connery standing there.

The Magnificent Seven, me with Chris Bonnington, Sue Lawley with a cardboard cut-out of Ronnie Corbett, Gary Lineker, Virginia Leng and Frank Bruno, 31 December 1989. *Trinity Mirror/Mirrorpix/Alamy Stock Photo*

John and I with the famed Golden Rose of Montreux for our *Four Seasons* film.

The moment of truth: with my manager, John Stanley as Michael Aspel delivers his surprise of the 'Big Red Book', *This is your Life*, 14 March 1990. I was caught at Abbey Road Studios.

World Cup harmony, June 1990 in Sardinia. *Back row:* Gazza and Chris Waddle with my fiddle. *Front row:* Brixie, Gary Lineker with Brixie's guitar, me, and Steve Hodge of Aston Villa.

Disharmony with Gary Lineker.

Above left: With Klaus Tennstedt when we were recording the Brahms Concerto at Abbey Road Studios, 26 August 1990.

Above right: The Variety Club Show-Business Personality of the Year Award, 5 February 1991. *Alan Davidson/ Shutterstock*

Above left: After the award I was whisked away by private jet for a charity show performance in Birmingham for Princess Diana, with George Martin. *Shutterstock*

Above right: Winner of the Classical Recording category at the 1993 Brit Awards, 16 February 1993, at Alexandra Palace, London. *Shutterstock*

On 24 January 1994, I presented Stéphane Grappelli (my musical Grandad) with a special cake to celebrate his 86th birthday. *Simon Kreitem/Alamy*

Doesn't look like it but unfortunately is more intelligent than many record company employees. *janecat/123RF*

With Peter Norris, 1996. *Michael Ward, courtesy of The Yehudi Menuhin School*

The
Kennedy
Experience

Left-handed Jimi trying his skills on the violin. *Inset:* My album from 1999.

I got into Jimi Hendrix pretty early. Like Beethoven he was powerful, trance-spiritual and based on solid strong rhythm. I was attracted to the freedom of his music and that he completely transcended the black/white thing, something which seems beyond the capability of many of today's artists and political commentators.

Above left: With Agnieszka and Sark, 1999. *Richard Young/Shutterstock*

Above right: The Classical Brit Awards, 5 May 2000, hosted by Sir Trevor McDonald. Sir George Martin presenting me with the award for 'Outstanding Contribution to Music'. *Shutterstock*

Back to the old days busking outside Kensington Underground Station, 31 May 2001, in aid of *Big Issue* magazine. *Julian Makey/Shutterstock*

With the Berliner Philharmoniker.

With The Who. The rehearsal was at Nomis Studios, Sinclair Road, West London, Wednesday, 24 March 2004. Daltrey was so considerate that he even gave Sark some earplugs. Treating him like a friend (a four year old friend!) he said: "You probably haven't heard us before, we're pretty loud. You put these earplugs in like this...."

Playing 'Baba O'Riley' with The Who, at the Royal Albert Hall, Monday, 29. March 2004.

I started playing and the magic infused and transcended everything. I could see Daltrey getting right into it and Townshend supported me in the build in a way that no other guitarist could. There were a couple of windmills, he gave more and more and my solo went more and more power pagan. I was carried away by the collective power of the band and the solo was a triumph! I even finished exactly together with Townshend—our last flourish completely synchronised.

With Donovan in Muzyczna Owczarnia.

Nicolas Pflug got me a muvva of a band to play with, a true Aristocrats of Jazz line up. Ron Carter (bass), Jack DeJohnette (drums), J. D. Allen (sax), Joe Lovano (sax), Lucky Peterson (Hammond), Kenny Werner (piano) and Danny Sadownick (percussion).

With J. D. Allen working on *Blue Note Sessions*. My three favourite songs on this album are 'Stranger in a Stranger Land' (subtle and beautiful work from Kenny Werner and Danny Sadownick), 'I Almost Lost My Mind' and 'After the Rain'.

Posing during a photo-shoot and press conference, Santander, Spain, 10 June 2005 to present my concert with my Polish Chamber Orchestra at Cantabria's Festivals Palace the following day. *Esteban Cobo/EPA/ Shutterstock*

Launching the first ever Dr Who Prom, Royal Albert Hall, 9 April 2008. *Shutterstock*

With Jeff Beck at a BBC Promenade concert in the Royal Albert Hall, London, on Saturday 26 July 2008.

With Jon Lord, September, 2010. Jon was humble, a good storyteller but not a gasser and ... WHAT A FUKKIN' HAMMOND PLAYER!! ... What made him one of the leaders amongst even this select group was his song writing and his soloing and of course his Deep Purple bandmates, none of whom could be called slouches! *Photo: Mike Maass*

With Agnieszka at the 15th South Bank
Sky Arts Awards hosted by Melvyn Bragg,
at the Dorchester Hotel, 25 January 2011.
Shutterstock

In Aston Villa colours at
St George's Hotel, London,
2 August 2011. *Shutterstock*

At the Royal Albert Hall, 6 August 2011. Fats Waller followed by Bach. *Wikimedia Commons, courtesy Paul Hudson*

Prom 34: at the Albert Hall, 8 August 2013. The performance was by the Orchestra of Life with 17 members of Palestine Strings, featuring the Saad family. Their father Zaher sat in the audience. He said: "When Mostafa played and Ghandi sang, my heart was beating fast...."

At the end of the concert, Mostafa returned to the stage to play my song Melody In The Wind, 15 years after Grappelli recorded it with me.

Mostafa Saad, who returned to London and performed again with me, this time at the Bethlehem Unwrapped Festival at St James's, Piccadilly, January 2014.

Nigel Kennedy Presents 'Bach Meets Fats Waller, Hamburg, Germany, 24 April 2013. *Action Press/Shutterstock*

BBC Radio 3 at The Southbank Centre, 24 July 2014. *Wikimedia Commons, courtesy Steve Bowbrick*

On his Twitter site Jack Grealish says "What a legend this guy is. So talented, was great to watch him live last night." The event was on 31 January 2016 at the Symphony Hall, Broad Street, Birmingham. Performing an acoustic version, titled 'The New Four Seasons', we took the audience on a journey through the seasons with new interpretations of the music while keeping the Four Seasons at its root. The first half featured 'The English Collection'. *Photographs by Graham Young, BPM Media*

With Jean-Luc Ponty at a gala concert at the Royal Albert Hall, 14 March 2017. *Shutterstock*

The same day, 14 March 2017, Robert Plant joined me on stage after 11 p.m. and we performed 'Hey Joe' and 'Kashmir.'

In concert with Julian 'Das Kid' Buschberger, Poznan, Poland, 8 May 2017. *Waldemar Wylegalski/Prs/ East News/ Shutterstock*

Deutscher Radiopreis 2017, Hamburg, Germany, 7 September 2017. *Michael Timm/Face To Face/Shutterstock*

Playing Gershwin at Ronnie Scott's, 2018. *From left to right:* Beata Urbanek-Kalinowska, Tomasz Kupiec, Rolf Bussalb, Howard Alden.

Ronnie Scott's 60th Anniversary Gala, Royal Albert Hall, London, 30 October 2019. *Richard Young/ Shutterstock*

Live at the 26th Summer Jazz Festival in Krakow, Poland, 10 July 2021.

Huxley, our dog.

The Aston Villa team of 1899 that won the First Division and the Sheriff of London Charity Shield (shared with Queen's Park).

"Well 007, that's the thing. No one in London or Lancashire really knows if Birmingham exists or not, but in case it does we must protect its population from being obliterated by people's minds. The inhabitants of Birmingham are called Brummies, if they exist."

"I'm ready, boss. Which way do I go?"

"Steady, 007. Everything I've been telling you is just background information. What I'm going to ask you to deal with is the following. There is an even more insidious plot to destroy Aston Villa and all Villa fans, if Birmingham exists."

"Well I never, M. And how do 'they' intend to do that?"

"The politically correct corporate propaganda weapon in question is called VAR, video assistant referee. It is a replay device designed to ruin the flow of the game and the fans' enjoyment of it. VAR prevents the paying public celebrating a goal while a Manchester United fan decides the score in London (because that's where most United fans come from), and makes them feel subservient and unable to express their feelings. This globalist tool makes working people feel powerless which is what the globalists want. Everything is connected—if there are no working people in Birmingham (if it exists) then the work can be done by slave labour in poorer countries—who then make the shirts, trainers and boots—which the players and the fans wear—but at a marked up price which is difficult for honest out of work working people to afford. 007?"

"Sorry, didn't mean to yawn, Sir. I can't wait to get into action, M."

"That is not all 007. This VAR propaganda conditioning weapon is in particular being used against Aston Villa and that is why more than half of Brum is in peril, if it exists."

"I presume Brum means Birmingham. I am ready for action, and now that I am portrayed by Daniel Craig and have a previously un-portrayed aggressive streak, I am ready to be as barbaric as necessary. I will do whatever it takes to rescue football in general and Aston Villa in particular if Aston exists."

"There are lesser teams in Birmingham as well, 007. Please rescue those and the whole city also, if it exists. This cunning but dumb VAR device was invented in Holland and is now kept and operated in Stockley Park, West London. Please now go and see Q to pick up the latest secret weapon developed especially for this fearsome task…"

"… Hello, Q. Can I have my new bomb, please?"

"Hello, 007. The device I've developed for you is completely new and is not a bomb."

"Oh, what a shame, Q."

"What I have designed is an all in one rat deterrent—truth serum—ultrasonic ray disguised as a vegetarian. The vegetarian disguise will enable you to get this device into any opinion censor's premises. The ultrasonic ray scatters all the particles of the VAR machine into outer space throughout the whole cosmos. The truth serum will nullify the media types and any other know-alls in a preachy mood. The rat deterrent will nullify the bourgeoisie globalists. By the end of it

Birmingham's existence will be unquestioned, football will no longer have to naffly be called 'the beautiful game' and to top it all not one person will be hurt."

"Shame."

"And Aston Villa will get fair decisions and will be recognised as the true inventors of the physical and not so beautiful game. Another side benefit and effect of the anti-VAR is that all foreign club owners will disappear and then reappear, with no bank accounts, all simultaneously in a one-bedroom flat in Scunthorpe which they can then sell and share the proceeds between them."

"Crikey Q. You've made a good 'un."

"Two things, James. The vegetarian disguise is functional unlike a real vegetarian, so it can walk with you from one destination to another. Also, don't feed it meat because it will break your cover and the machine might break out in hives, or puke or something...."

(Of course, the above sequence should've happened in real life and would've made the world a much better place, but folks, sorry, it was just another of my dreams.)

My First Game And Early Days

I started watching Aston Villa on the 4th of January, 1969. I was a plastic fan before that having only read about them in the paper or hearing Villa's name during the scores on the radio (despite regular attendances of 40,000 we were never on the TV and were in the lower reaches of the Second Division).

I was taken to the game by Philip Waddy, he was a few years older than myself and was the son of a doctor who was one of my stepdad's colleagues. Philip changed my life, he might not remember me but I remember him. Villa were playing QPR in the third round of the FA Cup and Philip had two tickets. When his folks had been round ours his mum had inadvertently pissed in one of my parents' favourite velvet chairs so the Waddys were probably trying to make up for it by having Philip take me to the game. I believe that destiny makes good people Villa fans but there's always a small chance that without the chair pissing I might not have become a Villa fan, at least not as quickly. These two tickets were gold dust because the FA Cup is the most exciting competition in football. You either win and go through to the next round or you lose and you're out on your arse until next year. The Cup is the opposite to all of those TV orientated European and international competitions in which you see so many shit teams none of which have the good grace to simply fuck off. These teams are like huge facial warts, not only do you not want them there but they also take far, far, far too long to go away. No endless string of meaningless games in the Cup, if you don't give your all you're on your way home.

The first impression I got was well before the match on the way to the ground. All the buses were absolutely jam packed, same with the trains, all full of Villa fans with proper horizontal bar claret and blue scarves and same style bobble hats. Badges also featured on scarves, hats, jackets and jeans. Everyone was smoking (boring tobacco) because people had a choice of what to spend their hard earned dosh on and how to spend their well-deserved leisure time without the pseudo-morality of some killjoys fucking it up. There was an expectant buzz everywhere. Even outside Villa Park one could cut the atmosphere with a knife. There were long lines queueing up for absolutely everything, classic gristle and pulp burgers, fish and chips, match day programmes, merchandise like badges and scarves. A lot of people had little wooden boxes with a handle on them, I'd find out what those were later. On the streets it was obvious that there was no 'beautiful game' bullshit around—this was THE PEOPLE'S GAME.

The extra buzz around the game was because the legendary and charismatic Tommy Docherty had just been appointed Villa manager. The Doc has unfortunately passed on while I've been writing this book but "Oy, Doc … you up there! Thanks for bringing our club back to life. You made sure that I became a Villa fan and what killa times I've had with the club since then. Cheers, mate." Basically The Doc represented a way forward for a club which had previously been stuck in the doldrums. Even though we were languishing near the bottom of Division 2, Docherty brought a fresh wave of optimism with him and I remember him saying "Villa have amazing support. If you hung 11 Villa shirts on a washing line five thousand fans would turn up to watch them!"

We walked along Witton Lane, the scene of many a good rumpus in the future, to find our turnstile. Even though it was a corrugated iron roofed shack the Witton Lane Stand was posh because it was seated. (Thereafter it was going to be standing for me until Thatcher's largely successful attempt to destroy football (and the working class as a whole) resulted in the right to stand being abolished). Anyone who's been to a game knows the amazing feeling one gets going up the stairs and then entering the spectator area. The whole panorama opens out before you in a breath-taking wash of energy, light and sound, the green of the pitch—the whole image and noise almost touchable across the huge space. There's also a more than literal sense of arrival, it's match day!

The players came out of the tunnel and were greeted by the roar of the 40,000 crowd. The claret and blue shirts looked so much classier than any of the other boring colours that we see all too often. It was at this moment that I found out what those wooden box things were, they were football rattles. They made a sound like a giant mutant cricket on steroids attached to a thousand maracas—and the sound of them all going at the same time was well and truly something else. It wasn't long before I got one and painted it up proper claret and blue. There was an electric atmosphere in the ground, the kind which some football fans know but which no one else has experienced in any other sport.

We won 2-1 with goals from Lionel Martin and Brian Godfrey. The crowd, as much as anything else, lifted Villa to victory. The vibes coming from The Holte End, 28,000 in one stand alone, was something I'd never experienced before—so much more powerful than any gig I'd been to. I was one of many new fans that Tommy Docherty attracted to the Villa. These were exciting times for the club and the beginning of a new era. Even though we got relegated to Division 3, Docherty brought in a fair few great signings who would later deliver phenomenal results for Vic Crowe, the next Villa manager. These players included Bruce Rioch, Chico Hamilton and Pat McMahon. Docherty also started the negotiations for Andy Lochhead who would become another Villa legend. Vic Crowe would oversee us getting promotion from Division 3 with a record number of goals scored in front of huge crowds the like of which have never been seen in that division before or since.

In the coming games I stood for a few on The Witton End, I preferred standing but anyway wouldn't have had the money to sit. We called The Witton End the mound end because, although it was stepped terracing pitch side, the back of it was just a mound of rubble which one could foot ski down to get out at the end of the game. If one slid down on one's backside it would make a black stripe badger style on the back what with all the soot and rubble that constituted the mound.

Segue to the Thatcherite Decimation of The People's Game, because having watched the game for a fair while, I've seen the changes that globalisation has enforced on the game to ensure profits for some goons who hardly ever set foot in the country (UK) let alone Birmingham.

Inevitably I gravitated to The Holte End, all the best songs and most partisan support was on The Holte. Each of the 28,000 individual people became one huge muvvafukka and it was muvvafukka to be part of one huge muvvafukka like that muvvafukka. (Of course, what the Thatcher goul was most frightened of was loads of people joining together to be one huge muvvafukka). I would say to you that if you've never stood at a game you've never really been to a proper football match. I'm sorry that you've been deprived of that amazing experience but having to sit at football is akin to being told you have to sit in your allocated seat all night at a rave. I suppose it's just another of those civil liberties or flexibilities so many of which have been taken away from us.

There was a police created disaster with tragic fatalities at Hillsborough (1989), there was a cock-up regarding fan segregation at Heysel Stadium in Belgium (1985) and there was a horrific fire at Bradford City's Valley Parade (1985). None of these tragedies have any connection with whether people were sitting or standing. All of the false conclusions regarding these sad, sad events are an example of Repeat A LIE, The Truth Will DIE. For instance; here are some truths which are very different to the normal bleating that we are force fed:

HILLSBOROUGH—disaster happened because of dreadful irresponsible policing, not because of standing.
REMEDY: Proper policing and proper justice for the Liverpool fans' families who were so tragically affected.

HEYSEL—disaster happened because of lack of proper fan segregation and
UEFA's refusal to change from that dump of a stadium, to one which was fit
for purpose, despite both Liverpool and Juventus requesting it. Barcelona's
Camp Nou and Madrid's Santiago Bernabéu were both available, for example. This ground was actually crumbling and people without tickets were
kicking holes in the walls to gain entrance. Liverpool fans are among the
most sporting in the world so it was despicable to blame the above two
tragedies on their behaviour. I remember being the only Villa fan on the
Kop fully decked out in our colours and there wasn't a spot of trouble, and
the Scousers are the only fans I know who applaud the away team.

REMEDY: UEFA should stage games in proper stadiums and be diligent about
fan segregation. Standing had nothing to do with this tragedy. The charges
of manslaughter against 14 Liverpool fans should also be made against the
UEFA officials responsible for staging the game.

VALLEY PARADE—this catastrophe happened because an Ozzie dropped a lit
fag and the stand was made of wood. The turnstiles were locked so no one
could get out. Standing had nothing to do with it.

REMEDY: Make sure that grounds are made of non-flammable material. Don't
lock people in.

The main freedom that people had taken away from them by the governmental
or football authorities on these occasions was to be able to go and watch a match
in safe conditions, live to tell the tale, and in the case of Hillsborough and Heysel
that the truth be told instead of being slandered. Lesser freedoms were then taken
from us football fans at large, and if you let governments chip away a little bit at
a time at our civil liberties through lies and deceit it doesn't, perhaps, take long
for our 'freedom' to be compromised very seriously. We used to live in a far more
tolerant society than the one we live in now which seems to be full of little moral
dictators telling us what we cannot do.

These disgusting false accusations against Liverpool fans (when a decent
human being would have extended sympathy) have then had a kick on effect
against rights and freedoms we all used to have. For instance, we used to be
able to go to a game with no advance planning, meet up with 12 to 15 friends
and then all go and stand and sing together on whichever part of the terrace we
decided, and have a smoke if we wanted.[26] Imagine the organisation and cost
involved in getting 15 seats together on the morning of a match, even if it were
at all possible. One has to be in Walt Disney's Fantasia to imagine standing or
smoking is a threat to crowd safety or that spontaneously going to a match would
make the world explode. Anyone bleating on about the game and how "it's safer

---

26 Dear reader, even if you are very sensitive, please don't cry! It's just an opinion of mine that
one should be able to smoke where one wants. Far be it from me to think I should be able to
deny someone the freedom to go away if they don't like it.

Nigel Kennedy: Uncensored!

now" needs to be sat down in a kindergarten and have the facts explained to them instead of the factoids.

FACT: Attending a game is now safer because the police behave better.

FACT: One could smoke and the game would still be safer because the grounds are now made of concrete (which, according to Zweistein, is less flammable than wood. Dreistein says it's completely non-flammable).

POSSIBLE FACT: A nanny state is shit if it only exists to satisfy people's desire to play nanny. Can't we leave nannying to the nanny goat family? Goat milk is great but not when it's poured all over innocent people's heads by a dithering rugby loving Tory lackey.

10 INCIDENTAL FACTOIDS (Repeat The LIE, And The Truth Will DIE)

FACTOID 1—Football attendance is safer because of Tory and UEFA instigated changes.

FACTOID 2—VAR helps improve the game and makes it fairer!

FACTOID 3—The history of football statistically and otherwise only started with the advent of the Premier League and Sky TV.

FACTOID 4(a)—It's necessary to have more than one type of away shirt.

FACTOID 4(b)—A different away shirt is completely necessary when the home team's colours are not the same.

FACTOID 5(a)—Horrid new personality free stadiums are better than the old ones in the community.

FACTOID 5(b)—That every 'stadium' should be called Allianz, Emirates, Etihad or Red Bull.

FACTOID 6—It's better for fans to have ground sharing enforced rather than having their own stadiums.

FACTOID 7—Games rearranged for Monday night are great for away fans because they benefit TV companies.

FACTOID 8—One is a football fan by watching games on TV, couch potato style.

FACTOID 9—Great players or managers should be sacked or suspended for knobbing a bit.

FACTOID 10—Loan signings are loyal and great for team spirit!

FACTOID 11—Pay channels need to have adverts on as well as taking our money.

FACTOID 12—I did say 12 factoids, I did say 12 factoids, I did say 12 factoids, I did, I did, I did, I did.

Thanks for bearing with me. It seems that I've been on about the toffs' gentrification and globalisation of THE PEOPLE'S GAME, OUR GAME. This subject was inevitably going to find its way into my book at some point. I hate seeing the things we love being destroyed for political gain or profit. Every fan of the game has had to pay in numerous ways for the penalties imposed on the game (and us fans) as a cover-up for the police, for Thatcher's vendetta against the working class or for globalisation by stealth. Villa fans are paying just like anyone else.

These decimating changes have really detracted from our match day experience. Now we can no longer just roll up to the ground and stand with some mates for a quid or so. The seats are very costly and if our arses aren't permanently locked to them we get ejected (I love away games because 3–5,000 fans standing are rather difficult to throw out *en masse* and Arsenal's bourgeoisie cushioned seats become particularly irrelevant!).

Oh yes! And after having all of those rights of enjoyment taken away from us the final nail in the coffin is that we are no longer even allowed to spontaneously or exuberantly celebrate a goal!! Now we see the goal go in, jump, but then have to wait for a VAR nerd to decide if he wants us to score, and if he's in a good mood we can then celebrate his kindness in letting us…not exactly the same thing. Fake, man—FAKE! The authorities have surpassed even themselves for stupidity with that masterstroke…!

Someone has to say this stuff, particularly when so many who are involved in football would endanger their livelihoods by criticising it. Fans are the most important but most ignored ingredient of the whole caboodle. I've almost got it all out of my system now but you're not getting away without a couple more factoids.…

FACTOID 13—All the musical interruptions are better than our crowd noise.
Mini Factoid 13—Some people like it! Come on, muvvafukka, fukk off!
FACTOID 14—It's fair that players and managers can be fined and suspended for
      bringing the game into disrepute while the authorities (refs, VAR, UEFA,
      FIFA) get away with dragging the game down much further.

READER: Mercy, Nige … mercy.
   ME: OK. I'm finished now. Back to some nice stories about the Villa…

ASTON VILLA (1) 2	MANCHESTER UNITED (1) 1	23 December 1970
Lochhead 37	Kidd 12	
McMahon 72		Att. 62,500

(League Cup Semi-Final 2nd leg)

Being a prisoner of The Yehudi Menuhin School of Precocious Talented Brats I hadn't got to too many games that season. Having become good enough to get into the school orchestra was obviously another huge setback because orchestra rehearsals were held on Saturday mornings, making it impossible for me to get to Villa Park before the second half and even then I had to be lucky. Also my folks had to be able to afford my train fare which wasn't that often. If Villa were playing closer to the school (in or around London) I had a chance to make it for the whole match. I had managed to make it to see us beat Fulham 2–0 at Craven Cottage which was memorable for three reasons: It was a win, Chico Hamilton scored direct from a corner (I'd never seen that before) and where we were standing one could see the Thames flowing by behind one's shoulder. We didn't look at the Thames much except at half time.

Now it was the Christmas holidays so no fukkin orchestra was going to stop me seeing what turned out to be one of the best games I've ever seen. In fact, the best. It was the second leg of our League Cup semi-final against Man Ewe. They were meant to be some kind of gods or something while we were languishing like dead minnows in the Third Division, but for some reason we were muvvafukka optimistic and knew we had a great chance of winning this. I should point out that this was an era when no team would think they were so grandiose and above the fans that they didn't want or have to compete for the Cup. Every player wanted to play every game and every manager wanted to play his best eleven every game.

A couple of months earlier we had lost at Halifax in front of fewer than 6,000 people, now we were going to play Man-Ewe at Villa Park in front of 62,500. United had a team of stars like George Best, Denis Law, Bobby Charlton and Brian Kidd but we had Andy Lochhead, Pat McMahon, Chico Hamilton and Willie Anderson. Willie Anderson's claim to fame was that as a member of Man-Ewe's youth team he had been George Best's roommate, played in the same position as Best but had been considered second best (without a capital B) and Man-Ewe had let him go. Now here he was playing in front of more than 60,000 diehard fans with maybe a little bit to prove. There were, however, eleven amazing stories all on the pitch playing for the Villa and there were 30,000 amazing stories featuring all of us on The Holte End that night with the best ground in the UK packed to the rafters. All of those incredible stories came together for the greatest possible common cause, helping Villa beat Man-Ewe.

I don't know if you can imagine what a standing crowd of 62,000 is like, all proactive, compared with a sitting crowd of 40,000 odd, all inactive. To tell the truth, there's no comparison. Certainly on that night our crowd was an unstoppable force and maybe had as much to do with the result as anyone on the pitch, apart from Andy Lochhead, that is.

The match was under floodlights which amplified all the positive energy in the ground. Whatever was going on outside just didn't exist. Being in the middle of The Holte End was like being part of one huge muvvafukkin' feelgood beast. 'United' were supposedly big time but we had a feeling that tonight we were going to have 'em for breakfast. It might have seemed that we were David against Goliath but there was a whole lot of David around for that game.

In the first leg Andy Lochhead had scored twice but the wanker in the black had disallowed one of his goals for no reason (apart from, maybe, that it was against United). Man Ewe[27] had got a late equaliser so everything was set up for a monster. The winner would take all and assume their rightful place in the final at Wembley.

---

27 Oops! Sorry! Don't know what to call them because United means Leeds, Sheffield or Torquay.

As the players came out of the tunnel the roar of our crowd must have been ominous for the Man-Ewe players. We must have lost the toss because we would, like always, have chosen the advantage of playing towards The Holte End, with its mammoth bank of home support, in the second half. As it was, there was another killa roar as Villa kicked off towards us in The Holte End and every time we got the ball the whole ground erupted. Us fans were the magic carpet carrying the team to victory, we were also the power which enabled our team to completely outplay their opponents and make them look like yesterday's men.

Despite our dominance, on their first attack a moment of individual brilliance put us 1-0 down. Brian Kidd received and controlled the ball outside our area, went past two of our defenders in one smooth movement before calmly rolling the ball past John Dunn into the net. Was this going to be the wind out of our sails? NO! All of us in the crowd revved up the volume even louder and our brilliant team was lifted to even greater heights. Every time one of our players won the ball the whole ground erupted. Even when play stopped for one of the Man-Ewe players to be treated for injury all of us lot started a chant of VI-LLA... VI-LLA...in a deafening crescendo.

Brian Godfrey was leading the team by example, and not long before half time he put in a perfect cross and there was Andy Lochhead's bald pate to head it in. Fukkin' 'ell, the noise! And then Lochhead's song. An-dy / An-dy Loch-ead / Andy Loch-ead In The Air / An-dy / An-dy Loch-ead / An-dy Loch-ead's Got No Hair!

The whistle went for half time and we all knew we were at one of the most exhilarating and historic matches we were ever going to see. Hardly anyone left to get a pie, we didn't want to miss even one second of this game.

The second half kicked off with us attacking The Witton End. Man-Ewe had stars but we had character. Then there was the crowd to reckon with, I've never seen a crowd make so much difference to the result of a match. It was another cross which killed Man-Ewe off. Keith Bradley put a long ball into the box from the right, Lochhead headed it on to Willie Anderson on the left, Anderson put in a perfect cross against his old team and Pat McMahon rose confidently to head firmly past Rimmer to make it 2–1 to The Villa Boys. This all happened miles away at the other end of the pitch from The Holte End where we were standing but there's no way I'm going to forget a millisecond of it. It was pure cacophony until the final whistle after which—PANDEMONIUM! We were the Third Division minnows to whom no one gave a chance and now we were well deserved giant killers. Vic Crowe was building the future of our club and maybe he was a vastly unsung hero, looking back with the perspective of history. But this match left a great, great feeling to this very day and more than matches up to anything I've seen since.

That season we finished fourth in Division 3 (missing promotion by a fair few points) and gave a great account of ourselves against Spurs in the final. If a superb long shot from Chico Hamilton had gone in instead of hitting the bar we could've been the only Third Division club in history to win the competition. The next season we won the Third Division with a record 70 points.

Meanwhile, after beating the Harlem Globe Trotters, sorry, I mean Man-Ewe, the dancing went on well into the night and morning ...

So there you have it. That's what it's like to go to a real match and that's why football became the most popular sport in the world. Aston Villa are the prime reason why football reached into every household in the world, unless inventing the sporting league system had nothing to do with it??!!...??

My Relationship with Aston Villa

In my particular case, when I was a young guy studying primarily what one could identify on a good day as classical music (but on a normal day as classical neuroticism) it was a true blessing for me to have an outlet in which I was surrounded by normal, honest, hard-working people who did 'proper jobs'.

Classical musicians, classical record companies, classical reviewers, etc, etc, were more often than not, up an ivory tower methodically and thoroughly exploring deep into their own sphincters by indulging their holier than thou attitudes, mainly at the expense of the completely uninterested taxpayer through Arts Council grants, the BBC and suchlike. My inbuilt bullshitometer always went into the red danger zone whenever I was in the proximity of these types of people, so I already knew that I was going to have to do something about it to prevent my life going down that particular toilet. Football and jazz provided me with a much-needed involvement with the real world. They both involved normal people without all those unpleasant airs and graces.

One game at the Villa and I was bonded to the club for life. This is the same for every Villa fan, it's one giant family. Marriages can come and go, jobs (after Thatcher) can come and go but your club is forever. My bullshitometer immediately goes into the red part of the gauge when I hear some bollockless neutered kat say "I used to support Aldershot but now I support Man Ewe..." or some krap like that. Even my own kid had to support Villa unless he didn't mind paying rent. I remember someone mentally challenged gave Sark a Man Ewe David Beckham shirt and he really enjoyed the ceremonial burning of it in the garden. Paraffin is great!

As I was saying before, Vic Crowe built the solid foundations which enabled us year by year to get back where we belonged, in the higher echelons of the game. Ron Saunders was the man to take over from Crowe and he steadily achieved those objectives to the highest extreme imaginable—winning the League in 1981.

As our team progressed upwards in the league we also progressed upwards in the combat league. My shitness and lack of interest in regard to all the boring academic fodder meant I didn't need to be Einstein to figure I was going to be a musician. I was good at music so my path was obvious, at least to Me Myself and I.

Not so obvious to Margaret Thatcher when in an earlier year she had come to inspect us lovely brats at The Yehudi Menuhin School when she was minister of education. She had told me very sanctimoniously that I would need my O and A levels in the future. I had told her that only mediocre musicians needed bits of paper as qualifications, it was their sound which got good musicians their jobs.

What with my involvement in music I had to protect my hands so I developed a fairly good head-butt which delivered me from evil once or thrice. Quite often there would be running street battles around the ground and Witton Lane was a real number in as much as it was so narrow that if there was a face-off the only direction was forward. One such situation happened with Man Ewe.

We were walking up Witton Lane towards The Holte End from Witton station and we got word that Man Ewe were coming in the opposite direction (from Aston Villa Leisure Centre where their coaches had dropped them off). They were coming towards their North Stand entrance so we were head on. About 3,000 of us against 3,000 of them. Witton Lane was only about 10 metres wide so there was nowhere to fuck off to. Even though we didn't have Eisenhower or Churchill as our military commander our mission objective was pretty clear, get to the other end of Witton Lane with as few losses as possible. The Ewenited objective was the exact same but in the opposite direction. This was not going to be a meeting of minds but of fists and craniums (just as good as crania, my learned friend).

My problem was that I was at the front. It felt great leading the line until I saw the 3,000 other cunts coming at us. I suddenly would've loved to make a French retreat but with thousands behind us in such a confined space that was impossible. Anyway, the loss of face would've been permanent. A few seconds after seeing the enemy a collective instinct started us all running at them—it was the only available option. We made the Māori Haka look like ballet dancing wusses. Once the two endless banks of combatants met I decided to risk my right with a huge punch more telegraphed than a right wing national newspaper, at a run I then followed up with my master head-butt on the next geezer (this head-butt left me with an extra growth of healed bone on my forehead which I still have to this very day). I was through the first two rows which meant only about 2,900 to go. I definitely didn't have it in me and noticing I was now on the side of the road next to the fish and chip shop I darted in there. Now safe I could see from my vantage point that all the momentum on each side had been lost. Being at 'the front' now merely consisted of about 200 people in a free for all and maybe a couple of thousand puzzled bastards stuck behind watching and thinking "WOT D FUCKK?" It's random fiascos like that which make a game memorable. Gradually the ones who didn't want to be involved dispersed in the directions they'd come from and in about 15 minutes the whole thing had petered out (that would be five rounds of boxing with no breaks). The police had been nowhere to be seen which was better for everybody concerned. If they had piled in with their lovely little truncheons the casualties would've been far worse. I can testify to that in my chapter of adventures with the police.

Being kind of 64ish now I've noticed that there is a pathetic form of moral censorship currently going on (and on and on and on) in our so-called free Western society. Nevertheless I'm going to maintain my right as a hard working tax paying citizen to hold and express opinions which might be different than the ones assigned to us by the unelected moral authorities who try and shame us all into spouting out the same opinion as them. I like opinion based on fact, so the opinion coming up is one of that kind. I would propose that:

1. (fact) 20 years of good old-fashioned football hooliganism didn't notch up even a fraction of the casualties or fatalities achieved by the police in less than a couple of hours at Hillsborough (the failure to take responsibility but instead to tarnish the reputation of Liverpool fans and football fans was disgusting and was strangely coincidental with the Thatcherite government's hatred of the working class). Add to that the culpability of the Union of European Football Associations for the Heysel Stadium tragedy (the stadium they were warned against using because many parts of it had deteriorated so badly that people could kick through the walls to gain illegal entry when other great stadia were available for the fixture) and my point is incontrovertibly proven. The authorities were responsible for both these problems and followed up not with apologies but with callous cynicism.

2. Hooliganism kept the bourgeoisie globalists and TV companies, etc., away from football which was a very, very, very good thing for real fans.

3. The tribal feeling of football made it far more exciting, far better than the sedentary involvement currently in vogue whether it's at a match or in the shape of couch potatoes at home.

4. More please. Pitch invasions are great and have never harmed anyone except those of us who have had to listen to the namby-pamby indignance of the TV commentators whingeing through the TV at home. As Johnny Lydon would've said: "It's a farce!"

Villa Inspire My Career

Meanwhile, Ron Saunders was guiding the Villa further and further upwards. We had won the League Cup twice and he was methodically piecing together a team to take on everybody and anybody. Jimmy Rimmer, Kenny Swain, Ken McNaught, Allan Evans, Colin Gibson (or Gary Williams), Des Bremner, Dennis Mortimer, Gordon Cowans, Tony Morley and Brian Little were all ready to rumble. The final piece of Ron's jigsaw and an absolute masterstroke of a signing was Peter Withe. As a centre forward Withe was a physical, hard-working regular goal scorer so it was going to be fascinating to see how he combined with our sublime sensation Brian Little. Unfortunately a tragic injury problem put out Brian Little so who would be Peter Withe's strike partner? GARY SHAW! SHAW! SHAW! This young genius scored loads of goals in his phenomenal partnership with Withe, he was way above England quality. What made things even better was that he was a Brummie Villa fan living the dream and of course ... we won The League.

In our championship winning year my career was doing badly enough that I had time to get to plenty of games but well enough to afford the petrol to get up to Brum and back to London. Seeing so many virtuosos on the pitch going about their business with incredible commitment, pride, awareness, enjoyment and flair plus Ron Saunders' hard work ethic definitely inspired me to apply myself wholeheartedly to see what I could achieve with the same attitude. I worked like a muvvafukka and enjoyed the results. As with Ron Saunders taking a few years to assemble a better than world class team, it took me a few years before I got the ingredients right for communicating world class music with the right number of people at the highest possible level. Like what I saw on the pitch from the Villa I learned how to pace things, to be able to give my best in the last minute of a gig and to adjust to whatever circumstances I found myself in.

Football Explanation—Where Are The Music Stories?

In this book of various recollections of my life there seems to be a lot about football. I've figured out why. I've had a very long period in my life doing over a hundred gigs a year, and if one counts the travel to and from the towns and countries where I've been playing it doesn't leave a lot of time off in between. In what little time I've had off I've gone to Villa Park or to away games.

Football is a great cure for the obsession, self-obsession, self-criticism, self-improvement, display of self, meeting of self with the vibe, any old self etc., etc., etc.

I don't remember what happened musically in gigs which happened a long time ago because I'm obsessed primarily with doing an even better gig the next time. There's nothing worse than a smug, complacent self-satisfied artist who's full of themselves because of what they've done in the past. That's a bit of an insult to us in the audience who are there now, we don't care about yesterday.

Also every morning, day by day, I start by playing Bach (as a meditational activity combined with improving my chops) and end up writing new music. Music consumes me and sometimes it's a bit of an inward trip, with every little decision seeming, possibly, a bit more important than it really is. Music is a beautiful creative life in which no one tells you what to do but one lives very much in one's own world. However altruistic and considerate to other people the picture is that I'm trying to create, being the bandleader it's I who am the centre of attention and for whom everyone is working. The people working for and with me range from my musical colleagues to soundmen (they seem to be blokes most of the time[28]), drivers, tour managers, managers, personal assistants, quite a lot of peeps and it's all centred around me.

Going to the football it's all about the team and I'm just one of 30–40,000. It snaps me out of all the above so I'd say, mental health wise, it's essential.

Live music is all about NOW and it's an everlasting NOW. I can't remember what happened musically in my performances except for the most recent one or two—tonight's performance is the only one which matters. Dwelling on past achievements or failures is not the right way to go about being a musician or any type of artist really. So since this book is about my thoughts and reminiscences and I'm not into dredging up past gigs of mine this is what we've got! I'm also not writing about smooth, uptight, grasping, ambitious people who pretend to be humble so that cuts out most of my dumbfukktor stories.

There are parallels between live music and football which might explain my love of Aston Villa and the golden era of the game they invented.

Parallels Between Football And Live Music

Football: is a team sport which happens at the given moment. A large part of a good result comes from reacting to what is going on. It's not all just a preconceived plan.

Live Music: is a team collaboration form of art which happens at the given moment. A large part of a good performance depends on reacting to what is going on (from colleagues and audience). A performance is not just a preconceived plan, although listening to some of my Classico comrades might just convince you otherwise.

Football: An individual can be very important but never more important than the team. Some refs might convince you otherwise.

Live Music: A soloist, singer or even more likely a conductor might think they are very, very important but they soon sound like an idiot (or look like, if it's a dumbfukktor) if their colleagues on stage stop playing.

Football: The crowd are what makes a match a special occasion. Without them it is just a practise match.

Live Music: The audience are what makes a concert special. Without them it would just be a rehearsal or practise session. If the audience aren't there it is like an electric circuit with one component missing—there is no flow of electrickery.

---

28 I would never be guilty of the discrimination of positive discrimination, I'm there to give the best possible value for money to the important people, the audience. Meritocracy wins every time in my band set up. Please don't cry.

Football: People go fukkin' mad about football
Live Music: People go fukkin' mad about music

Football: Football is 70% perspiration, 30% inspiration
Live Music: Music is 68% perspiration, 32% inspiration

Football: Amateurs always think they know better than the professionals
Live Music: Amateurs always think they know better than the professionals

---

Football: is an escape for the crowd from the problems and pressures of everyday life.
Live Music: is also an escape for the audience from the problems of everyday
life—it is essential for us performers not to depress the poor audience with
our own problems.

So we're coming to the end of my football chapter … but I can hear you saying
"Oh, no … surely not. He's hardly got started yet … please don't let it end…."
And who am I to disappoint you? Only because of your request, I will satisfy your
wishes, OY! Hands off! I didn't mean that … Just a few more football memories,
at least they could be loosely described as such.

The Man Himself, Doug Ellis

Things started happening for me … everything was going well. I had worked hard
and I was like an equivalent musical mix of qualities embodied by Paul McGrath
(top class reader of What's Goin' On), Sid Cowans (sorted and creative in midfield
like Riders On The Storm), Tony Morley (who would leave defenders Dazed and
Confused) and Gary Shaw (whose finishing was pure classical). The success I
started to get led to me being asked to do quite a lot of interviews. What with
Villa getting so little publicity even when winning the League and the European
Cup I decided to mention them more than necessary wherever I went. At some
point I was on a Radio 4 show talking about … ermmm … myself and … ermm
… VILLA! … no, not Man Ewe … VILLA! It just so happened that Doug Ellis,
the Villa chairman, was listening and heard this violinist geezer talking about his
lifelong love of a club which was from neither Lancashire or London. This ended
up with Doug inviting me up to Villa Park to receive five honorary shares in the
club and for many years I had an open invitation to watch the games from the
directors' box. This was a completely new experience for me … I had to wear a
tie! I would never have done that for anyone in any other social circumstance
and before long, making a bit of an effort without a tie was OK for Doug. He
probably understood that a fair few musos can be forgiven a bit of social ineptness
based on the fact we can bring something else to the table instead of sartorial

elegance. During my visits to Villa Park as Doug's guest I met so many unique and inspirational people to do with the club.

Doug Ellis loved Aston Villa. He was chairman and owner of the club for over 30 years and there wasn't a second going by when he wasn't thinking about Villa, mind, heart and soul. There are always discussions about any chairman but I can't imagine more dedicated, stronger or more passionate devotees of any club than he and Steve Stride, his right hand man and Operations Director for the whole of Doug's very long tenure.

It wasn't often that Doug could really relax but in the summer he would holiday in another villa (not the great Aston Villa) in Spain. I remember going and joining him there for a couple of weeks with his lovely family. Heide, his wife and Ollie, his youngest son, made me feel really at home and were fantastic hosts. We also had a great time on his yacht. Despite not being able to swim I lived through it.

Doug Ellis had made his dosh by starting the first charter flight company to offer flights from cities outside of London. This enabled people from normal cities to have the same choice of holiday as the Londoners. I remember him showing me a great picture of him on the runway kicking the tyre of the first passenger plane he bought—in the '50s.

Some people never forgave him that he had previously been a director of Birmingham City, but the context of this ghastly crime was that he had been turned down flat by a snooty and archaic Aston Villa board when applying to become a director, and of course inject some much-needed cash into what was a badly ailing club. He had, apparently, been kept waiting in a dingy corridor (doodling pictures on a grimy unclean window) until a door opened and he was summarily dismissed as not being required. It was after this that he became a director of the Bluenoses where, he said, he learned exactly how not to run a club.

We spent quite a lot of quality time together and, unlike his successor, Doug never, never, ever missed a match. The boardroom was a quaint situation. There was a middle area where all the guests were allowed. The directors' room on the left, all men, no women allowed. The women's room on the right where I wasn't sure of the policy although they always invited me in to play a song or have a drink or most often both. Getting to the boardroom was great because the corridors were lined with large pictures of all the great moments from the club's history. As well as incredible geezers from the world of football I met a few great musicians. Roy Wood (one of the originators of the Birmingham scene) Gerry Marsden (Gerry and the Pacemakers), Geezer Butler (Black Sabbath and Deadland Ritual) and Barney Greenway (Napalm Death) come to mind although thinking about it I actually met Barney on the terraces.

One of my greatest honours was when Doug inaugurated me as Senior Vice President of the club, a tenure of seven years followed. It was at a time when most rockstars were tight lipped about football, maybe because being associated with the game might not have been good for a squeaky clean image. Nowadays the game couldn't be any cleaner if we all drank a bottle of Domestos.[29] I was quite indignant about Villa and the whole of Birmingham being kept a secret by the media so became pretty loudmouthed in my REmediaL efforts. That I was a walking advert for the Villa in the middle of the London/Lancashire quagmire probably had a lot to do with my appointment.

I enjoyed my time being involved in the club in that way and did anything that was asked of me. Judging Miss Aston Villa, for instance, was a huge sacrifice. Just as difficult as it was for all those women who were made to go and see The Chippendales ... (thought I'd throw that in before some addled amoeba cries SEXIST!). It was also a huge imposition to have to present awards to my heroes at the player of the year awards. Man, that was tuffff.

Despite the very real privilege of being a guest in such exalted circumstances as the directors' box I started to miss the release that match day gives you when you are surrounded by other noisy passionate fans. When reacting to the events in a match it was too difficult for me to sit there like a dummy from Madame Tussaud's. Things like the ref or the opposition quite often made it necessary to shout, using some choice fukkin' words. Then there was the high of 'singing' the Villa songs. There's nothing like the sound of The Holte in full voice. My decision was to go and sit with my friends in The Holte End for the match and be as animal as needed before joining Doug and the upper kats after.

Having seen what Doug had to put up with I never wanted to be owner or part owner of Villa. Aston Villa are much bigger than myself and I prefer it that way. Anyway, I'd learned from looking at Doug's situation that there were always going to be a good 90 per cent of backseat drivers, knowing a better direction for the club but not able to pay for the car.

There were quite a few occasions where I could've made shitloads of dosh by going down a completely naff career route playing totally shit music, and could've made enough jelly roll to become involved at least as a part owner. My life had always been about doing what I wanted as long as it didn't hurt anyone else. My credo from then to this very day was "Don't listen to the killjoys and don't be one." Doug did, for a while, try to mentor me into becoming a smooth(er) boy but I wasn't ready for it. A couple of years later he admitted that he was quite envious of me being such a free spirit so I took that as a very welcome vindication from him. He accepted me for being myself and no longer tried to steer or influence the way I went about things. I was even allowed to bin the Etonian noose, oh, I mean the tie....

The other thing I would've found impossible would've been having to suck up to people (or liars) like UEFA rebranding the European Cup (which had been for champions) as The Champions League (which since then has, despite the grandeur of its name, mainly been for also rans) and staging unsafe events,[30]

---

29 Cry babies. Please don't try this at home.
30 I'm referring to Heysel, for instance.

Sky Sports and The Premier League by renaming Division 1 and most of the time pretending that the history of the game started with the advent of the silly name—they were both (and still are) also complicit in rescheduling matches for broadcasting reasons instead of respecting the supporters' traditional rights of being able to get to a match. Monday nights, for instance, will never be an away fan's dream, nor will a 12:30 kick-off. All the above are stupid and selfish ideas which would never have got a flowerlike response from me. AND ... how to deal with slimy agents who weevil in and undermine the loyalty of players to the fans who pay to watch them? "My young boy, you can't imagine how much money you'll make if you leave the Villa and go to Man Ewe..."

No disrespect to Doug or anyone else but I never would have been able to appease the bastards who are fukkin' up our game for their own selfish gain. In short, I was and always will be shit chairman material. I'm a fan and that's it.

On a lighter side, Doug Ellis was known amongst the football community as Deadly Doug. This was because in a relatively short period of time Deadly had sacked loads of managers. In a tongue in cheek riposte Doug had said "My reputation is unfair. Out of the 13 managers I've worked with I only sacked 11 of them."

One day I drove from Malvern to Tewkesbury to get a little Bulldog puppy. He was a great little critter who grew into a great bigger critter. Once I got him home I had to choose a name for him. I would have liked to name him after a Villa player but it was the beginning of the evil called football agents. Agents grab a percentage of transfer fees amongst other things. It is in their interest to unsettle players so that they can commission the resulting transfer fees which they make as big as possible. I would love to have named my critter after Dwight Yorke, for instance, but the agents had a created a shituation of here today, gone yesterday with all the good players. It was clear that Dwight was being unsettled and before I knew it I would've had a dog named after a Man Ewe player. Not exactly a dream come true ... and you can't burn up a dog like you can a Man Ewe shirt.[31] So my dilemma was as follows—with agents around no good player was going to stay at the Villa so no dog name. Also no manager was going to last long at the Villa with Deadly being chairman. That was it! DEADLY! I named my dog DEADLY! Deadly Doug wasn't going anywhere and would always be synonymous with the Villa. I had a great name for my doug—I mean dog. DEADLY DOUG ... DEADLY DOG. Up The Villa!

Of course, I wouldn't have met any of the players who I am going to be writing about next if Doug hadn't introduced me behind the scenes in the first place. So thanks, Doug, for making my book a little more interesting! And of course, you will be remembered always for your contribution to the city of Birmingham and to Aston Villa in particular. You were definitely one of sport's larger than life characters.

---

31 Oy! You whingeing cry babies. I look after my dogs brilliantly and would never burn one—so don't be silly trying to haul me in front of animal rights groups!

As you may have gathered, Doug is unfortunately no longer with us. One thing I'll regret for the rest of my life is being unable to have made it to his funeral. I had a family crisis here in Poland but would've loved to have been what little comfort I could've been to his family, and also to show the immense respect I had for Doug as a man and a friend.

What I learned from Deadly was to remain dedicated and that it's a good idea to keep one's fukkin' house in order!

Nigel Spink, European Cup Winner
And All Round Great Keeper

SPINK: Oy, Noige....

    ME: Yo, Noige....

    SPINK: I'm Nigel.

    ME: I'm Nigel.

    SPINK: Good to meet you, Nigel.

    ME: Very good to meet you, Nigel. Up The Villa, hero.

The scene: Aston Villa's Bodymoor Heath. A scruffy semi-punk-violinist type is vibing up to take penalties against a European Cup winning keeper who is probably the best in England, Wales, Scotland, Northern Ireland and even Ireland. The picture is even more incongruous because the punker is in his civvies from head to toe and wearing winkle pickers.

We walk towards the numerous football pitches where the Villa do their training.

SPINK: This is the pitch where we've just been training. I've just finished crosses and then some shot stopping. How about you take some penalties at me? That would finish my training for the day.

    ME: Fukkin'ell, alright, anything to be of some use around here *(if only...)*.

    SPINKSY: Great. Tell you what. Why don't you take 10 pens and we'll see how many you score?

    TERRY WEIR: *(the club photographer who had taken so many unforgettable pictures of the Villa over the years, there are also a couple of pap guys there)* This should be a laugh. Are you any good, Noige?

    ME: The answer is different depending on which Noige you're talking to....

I put the ball on the spot, take seven or eight steps back for the run up and then look at the ball, Spinksy and the goal. The ball looks OK *(it's pretending)*, Spinksy *(in his customary green jumper, no pansy colours[32] for keepers yet)* looks bigger than Shrek and the goal looks miles away, no bigger than a matchbox.

---

32 Not homophobia. Don't cry, my sensitive friends. Pansies are stupid colours and so are goalkeepers' jumpers nowadays—worse than Xmas prezzies.

I run up and kick the ball … thump, skid, squirt, grub … the ball rolls gently towards Spinksy who bends down to pick it up.

ME: Oh, shit.

SPINKSY: Oy, Noige, you're going to give me backache picking up grubbers like that … you've had one … NEXT.

My next penalty is much the same—tap, skid, squirt, grub, and the ball rolls gently towards Spinksy but this time I have deftly rolled it a metre to Spinksy's left. He takes one step to his left and calmly picks the ball up.

SPINKSY: Ow, my back. That's two … NEXT …

Things carry on like that. The ball has taken on a very obtuse manner and seems to have decided to squat my side of the goal line even though it obviously doesn't like me. Maybe it hates the net or loves being fondled by Spinksy's hands, it certainly seems very attracted to them. I imagine taking a bike pump valve to it and letting all its air out. It wouldn't be so puffed up with pride then.

Another problem is my lack of football boots and lack of grip. I can't get any purchase from the muddy slippery ground with my left foot in order to whack it in with my right. If only I had my football boots then maybe I could do a better job and excel in front of the cameras and the best keeper in Ingulund. Of course, I would love everyone to imagine that I am a truly, no I mean truly magnificent, great and sublime footballer. In reality the truth of the matter is that Tony Morley, Sid Cowans, Dennis Mortimer, Gary Shaw, Peter Withe (you name them)—even in high heels could still score a penalty. On second thoughts maybe it's better not to imagine any or all of them in high heels.[33] A dastardly and gruesome thought worse than a nightmare. What I'm saying is, to be honest, that I am a truly and despicably shit footballer who even when I'm playing for my own team am always put at left back because no one else wants to play there.

Things have progressed to 0 out of 8 penalties (not) scored, my only moral victory being that I haven't yet slipped onto my arse which in these particular conditions seems like a splendid achievement. Spink has had nothing to do and the photographers have also started to look a bit bored. Then, KAPENGWE! I know how to improve things.

ME: Oy, guys. Check this. (*I walk to the goal line to get my idea over, they all listen, including Spinksy*). This is becoming really boring for you guys and you haven't got a good photo yet. How about this? I'll shoot just inside your right hand post at waist height, Spinksy, then you can dive full length, Lev 'The Black Spider' Yashin style, and it'll make a great sodding photo. We need a good picture for The Birmingham Evening Mail and if it's really good it might get into The Sports Argus. Alright, Spinko?

SPINKSY: Spinksy.…

---

33 Oh dear, my sensitive one, please don't cry. Yet again this is not homophobia or even trans-
phobia. It's just that I think footballers shouldn't have to wear high heels unless it's voluntary
and they've already come out as whatever they've identified themselves as.

ME: Sorry, Spinky, let's do it and not just have photos of you picking up back passes.

SPINKSY: Call me Spinksy, Noige.

I put the ball back on the spot, walk back further and prospect the goal. Spink still looks gargantuan and the goal looks like a five-a-side. This is going to take huge effort and concentration. I run in and whack it as hard as I can. Spinksy dives to his right as planned, not the Black Spider, the Green Spider. The ball bounces tamely to his left … into the net … I'VE SCORED!! I do a little jig punk style.

ME: Oh, yaeyeeeeerss!… Yeah, man. Where's my contract?

I stop celebrating before it becomes in bad BAD bad taste. I realise that I've cheated on a Latino level.[34] Well, not that bad, my acting skills are not good enough. There's still one more pen to go and I've scored 1 out of 9. The last penalty is a brutal return to back pass reality.

TUMP	SKID		PLOP, PLOP
SKUFF	– SCHLUP	– SQUIRT	– GRUB
BOFF		BRZZZ	FIZZLE

And the fickle little bastard ball has rolled safely back into its master's hands again like a pathetic little teacher's pet. Its name was probably Timmy, or Annabelle, or something.

SPINKSY: Don't worry Noige, son (*this is worrying because I'm a couple of years older than him. Maybe it would be straighter to both change our name to George and let George Foreman add us to his collection*). Some people have never scored a pen against me, and anyway, you're probably a pretty good violinist, or so they tell me.

Nigel Spink has a good understated sense of humour and a very unassuming no bullshit nature. As a player he was strong, fearless and had every quality that makes a great keeper. His first game of note for us couldn't have been of higher prominence. He came on as sub for the injured Jimmy Rimmer after about 10 minutes in The Real European Cup Final against Bayern München in 1982. We won 1–0 and he played a blinder. He was with the Villa for about 10 years and it was a huge advantage to our defence to have such a safe, reliable pair of hands behind them.

I played a gig in aid of Spinksy's testimonial year in Brum's main venue at the time, the Town Hall. Playing in Birmingham is always fantastic because there are always enough Villa fans in the audience and the Town Hall has an amazing

---

34 Dear cry babies, this is not racist. There is no denying that parts of South America introduced a sordid element to the game during the latter part of the twentieth century. Diving with no contact. Writhing in agony dying swan style but fit as a…fiddle within 20 seconds. A tap of the ankle resulting in a clutch of the face. Diving like in the Olympics with not a splash to be seen or reason to fathom. Unfortunately everyone has now learned the pathetic tricks. It's important not to do a history rewrite on this one. What's true is true. Facts are facts. Send them all to RADA as punishment is what I say.

history of the absolute best bands appearing there. Having said that, I can't remember a thing about my gig that night ... PARTY? I do remember Spinksy presenting me with a replica of his European Cup winning medal on stage and also remember many of the games he played for us. Fair does.

Nice one, Nigel.

Thanks, Nigel.

What Spinksy re-affirmed to me (particularly during The Real European Cup Final which was only his second game) was to rise to the big occasion by living the moment.

Paul McGrath

Oo—Ah—Paul McGrath,

Say Oo—Ah—Paul McGrath,

Oo—Ah—Go-o-od,

Say Oo—Ah—Go-o-od.

This song was introduced by our knowledgeable faithful at Villa Park long before it was culturally appropriated on behalf of Eric de Gaul by The Theatre of Has Beens.

Where does one begin with such a legendary and inspirational figure as Paul McGrath? The beginning? No, the middle. Paul had been playing for Man Ewe but he had knee injuries which made it difficult for his future in the game to be guaranteed. Man Ewe put together an insurance package of around £100,000 or so for Paul to accept on condition that he stop playing. This might have appeared generous but the fact was he had a choice. Either he accepted the pseudo-generous offer from Man-Screw or made them look like idiots for letting him go by playing supremely for another team for a long period of time. He chose the second option and I'm sure that by playing the game he loved for so many more years he earned a lot more than the paltry £100,000 odd that was farcically meant to last him for the rest of his life.

I think it was the beloved Graham Taylor who signed Paul for the Villa and he was a phenomenal signing.

The first thing that Villa did was to Taylor-make a training schedule which was suitable for McGrath's particular physical condition. This involved only doing set piece training on Fridays, the day before the game. This might've been unthinkable for some players who relied primarily on physical fitness to compensate for their shortcomings, a bit like musicians who get faster and faster techniques but have nothing to say in their music. Paul was the opposite of this. His positioning on the pitch and intuitive reading of the game meant he was always in the right place at the right time without having to run miles. He was always strong, serene and unflustered, and in common with the greatest of musicians everything seemed simple. It was amazing to see. A true genius doesn't blind you with science and technique (although, for sure, present day science and technique has blinded a lot of us to the possibilities of a real life with real answers).

The other amazing thing about Paul is that his academy of life on the pitch was pivotal in the development of two excellent defenders, Ugo Ehiogu and Gareth Southgate. They probably wouldn't have become half the players they became without playing and learning alongside God. Who wouldn't have learned loads? It was interesting that without his level headed guidance they both became a bit mentally deficient and joined 'Boro "TO WIN THINGS"!!!! The only thing they might have won by leaving was an extra dime or two. I was very disappointed that these two great defenders didn't carry on the McGrath tradition with us.

To put it simply I can't think of another player who has made such an impact on our club, and more importantly us fans (because the fans ARE the club, not owners, chairpersons, blah bla blah). Name me another player for whom the fans still sing more than twenty years later. Answer from fans at large … ermmm … BLANK. My answer would be Andy Lochhead, possibly, but even he wasn't sung for every match like Go-o-od….

(To Kumbaya)…   Paul McGrath My Lord, Paul McGrath,
                      Paul McGrath My Lord, Paul McGrath,
                      On The Piss My Lord, On The Piss,
                      Oh Lord, On The Piss.

Musos note:

Either version on the rising triad and the descending whole tone is acceptable.

Paul was a legend of the George Best mould. Both of them could completely and justifiably get away with shit that no one else could. The reason? Mega talent and their humble shy attitude. There were two classic examples involving Paul that I remember. One time us Villa fans made the trip to Exeter to see us play them away in the FA Cup third round. On getting there we heard that Paul had made the slightly longer trip to Dublin to finally get a decent quality Guinness with his mates. The shortage of good quality Guinness in England is downright disgusting so we all raised a sympathetic glass to him (more than a glass, naturally). The same disappearing act happened when Ireland had an away trip to Albania. No other player could've got away with that without a heavy fine and suspension but for Paul it only enhanced his legendary status and the Black Magic was in the line-up for both Villa and Ireland when he chose to come back. Guinness is black velvet and Paul played in a manner which was even smoother than that.

It is all the more remarkable that Paul was so supreme on the pitch and is to this day such a humble gentleman off it, when one thinks of all the disadvantages he had to overcome on the way to success. First he was allocated to foster parents and then he was orphaned all within his first few years.

Being one of the first (if not the first) home-grown black Irishmen to play for St Patrick's and for Ireland can't have come without its problems for him in his early days but he overcame these considerable challenges in his usual calm and self-effacing way. He became and still is the best player ever to have played for Ireland. His is a triumph for humanity and an inspiration for mixed race people everywhere, an inspiration for footballers, an inspiration for Ireland and, of course, a continuing inspiration for us at Aston Villa.

Paul has been to a fair few gigs of mine, whether in Brum or in Manchester near where he used to live. It is an honour that such an important man from Ireland and Aston Villa should come to a gig of mine.

I did a gig for (in aid of) his testimonial year and also wrote a song to honour him which was on an album of my songs called 'Kafka'. The number I wrote for him was called 'I Believe in God', and featured The Holte End singing 'Oo-Ah-Paul McGrath'. What a feeling that was, a packed Holte End towering above me as I recorded them from on the pitch behind the goal. That is a fukkin' sound, man. And all inspired by the greatest Irish maestro to ever play for the Villa.

What Macca reminded me was to be aware of everyone around me on stage, in the same way that he was aware of everyone on the pitch, to be aware of the bigger picture in order to tell who's going to do what next.

Cheers, God

Andy Robinson

We were having a decent party at my house in Malvern after the match and my proper friend Andy wanted to get a bit experimental. I would employ Andy to drive us to and from the home games because he didn't drink and I definitely did, particularly on match day. He had just driven us back, we had probably won because just by existing and having invented the league system for all world sport we will always be winners.

ANDY: Oy, Noige, let me 'ave a gow.

I had been playing tug of war with my aforementioned bulldog Deadly, who had a muvvafukka[35] grip on whatever he wouldn't let go of. His grip could only be prised open by getting your hand in his mouth, then he would relax.

ME: OK, Andy. Good luck. You know Deadly's a strong muvvafukka.

I pulled on the joint[36] in preparation for the entertainment but even a good spliff couldn't be seen as having been responsible for what happened next. I passed Andy the rope and he immediately got down on all fours at which moment, if it had been a beauty contest there would've been no obvious winner although Andy

---

35 In these ever so politically correct times this term could be mistaken for an endorsement of incest. It is no such endorsement, but to be on the safe side please if you have urges after reading this DON'T TRY THIS AT HOME. Also, please don't cry or be upset, dear sensitive one.

36 Animal rights campaigners, please don't cry. In some cases a joint is not a cut of meat which I wouldn't truly pull at, I'd carve it. This joint was fully veggie apart from maybe the glue on the paper. Don't worry. Be happy!

was drooling less. Maybe Crufts Rejects might've been more relevant—neither of them was inbred enough. Andy inserted one end of the rope into his mouth and the other end was enthusiastically accepted by Deadly, who wasn't going to let go. The battle of jaw and neck power commenced and was evenly matched for about seven or eight seconds but then there was only one contestant in it.[37] With a savage wrench of the neck and rope Deadly achieved a result and what did we see scurrying across the kitchen floor? Andy's teeth ... they were still chattering as they went, like some demented mix of one of those wind up teeth toys and an unpleasant rodent.

Andy picked up his itinerant gnashers and set about reinserting them.

ME: Oy, Andy ... shouldn't you disinfect them first? Here's a bottle of vodka.

| Earlier: | Baník Ostrava 1 | VILLA 2 | 3 October 1990 |

We'd beaten Baník 3–1 at Villa Park two weeks earlier and now we were celebrating having beaten them in Ostrava 2–1 in the return leg. We were travelling back to Ingulund the next day so we had plenty of time to herald our new goal scoring sensation who had scored in both legs ... central defender Derek Mountfield, and a 5–2 winning aggregate.

After the game a number of us went to the old town (almost all Eastern European cities have an old town which surrounds a central square) and entrenched ourselves in a bar to drown our happiness by drinking vastly overrated Czech beer. After a few hours, being in the bar turned into being on the bar as our dancing skills came into play while singing the songs of each player. Caruso (or any other Italian tenor) was completely surplus to requirements musically or noise wise. Despite our nifty and delicate footwork the barman, who had taken an untold amount of Czech shitters from us, enough for a new Fiat, got a bit grouchy and suddenly called the police with no warning just like the informer he might have been in his yesteryears.

The Czechs had been 'free' from the Soviet Union for less than a year, so even though there were changes afoot the policing techniques were still much the same as in the old days of fascism or unter-communism. When they arrived these particular little piggies stormed the bar à la Stalin,[38] and even though of lesser intelligence than a real pig they were pretty menacing and had plenty of bad intent. They had come in through the front entrance, were blocking it and already had their guns out of their dainty little holsters. That little mix of metal and leather made them look like pissed off bondage victims. There was aggression coursing through the air and the situation was plummeting quickly from being a lovely tea party to something

---

37 Animal rights alarmists, please don't howl or cry. Bulldogs love tug of war, it's good for them. So this is not an abuse of animal rights, unless you're talking about my mate Andy, that is.

38 I know Stalin was Georgian and not Czech, please don't cry, baby. I'm not trying to rewrite history, just describing the police action...bla blah.

a bit less refined. Each time the porkers advanced a step the hostility between them and us went up a notch. Then, just before the first blow was struck I heard:

"Oy, Noige, cumm out eeya, moite. We downt want yoe involved in dis."

The geezer beckoned me, I jumped off the bar and he knowledgeably showed me out of the back way thru the kitchen. That was my first meeting with Andy Robinson. He'd probably saved me a broken arm amongst a lot of other broken things. The heave-ho could be heard starting as we exited the building. So much for capitalism versus communism, same old police tactics, same old exploitation, same old everything, different name. In the meanwhile, while the capitalist/communist police went about it with the Villa fans I'd made a new friend for life. We went down the quiet back street, hid our Villa shirts and went into another bar—to be confronted by loads more Villa fans. Shirts back on, then.

Andy was a minicab driver before the insurance got to be too much and of course he was friends with many other people in the same trade. Sometimes about 15 of us would meet on The Holte before that Tory Moy-no-han banned standing, making it impossible to just meet up and stand together. Another clear disadvantage of seating was getting stuck between Andy and his mate Andy II. I've never heard anything like it. Their singing sounded like cruelty to animals on the Island of Doctor Moreau—you couldn't fault it for passion though.

One place you might not find Andy is within the echelons of the Aston Villa Hall of Fame, but he's a killa friend and without the fans a football team is nothing. It's the collective experience and memory which make something real, not (like at the time of writing) an empty stadium with canned crowd noise—what an insult to the real fans that a TV company thinks it can replace them at the touch of a button. An analogy equally horrible is the classical musos who get loads of little musos in different places, divide the screen into loadsa little boxes, then shove all the little fukkers in them and pretend it's an orchestra. The magic of an orchestra is the collective sound, not loads of little peewit mikes on separate musicians simultaneously. What an elaborate procedure just to make a wannabe do-gooder musician look needed and virtuous while patting themselves on the back. Of course, it's much easier for the media to be fooled into believing in something 'clever' rather than identifying something with soul and reality.

PLAYERS in same stadium, CROWD with people like Andy and I in same stadium = FOOTBALL.

ORCHESTRA musos in same hall, AUDIENCE in same hall = CLASSICAL ORCHESTRA GIG.

STUFF made just in a studio or only recorded = FANTASTIC CONCEPT ALBUM but MERCY, not by Classicos or people who think we need them.

ANYTHING ELSE = BOGUS, SELF-INDULGENT SANCTIMONY.

I've got a nickname for Andy, it's Mensa, because sometimes he comes up with some amazing clanger classics. For instance, when I was touring the homeland, by which I mean Ireland, I employed Andy to drive for me. I got all my fiddles, bags etc. ready to put in the car, opened the boot and it was full—nowhere to put my shit.

"What's all this, Andy?"

"Well, it's all my dress shirts and eveningwear to wear for your gigs. I want to look professional."

"Andy—where can I put MY stuff? It's probably beneficial for the audience, if not imperative, that I wear something on stage, what with Ireland being a Catholic country and all of that. After all, I'm not doing shows for sexist women to watch The Chippendales … and I'll probably need my violins."

I have to admit that Andy did look right dapper in his frilly shirts though.

On another occasion SKY Sports asked me to do an interview about Villa. This presented me with a big dilemma. Going ahead and doing the interview might've been seen as endorsing the merciless commercialisation and demolition of our sport so criminally[39] carried out by SKY, The Preen-ya-League and football agents. Not doing it would probably lead to yet another Liverpool or Man-Ewe propaganda segment accosting the viewers. On that basis it was the lesser of two weevils to go ahead and do it on condition that we filmed it on The Holte End with a dozen or so of my Villa mates sitting around me and partaking in the interview.

The Holte End and the whole of Villa Park are mightily impressive even when completely empty. Apart from the energy of all those memories and all the noise indelibly etched into every nook and cranny of the ground, there's also an air of expectancy. The whole stadium (sorry, dirty word, ground) feels as if it's in stasis, waiting to come back alive at the start of the next match day. There's also something in the contrast between all the inanimate concrete stands with empty plastic seats and the huge rectangular space of living glowing green grass which they surround.

It felt great and looked slightly comical on the long shot, 12 of us sitting together in the middle of the upper Holte End, the biggest stand in England, in a completely empty ground.

The interviewer started asking me some real heavy and challenging questions …

INTERVIEWER: Are you a Villa fan, Nigel?

ME: No, I mean YES.

INTERVIEWER: Do you like playing the violin and do you like playing lots of concerts?

ME: No, errrm, YES. Maybe I need a lie detector, Doctor.

INTERVIEWER: Are these your friends?

ME: Who? Yes, Almighty God Bless Them All And Each One Of Them.

INTERVIEWER: Do you all support Villa?

US LOT: (all rather obviously wearing Villa shirts) VI-LLA---VI-LLA---VI-LLA---VI-LLA.

ME: Tell you what, it's all a bit focused on me. Why not ask some of my mates something? We all have to watch what's going on here. (We were going through a prolonged period of mediocrity on the pitch).

39 Morally criminal.

There then followed a fairly decent interview with everyone explaining what it means to be a Villa fan, and there was some stirring reminiscences of some of our great players and matches from the past.

Then the fact came up that only about 20,000 had turned up at Villa Park the previous week for our League Cup match. That's when Andy came up with one of his all-time classics....

ANDY: WELL, YOU SEE, THE REASON THAT NOT SO MANY PEOPLE GO IS BECAUSE SO MANY PEOPLE BUY THE TICKETS....

Mensa had spoken and it was all a fair bit beyond our comprehension. We all looked quizzically at each other—what the fukk was that he just came up with? He'd surpassed even himself this time. (He always insisted that he knew what he meant. That means he was in a minority of one).

I stood up and terminated that bit by walking towards the camera and saying "CUT! DON'T USE THAT BIT."

Of course, when it came to airing the interview the only bit they used was … THAT BIT. Including me standing up and saying: "CUT! DON'T USE THAT BIT." Plus a snippet in which I called Andy Dad. To be fair it was funny and made good TV. The Dad bit had a long legacy. There was many a match day when someone would come up to Andy saying "You must be so proud of your son."

The last occasion which comes to mind right now was going up to the famous Sunderland Cup game at Roker Park where Mark Bosnich saved absolutely everything. We only had four shots and ended up winning 4–3. (Alright you clever bastard, so Bosnich didn't save ABSOLUTELY EVERYTHING but he was Absolutely Fabulous). Singing "We've Only Had Four Shots" for the last 20 minutes sent us into a kind of hyperventilated euphoria. Watching the match, though, wasn't the problem—getting there was. My girlfriend and I had decided to go up to Sunderland with Andy and his mates. We were in a minibus with Andy's cabby collective and were sitting in the back having a spliff. We'd left early so things were looking good, when the van suddenly veered off the M1. It was around 1 p.m. Before we knew it we were circling around the ground, right next to it. It was very eerie. Granted it was two hours before kick-off, but it was still strange that no one was there at all.

"Why's no on here?"
"Not a big attendance then."
"Maybe we're very early."
"Nothing's open."   } 12 cabbies driving around Elland Road
ANDY: What's happening?   thinking they're in Sunderland.
"What day is it?"
"I need to piss."

ME: (ignoring all the surrounding expertise) Look guys, I think this is Elland Road. We're playing Sunderland, not Leeds. We've got miles to go yet and we don't want to miss kick-off. We've no time to spare, fukkit.

One other thing, the chips were great in Sunderland, cooked in lard, the proper way. But the main thing is—if you want to go somewhere, always trust your local cabby.

Whatever Andy's skills as an interviewee, navigator, Olympian tug of war contestant, whatever, from all that time back in Ostrava we are friends to this very day. He is a number one Villa fan, a great friend and the next match I go to will be in his company. Like many people I know he has overcome incredible obstacles and hardships but unlike many I never hear a whinge from him. His heart of gold always shines through and I'm a lucky muvvafukka to be able to count on him as a friend.

What hanging with Andy has taught or reminded me is that hard work and generosity are not a hardship, they're normal.

UP THE VILLA!

Gordon Cowans—Sid

Gordon Cowans or Sid, as he is known by all of us at the Villa, is one of the most talented and humble people that I have ever met. There is absolutely no front to this man at all. If there is some monkey of lesser talent getting more recognition than me (which happens all the time) I would probably say so. Sid confronts and confronted that type of problem in a totally different way. He was there for his team mates, not for himself, but his individual contributions on the pitch were a phenomenal joy to watch. Not only did he have vision, he had the work ethic and skill to deliver it. Every decision he made on the pitch was for the benefit of the team and he was smart enough to make the right decision every time.

Every Villa fan with basic knowledge[40] would put Sid in the top three players to have ever played for the club, along with Paul McGrath and one other.

Sid's résumé is one to be merely dreamed of by most football players on this planet and he achieved it for his beloved Aston Villa, not by making a mercenary move to a club full of Judas types. Doing tiddlywinks and knitting competitions with posers like 'Los Galácticos' just wasn't his style. With and for us he won The League, The European Cup, The European Super Cup and The League Cup. Within a year he had been in the winning Villa team against Bayern Mün$chen and Barcelona, so those overpaid lovelies can shove all their easy earned cash up their arsenal. I have already pointed out that in their typically perverse way UEFA now run a competition called The Champions League (more like The Chump-Peons Shleeg) in which most of the participants are not even as high up the food chain as the runners up. It should be named The Also Rans' League if there was any honesty involved but such is the sly complicity of modern day football authorities. Sid won The Real European Cup for us when it was only for champions. Also rans had to run somewhere else, possibly to the toilet where

---

40 Every Villa fan has far more than basic knowledge, otherwise they'd be supporting another team.

they belong. Today's ambition? Let's try to finish fourth! That wouldn't have been good enough for Ron Saunders.

The only contemporary of Sid's playing in the same position who even approached his level was Glenn Hoddle (Ha! You thought I was going to say Glenn Campbell, didn't you?). Hoddle could spray around some very nice passes almost as well as Sid, but he didn't have the get in where it hurts and win the ball quality that Sid had. For pass making, dead ball delivery, ball winning and general effectiveness Cowans was the absolute finest of his day. He would have been the obvious automatic pick for England if it wasn't for the London-Lancashire bias which was even more rampant then (hard to believe) than it is today. Being completely two footed, intrepid and courageous completed the picture of his game.

The work he has done coaching must have been an amazing inspiration to the younger up and coming Villa players, continuing his legacy in the strongest possible way.

Sid has come to quite a few of my gigs in Brum and talking afterwards it is clear that he completely understands not just the skill and inspiration but also the hard work involved. It's our job though, whether in football or music, to make it look easy. That's why we all love Sid, he was inspired, incisive and direct but it never looked complicated. Never 10 passes in the box and a damp squib à la Arsenal, Gordon Cowans has been a great reminder and example to me as a band leader—to dictate the course of events but make sure that the other talented people on stage around me have a chance to shine. Sid brought out the best of his team mates and I really enjoy trying to do the same.

A great thing about football and cricket is that, unlike in American sport, you don't have to be brought up on a copious diet of steroid burgers and milk in order to succeed. Sid had a comparatively slight physique but he dictated games and ceaselessly opened up possibilities like a super intelligent human dynamo. Run Your Heart Out For The Lads was not a song he needed to hear. He had absolutely everything as a midfielder.

The measure of a human being is how they deal with the biggest problems. Sid's message to everybody when being diagnosed with Alzheimer's was so typical of him. He professed love for those close to him and also for his extended Villa family. He added that he is approaching his future life as a new adventure. He was still thinking of those around him rather than himself. Not only a great, great player but a GREAT, GREAT human being.

SID! SID! SID!

What watching Sid has re-confirmed to me is that it's not the recognition or the dosh which is the reward, it's the work itself.

Tony Morley

Even though Tony Morley was only a Villa player for four years his impact on our club was absolutely immense. Most wingers are kind of peripheral figures who hang around for a lot of the match until a glimpse of their fancy footwork catches the eye, or once every ten games or so everything might go right for them and they might jink around a bit and get a solo goal. More often than not they are the pretty boys of football—if they were a band they'd be called The Ornaments.

Tony Morley was a completely different proposition. Of course he had the pre-requisite speed required by every winger but what set him apart was a merciless sense of purpose. No pretty shit, every time he got the ball there just had to be an end result. He injected excitement and would exuberantly increase the tempo and flow of the move. As well as scintillating speed with innate awareness, sense of direction and unstoppable energy Tony was equally happy to cut in and create havoc or to get to the byline and put in crosses like candy for Peter Withe and Gary Shaw to profit from. Our Withe-Shaw partnership was a true muvvafukka but someone had to feed this two-headed beast with the correct diet. On a plate was the way that Tony fed them, he was the chef extraordinaire. The rugged Peter Withe and the Greaves-like Gary Shaw were given hors d'oeuvre, main course and dessert by Maestro Tony Le Roux Morley.

As I was saying, Tony's ability to cut in caused havoc for opposing defenders, he was also a lethal goalscorer because…HE HAD A FUKKIN' SHOT!

I think you know my feelings about the Chump Peons Zleeg, and that I don't have a lot of time for many of those preening prima donnas who play in it. SKY Sports and their ilk would have us believe that fitness and skill only came into existence with the advent of The Preen-ya Leeeg and The ChumpPeonsZleeg. Time for a reality check please, Mercy, Mercy, please stop selling a Fiat as a Rolls-Royce. Look at films of Tony playing and you just have to retract those lies. Maybe one difference is that the cotton wool some of these preeners are wrapped in is of better quality.

When we won The Real European Cup it was only *Real* Champions who were allowed to take part. In those days it was very interesting because each team was comprised of players from their own or neighbouring countries, therefore the different styles of the adversaries made very interesting contrasts, whether it was hackers from Barcelona, smooth boys from Italy whose heads dropped if they went a goal down, systematic and skilful West German teams, shit teams from Iceland or a mixture of skill and competitive grit from Ingulund. All of the above instead of expensive Spanish-Brazilian style teams playing cheaper Spanish-Brazilian style teams. The comparison between ChumpPeonsZleeg and The Real European Cup is like that of homogenised-pasteurised milk and fresh milk from the farm. Homogenised-pasteurised is safer but fresh is real and less boring. In Villa's winning Real European Cup campaign going to East Berlin or Ukraine was going into the unknown. Football hadn't yet been the victim of the rampant globalisation that we all are afflicted by today.

The reason I'm going on a bit about The Real European Cup is that without Tony Morley's crucial contributions we wouldn't have won it. It's easy to remember the sublime footwork and cross which led to Peter Withe's tap in to beat Bayern Mün$chen in the final—but why were we in the final in the first place? Largely because of Tony Morley's goals dragging us through two very difficult ties against Dynamo Berlin and Anderlecht. His two goals away from home in East Berlin and his goal against Anderlecht were what separated the teams in extremely tight contests. Without Tony's brilliant goals there would've been no memories from Rotterdam. Tony was deadly without a capital D (and only Maestro Morley will get the poignancy of that remark).

Tony's enthusiasm for football hasn't diminished one iota. He can talk all night about the game even with a plastic spastic[41] player such as myself. Tony is not shy but not a show off. When he speaks he displays the same directness and purpose as he did on the pitch and not a word is wasted.

What Tony's brand of football reconfirmed to me as an artist is that brilliance is kool as long as there is a point to it.

> Tony, Tony Morley, Tony Morley On The Wing,
> Tony, Tony Morley, Tony Morley On The Wing.

Jack Grealish

Once every two generations or so the world sees an absolutely exceptional football genius. Someone who can introduce magic to a game and change it single-handedly. George Best, Gazza, Pelé, no other legend has changed the course of so many games on such a frequent level, pretty much every game he plays in. Maradona might come close but Jack doesn't have to use his hands except for Gaelic football which I reckon Maradona was shit at. No disrespect to the rest of our players but we wouldn't still be in the Preeeeenya Leeeg if it hadn't been for Jack's incredible performances.

At the moment we have a bit of a killjoy as Ingulund manager and one gets the feeling that he would use any excuse at all not to pick Jack. So far he has been too good and the manager's hand has been forced even though it seems he'd prefer to pick far more boring players. Luckily for Jack it's not just partisan Villa fans who want to see him play for Ingulund, it's football fans, fans of good entertaining football all around the country. The shift that he puts in in every game means that there's no excuse to discount Jack as a luxury player either.

Another thing which is great about Jack—he's one of our own, one of the Villa family. He's Villa through and through. He's supported Villa all his life, his Dad's a Villa fan and his great-great-grandad won the FA Cup with Villa in 1905.

---

41 Dear sensitive one, please don't cry. Spastic doesn't apply to anyone but myself and I reserve the right to call myself spastic, elastic, bombastic or whatever I want. No one should take a fence unless they can fit it in the back of their truck. What? No truck? Shame.

And just in case you thought that perfection couldn't be improved upon, he's an Irish Brummie! His Dad Kevin and I have been to many an away game well before Jack was even born. It's like Jack is part of my family but without any of the pressure.

One thing for sure is that his magic puts a smile on everyone's faces every game—and if loyalty and unselfishness have anything to do with it Jack's character is second to none.

>Su-per, Super Jack,
>Su-per, Super Jack,
>Su-per, Super Jack,
>Super Jacky Grealish.

Just while checking this through before handing this book to the publisher, Jack has been put in the position of having to leave us for Man City. This situation, in my opinion has been forced by Gareth Mousegate's refusal to put Jack on the pitch for Ingulund at times which matter. Mousegate possibly wouldn't have chosen Best, Pelé or anyone else who had genius and could've helped us beat Denmark by more than 1–0. Entertaining the world is something this amazing group of Ingulund players could do but not during Mousegate's tenure. Defence, defence, defence, and amusement around the world.

None of us at the Villa begrudge Jack leaving. He has already displayed a loyalty beyond the comprehension of Mouthgate, sportscasters, etc. 19 years of being a Villa fan and playing for us have been priceless and unique. Maybe Mr Mousegate's team selection can follow the normal prosaic, predictable lines now that Jack is playing for a richer and lovelier team....

FRIENDS AND INFLUENCES:
GARY LINEKER

It's Just Not...

The Malvern Hills were radiant behind us. Echoes of Elgar, Bernard Shaw and Blessed Ethel deeply imbued within them. The previous week we had set off fireworks on Elgar's grave to celebrate his birthday—we celebrated in the moon and fireworklight, maybe he didn't, maybe he did. But now something different was about to happen. The hills waited patiently, as they have since a wee bit before Darwin and T. H. Huxley thought of anything. It was a perfect day, the sun shining in a blue sky, the bluish tint of the hills gradually turning green as the sun slowly rose higher and higher. Butterflies flitted lazily from one flower to another and the birds were singing. We were at Mathon Cricket Club and the idyllic scene before us was all one would hope to imagine about a beautiful game of English village cricket. Everything seemed suspended in a timeless existence—which leads me to brag proudly that I have played cricket with GARY SHAW. Chandra (my Sri Lankan Cordon Rouge chef mate) and I had got a team together but we were so shit that we needed a couple of ringers. Gary obliged me and in addition to himself brought along the amazing Warwickshire all-rounder Paul Smith. Gary was also a more than fair cricketer so with them two on board it would've taken some doing to lose. Another advantage we had was keeping an open bottle of vodka at the ready behind the wicket. If you've got a quality bottle behind the stumps you'll do your best to protect them by preventing them being skittled, plus you have a bit of fuel to keep you going between overs. In fact, if you're an American friend you'd love cricket. It's a low action sport which gives you the ideal excuse to stand around getting pissed (= drunk) all day. Cricket is very calming so one never gets pissed, in your American sense of the word, when in such a tranquil environment. Pissed but not pissed, one could say.

As extra motivation we had a DJ bombing out reggae and ska from the boundary. The right stuff to appreciate that type of music was also in the vicinity for those who weren't too weak to have it.

NAMBSTER: Oh, I'm on a natural high. I don't need drugs. Drone, bore, bla, moggo.

NORMAL: Oh yes you do. Just look and listen to you.

It's quite an apt saying regarding village cricket that "it's not winning, it's the taking part that counts."

But ... due to Gary and Paul ... we won!

Just to remind you, dear friend, that Paul Smith won seven trophies for Warwickshire when they were the all-stars of cricket, the best team county cricket had ever seen. Gary Shaw, of course, is one of the Villa family and, as previously mentioned, won The League, The Real European Cup and The European Super Cup with Villa in consecutive seasons.

As the shadows lengthened and a few pigeons settled on the outfield both teams enjoyed the results from the pitchside barbecue and planned out the rest of the night, signalled by a spectral moon trying to survive the waning brilliance of the sun (no, not that scummy Thatcherist paper which tried to defame the Liverpool fans).

Gary Loin Acher Lineker

It was the year 1990. The sun was beating down, the heat was obdurate with a vicious and suffocating undertone. We were a bit beat up from two connecting flights and the taxi driver was driving atrociously in a physically disturbing way, but it was all right because he was Italian. He was taking us higher and higher up the Sardinian hills on a dusty dirt road which struggled to justify even that description.

Brixie, my girlfriend at the time and I were in charge of chaperoning Michelle, Gary Loinacher's wife, during Ingulund's World Cup Italia campaign and Ellie, my PA, had hired a lovely looking villa up the hills not too far from Bobby Robson's training camp and hotel. We were going to look after Meeky and take her to the matches, suffering the hardship of having to watch the games and hang with Gary and the Ingulund team at opportune moments.

The taxi ride had been interesting. There wasn't much vegetation surviving on the arid wasteland that we could see out of the car windows, but the elevated view was good. A bit different to London.

The taxi driver suddenly screeched to a halt in a cloud of dust.

"Deeess iz-eeet, ma non tanto cornetto."

"What?" (Meeky).

"Where?" (Me).

"Why?" (Brixie).

"Deeess eeess addressa."

"Caaan't wee go furrrderr?" Whined Brixie.

The taxi driver must have been thinking "What a loada whingers" or "Shuddapayour face."

Looking around outside the car we could see an unfinished gulag constructed of breeze blocks surrounded by concrete mixers. One might have surmised that this shithole wasn't fit for human habitation but it WAS inhabited ... by a pack of mangy wild dogs who didn't seem at all willing to share their concrete kennel with us. They looked ready to protect it at any cost, their prelude being a lot of growling and bearing of gnashers. We didn't want their fukkin' kennel.

My chaperoning wasn't going well. I had the hottest property World Cup Italia wife and a whining American girlfriend on my hands and I was a bit short of ideas. In the end it was Michelle who turned chaperone. She called Trevor East, Head of Sports for ITV and he sorted us out for hotels all the way through Ingulund's involvement in the tournament. In return I did loads of situ clips and match comment stuff—luckily I had my fiddle with me because it helped earn our keep. Apart from being outclassed by the Super Irish in the first game Ingulund had a fantastic World Cup beating Germany in the semis on penalties. Sorry! I was dreaming ... naturally our efficient friends beat us from the spot like normal.

Interlude
Ye Oldeee Kitchen Golf:
The Rules, Etiquette And Bylaws

Apart from drinking champagne from the FA Cup when Gary Lineker won it for Tottenham (wrong team but great achievement and an amazing day. I've hardly ever been to games when I can just relax because Villa aren't playing!) there was one other standout achievement which both Gary and I are responsible for.

Now that the Olympic Committee are admitting all fukkin' types of sports for any old Tom, Dick and Harriet to play and win a gold, before we know it Greta Thunberg will have won a gold medal in the officially recognised Olympic sport of Man Made Globally Warmed Tiddlywinks. I reckon that 20 years ago Gary and I came up with a sport which the world is finally ready for and which would be totally suitable in this sensitive (oversensitive) day and age. After all, why should there be such a strong prejudice against househusbands and housewives that they have no chance to win a gold medal at ANYTHING? The answer to this problem is in the new sport we invented ... KITCHEN GOLF. Being as far ahead of our time as we were, this was long before the advent of urban golf, which in any case is heavily stacked against housebound people and very, very BBC-ish. KITCHEN GOLF has the advantage that all types can play: fat, thin, tall, short, any colour, any religion, any gender, any blah, blah, etc., etc., etc.

How this new testosterone steroid mega sport got invented was as follows. Gary and I were sitting at my kitchen table in Malvern. It was getting late so Meeky and Brixie had called it a day and gone upstairs to get some sleep.

ME: Gary, look at all those disgustingly clean dishes. What do you say we do something about them?

GARY: What mate, are you hungry?

ME: No, man. I've got an idea. You're a killa sportsman so you'll like this. It involves an eight iron because it's not too long to swing it in here and it has quick elevation of the ball. You're a killa sportsman, you know that shit.

GARY: What's the Mrs going to think?

Here's what we came up with, tried and tested by a member of the proletariat against a truly world class sportsman.

i. Find some fake tartan shorts American style in red and green, failing that true American pink.

ii. Utter the official greetings "anyone for Kitchen Golf?" and reply "yes, whip me brother/sister."

iii. Find a kitchen, this must be owned by one of the participants—restaurant or hotel kitchens are out of bounds.

iv. Find an eight iron—this trusted club is not too long to swing in relatively confined spaces and has good elevation.

v. Each participant should have their own golf ball for identification purposes.

vi. Locate a number of plates (10) stacked next to the kitchen sink (if you are a man you might find it necessary to practise locating the kitchen sink)[42]

vii. Toss a wombat[43] to decide who takes first shot.

viii. Remove any other sentient beings from the kitchen in the most masonic way possible.

ix. Place a golf ball at the other end of the kitchen from the sink.

x. Address the ball, take three practise swings and whack the ball with the eight iron at the plates next to the sink.

xi. Quickly shout "FORE!"

xii. Equally quickly take evasive action under the kitchen table to avoid the ricocheting of the golf ball.

xiii. When safe, creep out furtively from under the kitchen table.

xiv. Try to locate the sink.

xv. Tally up the number of broken plates, cracks and chips do NOT constitute a broken plate.

xvi. Respect and repeat the procedure (# i–xv) 3 x, each time having another Turbo.[44]

xvii. Appraise your scorecards. The participant with the highest score of broken plates is declared the winner, receives their gold medal live on BBC afternoon TV (BBC4).

---

42 Dear BBC and other politically correct whingers, please don't cry. I apologise for this disgustingly sexist joke against men. I wash the dishes at home, keep the kitchen tidy, and have become so good at it that I sometimes even get PRAISE! Washing dishes can actually elevate one's standing in the household.

43 Oh-oh…sorry.

44 Turbo = ⅓ vodka ⅔ champagne

This game is luvvy-duvvy wonderful in that it conforms completely to politically correct thinking. It just wouldn't do at all for physical excellence, talent or hard work to be an advantage. Absolutely no vulnerable group need to have their feelings hurt by not being able to compete because every individual has exactly the same chance of winning. This game also conforms synchronistically with capitalism and capitalist thinking in that it could not be moved further from meritocracy.

I hope Gary will join me in pushing for this wonderful sport to be fully recognised by the Olympic Committee. We would hope for support from the House of Schlommons, the House of Frauds, Mongress, the Bolshoi Ballet and sponsorship from IKEA, Titleist, Laurent-Perrier, Russian Standard and the unsuspecting British taxpayer through the BBC.

I can't remember who won the prototype test game because of the obligatory celebrations. I also don't remember either Meeky or Brixie saying "Very Nice Kitchen" the next morning.

FRIENDS AND INFLUENCES: CRACOVIA AND ST PAULI

I can't let a football chapter go by without mentioning Cracovia and St Pauli. That would be completely remiss and horribly unfinished business. These are my adopted teams in the country within which I live and the country I love and spend so much time in.

Cracovia

It was my first ever night in Kraków when, by chance, Agnieszka and I met the great trumpeter/composer Tomasz Nowak in a small club. He'd just finished playing and was packing up. He saw me and with exemplary manners which belied his Shrek-like figure and demeanour asked if I was that violinist blah bla. Once we'd established who each other were, a friendship developed for life. Our friendship involved jamming, hanging and smoking a good bit of recreational and going to the club he had supported since he was a little Shrek.

It should be explained that there are two larger teams in Kraków, Cracovia and the rich posers Wisła. They are situated across a park (the Błonia) from each other in much the same way as Everton and Liverpool being on opposite sides of Stanley Park.

Wisła being a military team for large parts of their existence, used to have an anti-Semitic recruitment policy which would have made it impossible for me to support them. As it happened Tomasz took me to Cracovia and the deal was done. Incidentally, Cracovia's recruitment policy was different, if you were good enough you played for the club, full stop. That we are called 'The Jews' by other clubs is a matter of pride although they are not intending to compliment us.

It was heart-warming, also, to see a good old-fashioned bit of football hooliganism. It's so much more preferable to see some good and bad than the bland corporate nothingness on offer today.[45]

---

45 My dear bleating, crying whiners, please don't cry. I of course don't condone bystanders being dragged into it. It's between the two sets of fans and the police.

My first years watching Cracovia were remarkably similar to my first years at Villa. Relegation to the 3rd division and then consecutive promotions to the top. Within ten years Villa had won The Real European cup. I hope it's not too long before Cracovia win The European Also-rans League.

It might seem strange or even perverse to start supporting a team which is at the wrong end of the table but as I've said earlier, it's the fans who make the team and not the other way round. Like with Villa, I've chosen the right team with the right fans.

PASY! PASY! PASY!

St Pauli

I haven't seen a game yet! I was introduced to the idea of this team of all teams by my friend Julia (who has been a fan of St Pauli since she was a little baybay—a state of affairs which hasn't changed). Then, when I saw the team on TV and realised they played in…BROWN, that was it.

I love St Pauli for a variety of reasons:

1. To play in the colour of shit is original, takes a bit of chutzpah and is fairly fukkin' great.
2. They are the rock 'n' roll team. The skull and crossbones logo is second to none.
3. (this should be No. 1) THE FANS.
4. They are NOT Hamburg SV, their smug, self-satisfied neighbours.
5. The St Pauli ground is not a fake stadium in the middle of fukkin' nowhere. It's in the middle of something that Bayern, Man City and many other clubs wouldn't know about … it's known as … let's think … wait a minute … oh yes, … a community!

St Pauli's players' tunnel is killa amazing, enough to freak out any away team—a phenomenal wall to ceiling to floor to wall to ceiling mural all graffitied on a black background with UV lights and everything. ARTWORK!

And I remember a phenomenal conversation with their chairman Oke Göttlich, we were talking about stadium renovation which was being done at the time and I said:

"It'll be great when you get back into Bundesliga 1."

"To be honest, we don't care…"

"What ☠?!" I said, aghast as if someone had stolen the crown jewels.

"Our ground is always full, we have a special situation. Our fans love us whichever league we play in."

Wow! What a revelation! The first person from inside football who put the fans first for REAL. All questions were answered in that one sentence.

Scha la la la la la la
WE LOVE FC ST PAULI!
FORZA ST PAULI!
St Pauli hat Kampfgeist der Gegner zeigt Angstschweiß St Pauli!
Ein Sport und ein Lifestyle nicht jeder kann reich sein St Pauli!

THE ART OF PUGILISM

I'm in a gym talking to Don King, the legendary American boxing promoter with the finger in electric plug socket hair. George Foreman can be seen in the background putting all of his unmatched power and bodyweight into murderous merciless blows received by a punchbag hanging from the ceiling. He is working like a giant human anvil. The punchbag is green, the walls are a faint green, Don King's hair and eyes look slightly green. I guess his dollar bills are also....green.

DON KING: Well, Nigel-hammad—it's true that The Great American Audience figures are down and that there's been a decrease in pay-per-view figures.

ME: But you're my manager, promoter and agent. You can see that I'm in great shape and have been doing brilliantly in training. No one gave me a chance against Ali and I beat him—I know I can beat Foreman as well and possibly without taking much punishment. So why are my viewing figures down when I'm on the verge of having beaten the two greatest heavyweight fighters of all time? ... OF ALL TIME??!

Foreman can be seen behind me taking a huge crashing right hook at the punchbag which goes flying, having been ripped from its ceiling attachments as if by a double-sized juggernaut.

DON KING: Well, Nigel-hammad—as sure as America is Great and Great Britain is GREAT-ish I think it has something to do with your starting to play that viol-dinn of yours at mass meetings like concerts. No one likes that kind of thing. It's just not proper black activism, Nigel-hammad.

ME: (*feeling deflated*): Maybe you're right, Don. Where do I go from here?

DON KING: Well, Nigel-hammad. You surely will and truly verily have to stop that viol-dinn of yours and focus. I think that maybe you should get more serious and much more into GREAT AMERIKAN MUSIC like Aretha Franklin... the unsurpassable James Brown or if you're really desperate even jazz would be OK-ish...

At this point the dream is suddenly over with the dog using his head like a giant canine anvil to whack my head off the pillow.

Dream 14 October 2020

I have always had a strong interest in boxing and have huge pity for those who are prevented from enjoying it by bogus opinions of the sanctimonious variety i.e. Me, myself and I don't think that he/she should be allowed to box (whine, whinge, preach) because he/she might get brain damage (whine, whinge, preach) et cetera et cetera et cetera et cetera. The aforementioned type of view could anyway only be proposed by someone who is starved emotionally or intellectually (or both). Pretty much every boxer outgrew their need of a nanny (or Nanny State) by the time they were 12 or 13 years old.

When I first went to New York to continue my musical studies I didn't have many friends, had been mugged twice, was suffering from culture shock and didn't have much to do apart from preparing for my violin lessons. I decided to take up boxing and went to a gym in the South Bronx. The whole idea was a bit of a fiasco.

In those days race relations were a bit different. Being the only white in the gym didn't help me. Both of the only two days I went in I was beat so bad I was shitting blood. Even though Dorothy Delay always said "that's lovely, sugar…" my violin lessons were equally futile what with not being able to move my fingers properly after my work on the punchbag. If I had had a modicum of talent for boxing I would have continued to pursue it but all I knew was that being hit hard wasn't all that lovely and I literally didn't have the stomach for it.

The example of Miles Davis had inspired me because of his continuous pugilistic involvement but from then on it was only his music which drove me forward.

Even though boxing wasn't beneficial for me in practice there are obvious parallels to be drawn between the life of a boxer and the life in music of someone such as myself. Nowadays techniques I used in the '80s are a prerequisite prescribed by "record companies" and promoters for a classico and they all follow like enterprising sheep—each sheep being described as uniquely innovative by their PR people. But when I started this more specifically enterprising way of communicating classical music I wasn't only out on my own—sometimes I also felt it. At those times I only had to think to myself "think of the boxers—all of their professional life they are preparing for the moment when they are well and truly OUT ON THEIR OWN in the ring. Boxers can face up to being out on their own in absolutely the most challenging death defying circumstances." When thinking about this it reminded me that mental molecule journalists or jealous snotty classicos were in reality very insignificant.

Another parallel even more obvious on a superficial level is in the training. Training for a fight involves repetition, study, discipline and muvvafukka hard work. Then in the ring (for a talented fighter) everything looks easy. You can't just rely on talent and one doesn't get special results without dedication and sacrifice. I've even gone as far as that no sex thing for periods of time in preparation for important projects or gigs and produced stunning results—except in bed that is!

The most important difference despite the parallels is that for a fighter after all that hard work everything can be over one way or the other in a couple of seconds. I know my gig will definitely last two or three hours and if everything isn't close to perfect, I'll get a chance to do better in a few days. My last thought on these matters of perfecting one's craft is that one rarely sees the boxer's courage, dedication and commitment reflected in a musician.

Muhammad Ali

Even though I only met Muhammad Ali for a couple of minutes, how could I recount anything about boxing without mentioning him?

Ali was a huge inspiration for those of us who were thinking "sod the status quo—I'm going to make things better by doing it my way". Against far greater odds than we will ever face (whatever colour or creed) and at far greater cost to himself he established a better world for future generations and for everybody around him.

I was introduced to him after one of the great all British middleweight world championship fights between Chris Eubank and Nigel Benn—Don King was also there. Before the fight I had played the national anthem in a way which disturbed and upset some of the more mentally fragile and limited members of the British public. To have met Ali at all was at least as important for me as it was for some others to meet the Dalai Lama or the Pope. Ali certainly did more to change the world for the better than the other two very estimable gentlemen.

In those days some of the Yanks had trouble with my name leading to some utterances such as Neeyell, Neeeggell, Nieyelle, Nigggle, Nyeyall, *et cetera*. Ali pronounced it perfectly and as with everyone else he talked to he showed a lively but calm interest, treating everyone with respect and as an equal. There were a lot of the boxing fraternity in the room but he treated a fukkin' violinist as being just as important as everyone else.

It strikes me now that Ali was an ultra-intelligent and irrepressible living example of Black Lives Matter instead of a bourgeoisie talking one. In a crucial era he rejected the name forced on his family by slave drivers and was a living embodiment of the fact that intellect didn't only reside between the ears of white people. He also enabled all of us to realise that black culture was as evolved and as important as any culture in the world—my listening collection would actually denote that it is far superior ...... to this very day!

In my opinion a very large part of the legacy of equality is owed to Ali, who was one of the few celebrated personalities who talked about anything which mattered—and in a smart way which completely avoided the realm of the egghead.

In the ring he had an extraordinary movement and balance. On a level with Jack Johnson, he was unhittable but at the same time dictated the course of the fight with his innate tactical awareness and stamina. He was able to keep his body and brain working for the full fifteen rounds—no lame twelve round fights in those days!

He was a unique fighter but what made the most significant mark on me as a kid and up until this very day was his strength outside the ring. The strength of his principles. He was a leader people looked up to all over the world and the best president Amerika never had.

"White people sending black people to fight yellow people to protect the country they stole from red people."

"No Vietcong ever called me nigger."

I remember not completely understanding why Mohammad Ali became the most famous conscientious objector of all time during America's capitalist attack on communist Vietnam, and not understanding that the success and definition of capitalism depends on a very few people owning and controlling all material wealth at the expense of the lives of other unseen people living shortened exploited lives out of sight and far away. But the way he put it made it as clear as a flash of lightning. I needed this type of education at the time and Ali through his succinct, brilliant and entertaining quotes was the only one giving it to me in a clear and palatable form.

At The Yehudi Menuhin School there was no differentiation of or by race. Jewish, Indian, Singaporean, Caucasian et cetera were all the same. There were, however, other issues: fatism, shortism, skinnyism, ageism, shitmusicianism but on the whole preferences or judgements would be made on the basis of character. It was hard to believe that there was a world out there which worked in a completely different way.

It turned out that Ali's principles cost him many of his prime boxing years in prison during what would have been his peak in the ring. Before him Jack Johnson had also lost many of his best years due to a completely unjust and racist sentence. The fact that Ali was a man of his word didn't just cost him his freedom but millions of dollars as well. It was invaluable as a young brat violinist to see and learn of someone whose word was more than noise. His eloquent pure reasoning is something I feel so privileged to have been aware of when I was growing up.

"Impossible is just a big word thrown around by small men who find it easier to live in the world they've been given than to explore the power they have to change it. Impossible is not a fact. It's an opinion...."

Sean Connery

I am writing this boxing chapter as of 31 October 2020 and have just found out that Sean Connery has sadly passed on. I met him once so you can now have a little break away from boxing while I tell you about that time ...

Two thoughts immediately occur to me:

1. There is a tenuous connection with this chapter in as much as two of Mr Connery's earliest acting roles portrayed boxers (in the TV series *The Square Ring* and the lead in the TV play *Requiem For A Heavyweight* which had been played by Jack Palance in the original American production).

2. The BBC obituary on their website was horribly condescending and sanctimonious. In their endless and increasingly pathetic attempts to be politically correct-ish they described Mr Connery's Bond films as museum pieces featuring non-consensual sexual advances and therefore not valid as relevant films today. Well … Here's some non-consensual sex for the BBC … BBC—FUCK OFF!

Anyway, as it 'appens (a quote from one of their favourite personalities—oy Jimmy), when I'd had enough of The Juilliard School of mediocrity and was back in London, before anyone knew of me apart from my friends and myself, somehow Sean Connery was at my door ringing the bell.

I was renting a small one-room building in the garden of a much larger house at 11 Rosslyn Hill. That evening I had become acquainted with a girl I met on the street dressed as a clown who was getting a bit on my nerves because she was talking rubbish far too much. BRRRRINNNG!!

ME: Ha! I wonder who that can be.

GIRL: Blab la bl' blahhh blah … a a a a a.

I go and answer the door and, fuck me, it's Sean Connery standing there.

ME: (*very originally*) Hello …

MR CONNERY: Hello, I'm sorry to bother you but do you know the way to number 12? I don't seem to be able to find it.

ME: Yes. There's no logic to the numbering on this road so it's complicated. I can show you the way but would you like to come in for a glass of whisky first?

MR CONNERY: Um … Well, of course, alright.

I show him into my place through renegade dirty clothes et cetera and we sit at my old '50s breakfast bar which divides the germ warfare kitchen from the rest of the room.

GIRL: (*oblivious of who he is*) Blablablaaablahb-b-blabla.

I pour three clean-ish glasses of Famous Grouse which had been given to me by my violin making friend a while before.

MR CONNERY: Very nice, thank you.

GIRL: Bleeb blah b-a-a-a bowglah weather.

ME: (*to Connery*) Nice one monsta (*a term of endearment I used to use in the early '80s which unfortunately got appropriated by loads of TV celebs a bit later*).

At this point I have a killa idea clear as a bell. Because the girl is still completely oblivious of the fact she is having a drink with Sean Connery alias James bond, *A Bridge Too Far* etc. I pull her aside and whisper to her "Don't you realise who this guy is? He's Sean Connery's stand in. He does all the stunts and love scenes in the James Bond movies. A flash of intelligence crosses the girl's face. She turns to him.

GIRL: Oh hello—it must be blah really nice bweeb and interesting working with Sean baabla Connery. It must bibe-be-be-beraan kool.

MR CONNERY: (*returns my wink with that amused twinkle of the eyes he was so appreciated for*) Yes, I really enjoy working with him—it's good fun. I do my best to be and look like him.

GIRL: Dweeb blaaaah bla bleeeblah nice.

A bit later I showed Mr Connery the way to number 12. I was really impressed that even with complete strangers that he didn't know from Adam he showed such an easy-going chivalry and sense of humour. A proper decent geezer. I hope his family are okay and that one of them might enjoy reading this bit one day.

Barry McGuigan

Barry McGuigan is a fighter whose influence and reach have extended far beyond the world of boxing. I can't think of any other individual who has done more to facilitate respect and peace in Northern Ireland and Ireland as a whole.

In 1985 Barry McGuigan became featherweight world champion beating Eusebio Pedroza before an absolutely packed crowd at Loftus Road football ground in West London. His ceaseless unremitting style led to him being nicknamed the Clones Cyclone. Clones after the border town of his birth. Cyclone after his unstoppable energy.

In addition to his incredible bravery in the ring Barry made a decision which was equally as brave about his pre-fight anthem before the Pedroza fight. Barry was both an Irish and British citizen. Rather than the impossible choice between 'Amhrán na bhFiann' (as Irishman) or 'God Save The Queen' (as a British citizen) he chose the beautiful song 'Danny Boy' which was sung so emotionally by his dad Pat McGuigan. This could have been taken the wrong way as a slight against either anthem considering that The Troubles were at their height. Either Catholics or Protestants could have been offended to a dangerous level. As it turns out the choice of 'Danny Boy' was a massively educated gamble and the public of both Christian tribes responded amazingly to the McGuigan family's honesty and maturity.

I met Barry as a co-guest on a British TV show called *Mrs Merton*. I played 'Danny Boy' for solo violin in honour of Barry's dad who unfortunately had recently passed on. Playing it just two or three feet away from Barry was a very moving experience. I play the song a lot wherever I go as an encore and it always connects in a unique way from Taiwan to Tipperary. I remember in Taiwan, for instance, the whole audience spontaneously hummed along with me. The McGuigans gave me an understanding of the social, historical and emotional significance of this song and that is why I now am able to give a deeper dimension when playing it to the public. It is a song for peace in the whole of Ireland given to me by the McGuigan family.

We became friends after that TV rendition and it is an honour to know such an honourable, natural and caring man. His son Shane, incidentally, is now one of the best boxing coaches in the world.

Frank Bruno

We're sitting at the dining table in Buckingham Palace, members of a group of high achievers which were called 'The Magnificent Seven'. We did various things which raised money and awareness for The Duke Of Edinburgh Awards Scheme—a charity organisation to enable young people to access experience outside their normal environment. The seven included Gary Lineker, Frank Bruno (the most popular British heavyweight champion ever), a lovely guy who played fiddle and four other cats so clever that I can't remember them. I'm sitting next to Frank and we are looking at the very poshly set up table with all the crystal glasses and the rest.

ME: Man … Those salt and pepper cellars would look nice at home wouldn't they?

FRANK: (*regards the heavy solid silver salt and pepper cellars*) Yes they would Nigel—where's Harry? Ha ha.…

ME: (*in a good soft-core bit of racial stereotyping not to be tried at home or on the freeloading BBC*) Tell you what—the best way to do it is if I have the salt, you have the pepper.

FRANK: Ha ha, Nigel. Maybe …. I know who could organise it. Where's Harry?

That's how surreal life was sometimes. There I was sitting at The Duke Of Edinburgh's table in Buckingham Palace talking with the heaviest handed champion Britain has ever produced. His jab was more damaging than most fighters' right hooks. How many of Frank's fights I'd been to—watching his jab hammering his opponents head back the best part of a metre. All of us British public love Frank in and out of the ring.

Kirkland Laing

We're making ourselves comfortable on the grand marble steps in one of the giant stairwells of the Royal Albert Hall, London. A venue which holds many an important memory from my concert career but at this particular moment it is Kirkland Laing's night. In and out of the ring his style is unique and relaxed. Hands down below the waist and leaning back to avoid punches (in the ring, you idiot! Get it together…). His offence from the hands down position flummoxes the opponent, coming from angles they've never experienced getting hit from before. Kirkland's leaning back would lure them in making them miss and overreach—then he'd get 'em.

Kirkland is a colourful unusual one-off character and was the first world-class boxer to wear his dreads bunched up to the back of his head in the Jamaican flag coloured wrap. On this occasion he's just beaten Rocky Berg and we're wondering who his next fight will be against. We'd been introduced by a Japanese mate of his who I had met in that great Lonsdale shop on Beak Street. Kirkland has shown himself to be world-class again tonight and is relaxed, happy to sit on the stairs in chilled out clothes very unlike those worn by some of his ringside spectators. He is quietly happy, natural and not full of himself. There is no entourage around him.

"Hey Nige maaan, gimme summaa dat szpliff maaan...."

I pass it to him. We get off our backsides and exit the venue, walking round it to get a cab. We end up in a friend's place—I can't remember where (possibly because of the fine herb).

What is so impressive about Kirkland is that he's his own man. He hasn't let any of the seductions of fame and success change him. I'm amazed that at the peak of his career he was able to embrace recreational downtime in a normal manner and then turn out superlative performances in the ring. He truly was The Gifted One as his nickname suggests. He was British and European welterweight champion and also went on to beat Roberto Durán in one of the shocks of the century. Oy Kirkland—you're TOP and a one-off mate.

I could go on and on but should probably divert to less interesting stuff like music and other things from my life before pensionerhood. Some other fighters I could have written about are: The Gentleman of boxing—Michael Watson/the master of defence Chris Eubank/the master of attack Nigel Benn/the tactical master in one of the best fights I've ever seen (against Canizales at Elephant and Castle) Duke McKenzie/and fighters I admire: The Klitchkos, Tyson Fury, Mike Tyson, Anthony Joshua, Billy Joe Saunders, Lennox Lewis.

ENCORES:
MY CONCERTO RECORDINGS

Ladies, gentlemen and other types of people (you know exactly who you are!), this next chapter is about the classical concerto recordings that I've made through the years. I've made a fair few, so if you find this a bit boring, please skip to the next chapter. If I find it a bit boring, I won't finish it and will also skip to the next chapter.

Making these recordings and playing the various repertoire in public has been a memorable part of my life but I have no idea if these reminiscences will be of any interest to you. Certainly, without my recordings there's a strong chance you wouldn't have this book in your hand. Without them and the promotion they received my gob wouldn't have found its way into half as many homes.

I will write about the recordings in chronological order until I grind to a halt.

Good luck!

Nigel

Elgar Violin Concerto in B Minor
London Philharmonic Orchestra
Vernon Handley, 1984

This was my first concerto recording. A year earlier I recorded two albums (on the same day!) for a record label called Chandos. We had finished recording Elgar's violin sonata much earlier than expected so I got a crate of beer in and my amazing piano partner Peter Pettinger and I had a good drink and improvised on jazz standards for a couple of hours. Unusually for a Classico in those days Peter was equally at home playing jazz or classical music. By the end of the day we had an extra album on our hands which I decided to call Strad Jazz, bearing in mind I was playing on a Stradivari violin. Chandos therefore got two albums for the price of one, or maybe the price of half if you look at the royalties I get! I just got my most recent royalty cheque … a whopping £12.50. Incidentally Peter tragically died from giving up alcohol so please don't try this at home.

In my opinion inanities like Stoptober (for weak brains to give up smoking) or Dry January (for weak brains to give up drinking) are pathetic not only because of their names, but also because a lame sheep-like mentality is the last thing anyone needs at any time, let alone when addressing important addiction issues … ermmm … back to Elgar!

What with the success of all my gigs and of the two albums mentioned above it seemed obvious that, residing in London, I should go on to record for the London based record company EMI. Obvious to everybody, that is, except the grandees at EMI. Reports coming back to me from my agents of the time, Harold Holt Ltd, were that I was not 'international' enough and that maybe I didn't have the right kind of sound for recording. Ironic that when finally being 'allowed' to sneak through their back door, my recording for them won pretty much every award under the sun. It also sold over 60,000 copies for those jumped-up buffoons, at least 10 times the EMI Fuddy-Duddy Classics average.

Elsewhere in this book I describe the anti-British prejudice which existed in the British classical music business. My Elgar recording was, in hindsight, the first step towards stamping out bigotry, not just making things a lot easier for myself but for every other British soloist in the future. Here's what happened.

Of primary importance is that I had found an original way of interpreting Elgar's violin concerto which didn't owe to Menuhin or any other predecessor. Most other soloists of the generation before me approached this work as a lovely long wallow, with some nice melodic bits interspersed with technical strain and struggle against Elgar's challenging violin part. I had found a way to de-prioritise the technical struggle and tap directly into the pathos of this unique concerto.

At around the same time I had the incredibly good fortune to meet and collaborate with one of my favourite conductors ever, Vernon Handley. Todd, as he was known by his friends, was an absolutely first rate interpreter of all classical music from every country, but in his humble unaffected way he had devoted his life to becoming the absolute greatest interpreter of music from the British Isles. Todd was the first to reach the level of Boult, Barbirolli, Beecham or Henry Wood in this field and no one has equalled him since.

We performed the Elgar concerto quite a few times and his relaxed endearing way with the orchestra was immediately apparent. It was also clear that he understood my approach which, unlike other soloists, involved the avoidance of turning this 54 minute concerto into a boring and endless rhapsody with a clever bit of violin playing on top. The architectural foundations of a building need to consist of more than a blob of jelly. Todd didn't just understand this, he was killa enthusiastic about my way of seeing the concerto and plunged into our work wholeheartedly. Almost immediately he wanted to record this music with me and despite the British anti-British despots at EMI he found a way of doing it. It was at very short notice.

One of those bellowing, braying classical singers had to cancel a recording session which Todd was conducting so he brought me in for two days to record

Elgar instead. I guess everyone benefited. Todd and I got to make a fantastic recording of Elgar together and EMI Classics, loath as they were to have me record for them, avoided having to pay a whole large orchestra not to play, and instead got a multi-award-winning recording. Sometimes, just sometimes, there's an advantage to leaving the back door ajar. (No, you idiots, don't try this at home!) Also, in my own little way, I helped a very small part of the public avoid being assaulted by the farmyard noises from Mars otherwise known as classical singing. Mercy, MERCY!

The recording session itself was memorable. The London Philharmonic Orchestra played beautifully—Vernon Handley's no fuss 100 per cent understanding of the score allied with his phenomenal baton technique produced inspired results. I played my very best knowing that I had comprehensive support from all the wonderful musicians I was working with. The London Philharmonic Orchestra were happy to see a British soloist getting a chance for a change and everyone could feel that something special was happening in the session.

The Elgar violin concerto is the longest concerto of the core violin repertoire but there is a line of development in this work which enhances and puts context to all those magic romantic moments of longing and triumph. Just as a three minute masterpiece by The Beatles or The Kinks can seem timeless, this 54 minute masterpiece can seem to go by in a flash if one can find the balance between logical development and personal pathos. Todd and I found that key to this concerto and used that balance to unlock it. In my opinion, the only other person to have found the key to the Elgar is Albert Sammons, but he recorded his magnificent interpretation of the concerto in 1929 before the advent of long play albums. His version with Sir Henry Wood is probably the best ever ... no, definitely the best ever. Needless to say Sammons was a great source of inspiration for me, primarily because of his inspired NO BULLSHIT interpretation of Elgar, but also because he was the only other English violinist who achieved the absolute top musical level. His history gave me an example to aspire to. At the beginning of my career there were all kinds of racist theories about what kind of background or genealogy produced great violinists and none of them pointed to the merits of being English–Irish! Sammons was a beacon in this regard as to what was possible whatever your race or background. Another thing I loved about Sammons was that he only had ten violin lessons and then taught himself. I think teachers or professors in any field are vastly overrated. I had amazing teachers but most of my student life was spent discovering that I didn't need them.

SILLY WIKIPEDIA TYPE FACT: My Elgar recording was the first classical CD to be released by EMI in Britain. WOOPIDOO!

RATING: There is no one alive who has got anywhere near approaching the level of my recording and neither have all but one of the dead ones. The recording by Albert Sammons and Sir Henry Wood, however, has more drive and just as much sensitivity. OK, so his recording is better than mine but I'm here and he isn't!

Tchaikovsky Violin Concerto D-major op. 35, London Philharmonic Orchestra Okko Kamu, 1986

Russian music has a passion, intelligence and storytelling narrative which is completely unique in the world of classical music. In his best works Tchaikovsky epitomises these qualities, bringing a rich simplicity to his orchestrations thereby enhancing the drama and character of his melodic gifts. There are no hidden agendas in his music.

Seeing as I'm anti-snobbery of any kind I can't help mentioning that Tchaikovsky's music is looked down upon by some pseudo experts as being somewhat below top level and this sets off my bullshitometer right off into the red. These pseudos try to discount this beautiful music because it has committed the cardinal crime of becoming phenomenally popular with classical audiences all around the world. FAR TOO POPULAR! If everyone knows and likes some music what use is a fucking 'expert' to tell us anything? In order for the 'expert' to protect his/her status it's better to pretend that something popular is SHIT in order to appear as if he/she knows more than us poor proletariat. Of course, this is sheer Wallyism. It seems that listening to any 'expert' on any subject ranging from global warming all the way to poor little music, there's always some inflated mouth ready to portray themselves as knowing better than us. It's all hot air and no substance, reminiscent of the emperor and his new clothes. Mind you, if we're to believe Greta and up to half the scientific community it won't be long before neither we nor the emperor will need any clothes.

For all you semi-intellectuals out there, Tchaikovsky is a great, GREAT storyteller and no great storyteller uses only five syllable words. Anyhow, whatever the mental midgets might say, Tchaikovsky is a REAL SPUTNIK.

As a follow up to my muvva of an Elgar recording my Tchaikovsky recording was a bit of an anti-climax. Playing a concerto as an extension of a composer's symphonic repertoire works in the cases of Beethoven, Brahms or even Elgar but it didn't work with Pyotr Ilyich Jock-itch. Unlike other soloists of the time I saw the Tchaikovsky concerto as symphonic and wanted to cleanse it of all the automatic technical virtuosity and unnecessary bravura found when listening to people play it. While this was a laudable sentiment partially formed by being provoked by the finger flicking "Me, me, ME! Look at how good I am!" approach of some soloists, the result was somewhat devoid of charisma. A concerto does, after all, feature the soloist so, without being obnoxious one shouldn't be too reticent.

RATING: In all of my concerto recordings I can honestly say that mine are at least as good as any of those by my contemporaries, but not this one! I can recommend two superlative interpreters of this work which beat mine: from the past David Oistrakh and from the present Maxim Vengerov. Both of these artists have amazing control of their sound, effortless technique and a comprehensively beautiful vision of the work as a whole. After hearing these two versions any others that I've heard, including my own, seem superfluous to requirements.

Walton Violin And Viola Concertos
Royal Philharmonic Orchestra
André Previn, 1987

André Previn was one of the most talented musicians around. He was right up there with his mastery of jazz and of twentieth century classical music.

I think the first time I played with him conducting was with the Boston Symphony Orchestra doing Felix 'Polite Boy' Mendelssohn's Concerto. Before rehearsing with the orchestra we were having a piano rehearsal, just the two of us, with André playing the piano, in order to decide how we wanted to interpret Mendelssohn's music. I remember I was playing like a kunt so at my request we improvised for a while on the beautiful jazz ballad 'Body and Soul' and left it at that. The gig went great so no harm done. Without the audience there's never the same strength of circuit through which the energy of the music can flow heart to heart.

The next time I found myself performing with Previn was in the repertoire of William Walton's violin and viola concertos. Having performed them in two London gigs we proceeded to record them in Abbey Road Studios, one day for each concerto. At some point the orchestra damager called a twenty-minute break, so rather than get frazzled queueing up in the cafeteria I thought I'd have a little power nap on the floor behind the recording desk in the control room. It wasn't much later when Previn and Andrew Keener (my producer) came in to listen to some takes, completely unaware that I was lying like a comatose bat behind the desk. The takes sounded pretty good and Previn remarked to Keener "Nigel's a money man, isn't he?" Keener replied ever so succinctly "Oooeeerrr..." (he's Welsh). I didn't know what the phrase money man meant but never considered myself particularly mercenary except when doing my best to make sure record companies, agents and promoters couldn't rip me off. After initial surprise at having inadvertently complimented me in my invisible vampire-esque presence Previn explained that it means someone who delivers the goods when it really matters. He obviously remembered that Boston performance and various other rehearsals in which I'd been saving it for the gig.

RATING: What with having managed to get one of the best Walton conductors ever to agree to work with me on these concertos I already had a head start. Previn's alertness, awareness of detail and subtle guidance of momentum made him the perfect man for this project. Then there was my ability to completely identify with the energy and harmonic idiom of Walton's music. The other clincher for this album's championship credentials is that I play both the viola and the violin concertos. No other monkey has done that on one Walton recording.

As far as the viola concerto was concerned, even though I habitually played five string electric and acoustic violins both with C strings I wasn't a viola player by trade. This didn't matter because it was obviously far more important to be a great Walton interpreter than a good old long in the tooth viola player, and anyway, I had seen Pinchas Zukerman play the viola and if he could do it I could easily do it. I had the same number of fingers and arms, for a start, and that boded very, very well. My suspicions were well founded and playing the oversized violin was no problem.

William Primrose was the greatest viola player ever so if you solely want to hear the viola concerto it's a matter of taste between him and I. He brings out the Britishness of the concerto with a great sense of forward direction. I bring out the wistfulness of Walton's melodies and because of my jazz background am better able to exploit the harmonic tensions and resolutions. Neither of us are challenged on a technical level. Primrose was also a great violinist but he never recorded the violin concerto. However, if you want to choose his version over mine my family still wins because my 'cellist granddad Lauri Kennedy recorded various stuff with him and they played countless gigs together.

Jascha Heifetz is the only other consideration when talking about Walton's fiddle concerto. His silvery sound and perfect but rather brusque technical control might be completely unsuitable for Bach or Beethoven but are perfect for this music. My version, because of my jazz involvement, is more harmonically aware so there are different things to enjoy in both my performance and that of Silvery Boy. Silvery Boy, though, doesn't play the viola concerto. So if you want both these great concertos on the same album recorded by the same artist, on the basis of a no contest, I WIN!

Bruch And Mendelssohn Concertos And Schubert Rondo, (Fuck The Keys And Numbers) English Chamber Orchestra Jeffrey Tate, 1988

I didn't have to be Albert Einstein to come up with this pairing of concertos. I could have been twice as good as our fiddle playing philosopher friend and been called Albert Zweistein but that wasn't necessary either. Even though every Tom, Dick, Harry and Yehudi had already put this combination of concerti on record before me, it was for a good reason. These two contrasting examples of romantic violin, for no intellectual justification, co-exist perfectly. Maybe not in concert but on record. Other soloists have tried 'cleverererer' combinations of one or other of these concertos on their albums with cleverererer repertoire but the sad fact of reality is that none of this cleverness has resulted in an album which is a more enjoyable listen for us at home. Normally this cleverness involves dredging up another inferior work by the same composer and replacing the second composer with it. We don't need a high Mensa score to realise that this results in half the album being ... shit. It's sometimes difficult for an intellectually hyperactive kat to comprehend that "What's not broken don't need fixing." Think of the poor audience instead of your own brain! Unless one's an Arts Council sycophant or a silver spoon monkey it's our friends in the audience (or listening at home in the old days) who have paid our mortgages to whom we owe something.

So, when EMI suggested that I record Mendelssohn and Bruch concertos with the English Chamber Orchestra it was a no-brainer. I had recorded The IV Seasons with the English Chamber Orchestra and went back a long way with both concertos which had been a part of my performing life from the very beginning.

Bruch Violin Concerto in G Minor

This was the first concerto I played in public, when I was around 13 years old. Before you get all excited about me being a prodigy I am very proud not to have been one. Nine or ten year olds who can play this type of stuff are a dime a dozen and their best trick is the disappearing act they normally do when they reach their early twenties.

The first London orchestra I played it with was The Royal Philharmonic. Playing the concerto with them was doubly meaningful for me. Firstly because I love the Bruch concerto and secondly on a nepotistic level because when Sir Thomas Beecham formed the RPO he chose my father to be the lead 'cellist.

The Bruch concerto is amazing because of its passionate, honest, beautiful melodic and harmonic content. The orchestration is also perfect for the violin and orchestra to be effective together, with rousing climactic orchestral tuttis. 'Experts' (please look up the meaning of the preceding foul word in the glossary I've provided at the front end of the book) often deem this beautiful concerto to be somewhat less than great. This is because they mistakenly rate developmental intricacy as more important than great subject material. The prioritisation enables these type of chattering classes to grind on like some crickets on steroids, endlessly chirping on about their irrelevant existence. One of my favourite concertos, this work has absolutely GREAT subject material. It's a joy to play and a joy to listen to.

The public, decent soloists and proper good orchestral players know that Bruch has written one of the greatest violin concertos of all time, and no killjoy can take that away from us.

RATING: I think this recording of Bruch is probably SECOND TO NONE, at least among my contemporaries—so go and buy it!

Alternatives (all unfortunately no longer with us): Isaac Stern, Yehudi Menuhin, Fritz Kreisler, Albert Sammons.

Mendelssohn Concerto in E Minor

I made my London concerto debut playing this concerto. It was quite an important gig made more so by the fact it was being shown on BBC1 TV. I remember the conductor Riccardo Muti getting the hump because in 'his' first orchestral tutti-frutti I got my Aston Villa scarf out of my pocket, let it unroll so that the audience could read the name of the most significant team in football history and then cleaned the resin of my strings with it while he preened his way through his bit. I can't remember anything about the performance, the magic musical moments are NOW, not yesterday. The scarf justified itself twofold in as much as my strings were clean for my next solo entry and because it was an Aston Villa scarf at least I remember one thing from that night.

Mendelssohn's concerto (OY! Experts, I know there are more than one but everyone with noodle knows which one I'm talking about) is beautifully written music. Simultaneously atmospheric and clear—never too heavy. One could say that it's light music from the classical genre.

Long ago I decided to stop playing this concerto in favour of more substantial repertoire. While not being as bad as Mozart or Haydn, Mendelssohn does get close to these two bastards in regard to over formality and excessive politeness. These three composers always remind me of Baldrick in *Black Adder*. I do however admit that Mendelssohn has enough good taste to avoid the sickly mannerisms of Johann Strauss (oh muvvafukkin' shit, that Vienna New Year's Eve stuff is so cringeworthily horrible!). A subsidiary reason why I found it necessary to stop playing the polite boy's music was the growth of my loyalty to the audience. People had started to buy concert tickets just to hear me play, not the orchestra or the stick waver (who more often than not can't play anyway). Audiences were starting to regard having to listen to the orchestra (and cunt-duck-tor) for the whole evening apart from 20 minutes during which I played, as not what they paid for and a betrayal of their trust. There were a number of occasions when the conductor's ego had shoved me into the first half (in order to take the limelight at the end of the gig) resulting in The Ego playing to a half empty hall in the second half. I could no longer allow a conductor's ego to shove me in the first half for a short time in order to allow them and the orchestra management to swamp out the second half with their boring, pompous overblown symphony. I literally received numerous complaints about that kind of shit from people a little worse for wear having preferred the merits of the pub to the merits of the second half symphony. As far as they were concerned they hadn't got their money's worth. A third reason was that, like an actor who in the end wants to direct the movies they act in, I considered it my job to present music to my friends in the audience the way I saw it. Putting false modesty aside it benefited my colleagues onstage, the audience, the music and myself that I took charge of things and presented beautiful music the way that I saw and felt it. It was also far more exciting for me and gave me far more opportunity to develop as a musician and as a performer than merely being the last piece in the jigsaw for some self-important kunt-duck-tor.

I remember being a bit incredulous when, as a student, my professor Dorothy DeLay told me that I had better ears and more knowledge of music than most of the kunt-duck-tors I would be working with in my future career. Fortunately (or unfortunately?) she turned out to be correct!

Question from hypothetical pub quiz:

Q. Which is less offensive for the audience—looking at the cunt-duck-tor's ugly arse from behind or my ugly face from the front?

A. I don't know.

Anyhow! The recording of the concerto went well and produced good results.

However there was one long tedious danger moment when the conductor got obsessed that he couldn't get two bars in the third movement together with the orchestra and was spending hours on this ensemble deficiency. We had an incredible amount of music still to record in the few hours remaining including the whole of the Bruch concerto, so I had to put an end to this self-indulgent faffing which was endangering the delivery of the whole album. Sometimes you have to get a grip on the antics of these conductors and this was one such time. A few years earlier I might not have had the confidence to see the bigger picture and direct the conductor towards the end result and away from obsessive minutiae. I think we got a very rewarding album made and am quite proud of it.

RATING: My version of the Mendelssohn is very, very good but an over fussy approach from the conductor stopped a more complete picture developing and curtailed some inspirational and improvisational moments. If God is The Big Picture and the Devil Is In The Detail the Devil won this time. Menuhin, Stern and Kreisler have left us with recordings of the highest spiritual level, transcending the technical and compositional minutiae which got over prioritised in our recording. Their interpretations are the yardstick.

CONCLUSION: If you can't find Menuhin, Kreisler or Stern get my version. It could well be the best of the rest. OOPS! I've just thought of my friend Cho-Liang Lin. His reading of Mendelssohn is aristocratic, poised, honest and unique … go and get his!

Vivaldi The Four Seasons
English Chamber Orchestra
Nigel Kennedy (Director/Soloist), 1989

Because the recording completely changed my life and the whole classical music business, I am devoting a whole chapter to it—but not here.

RATING: This recording was a breath of fresh air and a necessary antidote to the boring over mannerismed pseudo authentic movement which was spoiling and dominating the performance of Baroque music at the time. It was also an answer to the lugubrious and complacent habits relied upon in this repertoire by my contemporary colleagues from America and elsewhere.
  The public voted this album the best in the world with their hard-earned cash, and would anyone, including myself, be arrogant enough to argue with them? There is no better recording of The IV Seasons—go and buy it!

Brahms Concerto for Violin And Orchestra in D Major
The London Philharmonic Orchestra
Klaus Tennstedt, 1991

Brrrrring Brrrrring … Brrrrring Brrrrring … Brrrrring Brrrrring …
I pick it up … it's a proper landline, not one of today's brain burners.
ME: Hello …
EMI: Halleyooo …
ME: Hi …
EMI: Halleyooo …
ME: Umm. Who's there? Can I help you? (*Thinking: Obviously not financially*).
EMI: It's EMI here, we hope so.
ME: (*Feeling a bit like one of those psychoanalysts who are so prevalent where I live*). Well, what seems to be the problem?
EMI: Klaus Tennstedt is recording the Brahms Concerto in Abbey Road with The London Philharmonic Orchestra and Kyung Wha Chung …
ME: How fascinating and nice … (*Thinking: Well, I've got no idea what that's got to do with me. What are they calling ME for? Do they need someone to make tea? That's the only job EMI would give to a British violinist*).
EMI: It might seem so but Maestro Tennstedt has taken offence at something Miss Chung said about the woodwinds. He's walked out and is refusing to record with her.
ME: What an awful, awful shame (*Thinking: So what? Tuff*).
EMI: (*with a 60 piece symphony orchestra and Abbey Road paid for with no recording coming out of it*) Well, he said that he would like to record Brahms with YOU … can you come down to Abbey Road and record with him TOMORROW AND THE DAY AFTER?

ME: This is a bit irregular. You know that an artist would normally take a couple of months preparing a project like this and you're giving me a couple of hours (*Thinking: Wow, Brahms with the world's greatest living conductor, killa, he's renowned for being very difficult to work with, makes no compromise, but even if we don't get on EMI haven't lost anything. Anyway, there's no better conductor on the planet (dammit), so we could do an epic Brahms*). Let me think a while ... I'll check my diary ... YES!

EMI: What? ... do you mean you can do it?

ME: (*thinking back and remembering that I had actually played the concerto the previous month with David Lardi and The Haringey Philharmonic*) Yes, but, if possible, give me the morning to get prepared.

EMI: That shouldn't be a problem. Maestro Tennstedt doesn't like mornings anyway.

ME: (*ever so profoundly*) OK. See you there, mate.

That afternoon and evening I practised like a muvvafukka and by the end of the next morning I was ready to record the Brahms Violin Concerto one of the all time greats and the best orchestra in London. Maybe EMI didn't have much hope for the punk violinist to get on with Tennstedt or *vice versa* but they had nothing to lose.

As it happened Klaus and I hit it off great and, because I call everyone 'monsta', in our numerous future gigs together he referred to me as his Little Monster, and he was my Big Monster. Age before beauty. I became Big Monster's favourite violinist which was quite something considering that he'd worked with all the greats from Russia, Australasia and Central Europe.

There are some conductors who mouth or gesticulate every note—annoying. There are some conductors who solely rely on a pathos-free, smooth stick technique—a waste of space. There are some who talk a lot to the orchestra like a professor—ouch! Boring. Some who get and keep their jobs by talking smoothly with sponsors—ouch! Wankers. The Big Monster was none of the above. He was a consummate musician. Improvisational, inspirational, giving no less than 100 per cent at any given moment, his love of the music clear on his face—all of these qualities meant that the orchestra found it impossible to give him less than 100 per cent of themselves. There wasn't a superficial moment from his conducting EVER.

Tennstedt's unique honesty might have been at least partially connected with the fact he grew up in East Germany, a place that has produced so many wonderful people sporting a down to earth attitude unspoilt by rampant consumerism.

One of the prevalent characteristics of this album is the expansive view Tennstedt has of the first and second movements. I loved existing in and reacting to this world he created. Something else needing to be created was my first movement cadenza. A few years earlier I had heard a recording of Beethoven concerto by Gidon Kremer which I loved. In the first movement he played a cadenza by a composer called Schnittke (or something like that!) and one or two record company publicists made a lot of fuss about it. For me it only seemed an item of interest for a few nerdy students, even though I was a student at the time I wasn't a nerd and found the cadenza irrelevant to either Beethoven or cadenza playing practice. The standard cadenzas by Kreisler and Joachim for both Beethoven and Brahms were much better and on the spot I made up my mind. If one was going to depart from these two brilliant writers of cadenzas the only valid reason would be in order to write or improvise one's own, as was the custom up until the 1940s when the skills seemed to have foolishly been lost. With that in mind I decided to part-improvise and part-write my own cadenza. My great idea was to eschew the normal gratuitous technical pyrotechnics in favour of something closely related to Brahms' subject material. Reintroducing the practice of playing one's own cadenzas felt pretty enterprising at the time bearing in mind that no other violinist was doing it. The reward for my bravery was that after my recording, many other fiddlers followed suit and I am proud to say that original cadenzas have rightly become much more standard practice again.

It's amazing that one never knows what is around the corner. This album was made at one day's notice and soon after release more than a quarter of a million people had bought it. Probably 220,000 had been introduced to Brahms for the first time, with the other 30,000 already acquainted with his music. Bringing quality music to so many people with absolutely no compromise is one of my best achievements.

RATING: One can argue between Stern/Ormandy, Menuhin/Furtwängler, Kreisler/Blech or Kennedy/Tennstedt. Stern for his complete honesty, rhythmic pacing and expressive intonation. Menuhin for his spiritual and radiant melodic playing allied with Furtwängler's unprecedented emotional and architectural understanding of Brahms' musical form. Me/Tennstedt for our intimate, personal and magical view of Brahms' unique musical world. Which do you prefer—an orange, banana or mango? My recording is the mango ... sweet!... go buy it!

Beethoven Violin Concerto in D Major
NDR Symphony Orchestra
Klaus Tennstedt, 1992

This was a live performance which was televised as well as recorded. There are moments of applause, there are one or two noises from the camera dollies and some other noises. What one does get is the magic and energy of a live performance with Tennstedt and because there has been no comparable interpreter of the Central European repertoire in following years it is rewarding to hear what he brings to this music. I am also in hot shit shape. One doesn't get a studio recording but, to use boxing parlance, it is what it is.

Overall there are four recordings I would choose over this one.

Menuhin/Furtwängler: As with Brahms, Menuhin and Furtwängler probe deeper on a spiritual and structural level than anyone else has found possible.

Kreisler/Blech: Kreisler's radiant sound and his humanity makes this recording impossible to rate behind anyone else's.

Stern/Bernstein: Stern's truth, Bernstein's charisma and bold artist's inspiration. What a combination!

Kennedy: A later version under my direction. No conductor—fantastic! More rhythmic impetus in this approach, an original cadenza, one of my best albums. Done a fair few years later than my first version.

Listening to the aforementioned unique masters when I was a kid was like turning a light on in a completely dark room. Hearing these guys not only gave me the reason to stop playing classical violin but also to carry on. Even now, when I listen to them, they illuminate their subject material in a way no one else can and it's like hearing music for the very first time. Transmitting the joy of discovery is what separates the truly great artists from the very good ones. And of course showing how hard one's trying to discover something is no discovery at all!

Bach Concertos
Berlin Philharmonic Orchestra
Albrecht Mayer (Oboe), Daniel Stabrawa (Violin),
Nigel Kennedy (Director/Soloist), 2000

RATING: Baroque music faces a dilemma, especially Bach, being faced on the one hand by over fussy, over ornamental self-conscious stylists from the so-called authentic school, and on the other hand by the stolid, flaccid heavy handedness of the 'more modern' school. Both schools tend towards brands of self-infatuation which are particularly detrimental to the spiritual and structural qualities of Bach's music. In my opinion one completely misses the point of music if one becomes obsessed by oneself instead of opening one's awareness of colleagues, of the moment and the unique pool of consciousness which is revealed by top class music. Style before substance is a shoddy maxim in the musical arena.

I can, therefore, wholeheartedly recommend my recording for finding the truth of the music, largely from instinctively and intellectually forming an approach which was fresh and unsullied by either of the styles mentioned above. This recording features the best orchestra in the world with two of the best co-soloists in the world (Albrecht Mayer (oboe) and Daniel Stabrawa (violin)) who both came out of the amazing orchestra to play the D minor double concertos with me.

False modesty would be too close to the muesli eating 'authentic' school in my view, so quite simply, check this album. It's one of my best achievements, playing the most influential and substantial composer of them all.

Coming from the direct line of Georges Enescu (who rediscovered Bach when he was largely forgotten) and Menuhin (who was Enescu's pupil and whose name became synonymous with that of Bach) I fukkin' own this music and its legacy. My Land!

Vivaldi Four Seasons
Berlin Philharmonic Orchestra
Nigel Kennedy (Director/Soloist),
Daniel Stabrawa (Co-soloist) 2003

RATING: It was always going to be difficult to re-record the same repertoire and live up to the album which shook up the classical music world and changed it forever. It was going to take something special ... recording it with an orchestra unparalleled in the history of music, for instance.... This was an inspirational musical opportunity, and that they wanted to follow up our Bach album with this Vivaldi stuff was an incontrovertible endorsement of my qualities as a musician. It was a good stiff jab in the gullet for the pseudo experts who had tried to invent every superficial reason under the sun why my original IV Seasons was so successful. What their up-pointed noses prevented them seeing was that I played the music brilliantly, interpreted it in a way that was urgently needed at the time to rescue classical music from them and that people liked it and liked me.

"Rather simple, wasn't it Sherlock?"

"Yes, Dreistein, easier than times 3."

If you like the idea of the least boring violinist in the world playing with the most phenomenal orchestra, this is just what you need. An added bonus on this album is the concerto for two violins in A minor which I recorded with the superlative Daniel Stabrawa.

Vivaldi Concerti
Berlin Philharmonic Orchestra
Nigel Kennedy (Director/Soloist), 2004

RATING: Vivaldi wrote about 200 concertos for violin and I checked them all ... the vast majority of them are moribund shit. The concertos I have chosen for this album, however, are his best—well contrasting, melodically unique and with unstoppable energy in the fast movements. Fire, water, air but never earth. Making this collection even more vivid, my friends Albrecht Mayer (oboe) and Daniel Stabrawa (violin) each contribute to a double concerto with me.

I found this exploration, with my Berliner comrades, of more relatively unknown Vivaldi very rewarding. We really enjoyed making these recordings and that jumps out of the speakers abundantly. This is more music on the same level as our Bach and IV Seasons recordings. In other words SECOND TO NONE! Buy the stuff!

IV Seasons × 3 (XII Seasons?)
Orchestra of Life
Nigel Kennedy (Director/Soloist), 2015

The IV Seasons and, indeed, classical music as a whole are a weird one. No matter how many times I have played or recorded something, each time I pick it up again I always end up learning something new about it, gaining a new, broader and fresher perspective on the work itself and on music as a whole. I guess this is what keeps one's approach alive and stops musical life becoming repetitive.

Because the IV Seasons has seen me through a large part of my life, for this recording I decided to put a large part of my relevant musical knowledge back into this set of concertos. I have grown as a musician with these concertos and they have grown with me. The ways I applied this knowledge took the following forms:

IMPROVISATION: Instead of subscribing to the rather cliché simulation of how we imagine people improvised in the Baroque era (there is no conclusive proof about performance practice seeing that it would be a long time before Thomas Edison would be kind enough to be born), I applied twentieth and twenty-first century improvisation techniques, many of them my own. Also one example of whole orchestra group impro.

INSTRUMENTATION: In addition to the standard Vivaldi instrumentation I used twentieth century instruments such as acoustic violin, five string acoustic violin, five string electric violin, acoustic and electric guitar, Hammond, piano, Moog, vibraphone, marimba. There was quite a posse in the studio!

PERCUSSION, DRUMS and PROGRAMMING: What with jazz being the main evolved form of the twentieth century there had to be drums. Percussion was also an important element in order to enhance the traditional dance rhythms used by Vivaldi. To expand Vivaldi's world into the twenty-first century I was lucky enough to work closely with Damon Reece, the genius from Massive Attack. His programming was subtle and inspirational.

So there you have it. Elements of jazz, rock, folk, programming, improvisation and absolutely hip, top class playing from my own orchestra, The Orchestra of Life, all to bring Vivaldi's music into the present day in the way he would've wanted it. This wasn't one of those horrible 'modern' adaptations which turned Viv into an ambient non-event. Vivaldi still had his bollocks and mojo intact, in fact, never more so!

The IV Seasons is set to some rather mediocre poems (most likely by Vivaldi himself but not conclusively). What would've completed my new picture would have been to get new poems written for the music by a more relevant living writer (like Murakami, Kureishi, Zephaniah or somebody of that order) but Sony, in their wisdom and according to my damager at the time, decided against that. I'll have to save that for my fourth recording. The 4 × 4 Seasons sounds like a yuppie mother's car to do the 200 metre school run in!

Despite the Sony boss's arrogant lack of vision, this particular recording is even more full of the contrast (which is Vivaldi's trademark) than the versions I made previously. In my less than humble opinion, unlike other attempts to modernise the piece, this interpretation doesn't emasculate Vivaldi, it empowers him.

Go get it, Rover!

OK folks, I admit it, this is on the verge of becoming too boring to credibly expect someone to carry on reading this book. When writing of recordings I am inevitably drawn into reminiscences of the arrogance, duplicitousness, idiocy, wallyism, treachery, greed, dishonesty, misplaced ego, ineptness, you name it, that any independently minded artist finds themselves confronted by from every major record company. I could write a whole book on these mental midgets but it wouldn't be fair to you, my dear reader, and it would end up being at the expense of all the amazing things which have been my good fortune to experience in this life so far. To have had the luck to be born in Northern Europe with food on the table almost every day, education, the health service and in a war-free zone would make it exceptionally pathetic for this book to turn into an endless whinge about useless record companies and kunt-duck-tors (let's face it, it doesn't matter what your job, there's always going to be a halfwit behind a desk who thinks they know more than the person who was actually lived the life for real).

So I will change COURSE, like a HORSE, who doesn't like the prickly GORSE and will devote the rest of this book to all the less tedious or slightly amusing incidents I have been involved in. With all that in mind I will curtail all the hot air about the rest of my concerto recordings by simply doing my ratings. Just in case you like my kind of thoughts about composers, performers and the actual music I have already finished another book: *KENNEDY'S A to Z of MUZIK*, which you can get if you are prepared to wait a couple of years for it to be released.

MY ALBUMS

This lovely little chapter is about my albums, albums of my fukkin' music. I have loved writing, arranging and making music with my various bands. Here's what I think and remember about some of my own albums:

Let Loose
1987

Co-written and produced with Dave Heath this was my first original album. I was being Let Loose from my 'classical' work and from playing other people's stuff like Elgar, Brahms, Walton, Bach etc., and was now able to do something of my own with no restraint, hence the title.

I should point out that this album was released quite a long time before the very, very, very nice looking band from London took the same name.

Working with Dave Heath was great because he is a completely original composer who brings together the terrain of symphonic, pentatonic, modal, jazz, Celtic all onto the same planet. He is also one of my best mates. We dumped symphonic for this album but loads of other shit went into it. I had players of absolute class playing with/for me—Mitch Dalton, Andy Pask, Andy Barron, Jon Hurst, Ron Matheson, Guy Barker, Dominic Miller, Graham Ward and I think that's everybody!

As well as the original writing of Dave and I there's a version of 'The Way We Were' which I like because it's not anything like anyone else's cover.

It was concerning this album that I remember the first prejudice I received from a rock/jazz reviewer (hearing-impaired) who thought I couldn't be much kop because I was 'classical', and worse than 'classical', good at 'classical'. He/it said that I was copying the innovations of Miles Davis's album *Tutu*. This was a huge inadvertent compliment because I hadn't heard that album by the time we recorded *Let Loose*. That meant Nigel Kennedy = genius like Miles! And another quibbler scribbler bites the dust....

Music in Colors
Stephen Duffy feat. Nigel Kennedy (Yeah, That's Me)
1993

I love this album. It was quite natural that Steve and I should work together, after all we lived on the same street in Malvern, were both Villa fans and ... were both musicians (that last fact is probably the one that cracked it). As well as going regularly to the Villa we'd enjoy the benefit of dope rock cakes (or rock dope cakes) made in an exquisitely traditional manner by his girlfriend Kate and we'd enjoy the Malvern sunsets from the hillside. In fact it was on one of these evenings that Steve introduced me to the music of Nick Drake.

Steve is an absolutely great singer songwriter himself so it was no hardship to work on a project with him when he invited me. I really enjoyed learning a fair bit from working with Steve, from his song writing skills and studio knowledge. In fact, the work we did was right on it, stress free, quick and produced great results.

Obviously the song closest to my heart is 'Holte End Hotel'. This beautiful red brick building behind The Holte End was going to be destroyed and was written in the hope that this unique part of the history of Aston Villa and the industrial revolution would be allowed to survive. The song was great and reflected a lot of the feelings us Villa fans had towards the place. I'm glad it survived and it is now a drinking hole for us Villa fans prior to the match—not sure how much credit our song should take for that....

I've done some of my best fiddle playing on this album and more importantly Steve wrote some cracking songs.

Somehow the mental midgets at EMI, Parlophone or whatever they make the effort to call themselves, managed to fritter this album away.

I've seen that Gnarlophone have posted the album on YouTube and they've been nice/dumb enough to credit me with all the vocals on all the songs but one!

"Dunderhead, if you heard me sing at Villa Park you might change your mind about that credit—and what the fukkk did poor old Stephen Duffy do on the album then? Every now and then I play the violin, something I have a bit of a reputation for. It's a four string instrument normally held under the chin in Western society and it has a thing called a bow which draws the sound out of it. It's lovely."

N.B. My operatic appearances at La Scala, the New York Metropolitan Opera House and Covent Garden Opera House were all cancelled long ago due to serious quality concerns centred around my singing. Concerns not seemingly shared by Gnarlophone.

Kafka
1996

It was almost another 10 fukkin years until I was able to make my second album of original music. The success of my partnership with an ugly geezer called Vivaldi saw to that. It was either Viv himself or other guys who smelt of the same cloth who occupied my time because of my 'success'. Classical ruled my waves and it was always "A little bit later, Nigel, and it will be the right time for your own music", then another un-refusable opportunity would arise in the world of clarse. Finally I drew the line and this album appeared in my mind. It's some of the best work I've ever done, and in retrospect one can see that it was ahead of its time in a fair few ways and quite influential.

This album was a change for me after ten years of clarse grafting and what with my electric violin, the great collaborations and all of the songs being my shit, it was going to be viewed as a change by my listeners as well. Circumstantially all of my songs in this collection were about change, so there was a synonymity about the creative world of the album and my own situation.

What with change being the core element I thought of Franz Kafka's *Metamorphosis*, but ... METAMORPHOSIS ... sounded too much like a Lithuanian prog rock band or something. KAFKA was a much nicer word and reflected some of the humanity in my songs. I was keen for the humane aspect of change to be represented by my work, not the 'change' represented by the butchery that globalist capitalism calls progress. So *Kafka* it was.

The list of artists who came to record on this album was a muvvafukka: Danny Thompson, Stéphane Grappelli, Pino Palladino, Manu Katché, Naná Vasconcelos, Donovan, Jane Siberry, Stephen Duffy, Caroline Lavelle and those others called MORE. They all did a beautiful job, even the MORE guys. We recorded at Rockfield, the studio where Queen recorded 'Bohemian Rhapsody'. The piano that Freddie Mercury played is still there.

This book'll never end if I do a synopsis on every song so here are just five or six:

FALLEN FOREST: Double meaning. People assume I'm referring to criminal logging in Poland and Brazil. Maybe, but at the time I was also referring to the relegation of Nottingham Forest. One of my best melodies, when it first came to mind I thought I must have heard it somewhere else but I hadn't.

MELODY IN THE WIND: I wrote this for Stéphane Grappelli and it reflects his happy optimistic musical personality. It was a magic moment when he agreed to come and record this with me.

INNIG: My first recording on piano. An intimate song beautifully co-written and uniquely sung by Jane Siberry.

I BELIEVE IN GOD: Written for Paul McGrath's testimonial, he played like a God for the Villa. I recorded the crowd from behind the goal in front of The Holte End at Villa Park.

FROM ADAM TO EVE: There'd been some androgyny but I don't believe anyone had written a positive song about sex change before this song. Inspired co-writing and recording by Stephen Duffy and Brixeeee Smith.

TRANSFIGURATION AND LE SOLEIL LEVANT SUR LA SEINE: Both of these were very early examples of acoustic instruments and vocals played live over programming. Rare at the time this has since become commonplace.

I'd done some of my best work but unfortunately I had a manager at the time who seemed more interested in hobnobbing with the record company than grabbing them by the scruff of the neck (or by the pig nose ring) and dragging them towards success.

That's the only way. Money doesn't grow on trees and success doesn't grow in a record company, it has to be forced on them.

Anyhow, despite EMI's best efforts, I hope you get a chance to hear this, some of my best work.

Oh yeah, Oasis were recording in the next door studio and we hung out with them quite a bit. As we all know, they have a strong affinity with The Beatles. Well, one day Liam came into our studio and said:

"Hey, guys, I'd like to meet Ravi." He was excited to meet the sitar virtuoso.

I said "Sure, mate. He's right here playing darts."

Liam turned his ready to worship gaze onto yet another Manc playing darts. This particular Ravi was there to record some kora (African harp) for me. A really good player. Right name, wrong Ravi as far as Liam was concerned. Ravi Shankar playing darts is still a sight I like to imagine. Imagine?

Later in the sessions I arranged a drug infused football match against Oasis.

They started with 15 against our 11 and by the time we realised how many of them were on the pitch we were trailing. With 11 against 11 we did much better. In the name of all bad losers I reckon they should've been disqualified and the result struck from the record.

The Kennedy Experience
Nigel Kennedy plays Jimi Hendrix
1999

I got into Jimi Hendrix pretty early. Like Beethoven he was powerful, trance-spiritual and based on solid strong rhythm. I was attracted to the freedom of his music and that he completely transcended the black/white thing, something which seems beyond the capability of many of today's artists and political commentators.

At some point I'd heard a classical-ish string quartet playing 'Purple Haze' and while thinking "All credit to 'em for playing Hendrix on acoustic instruments" I also thought "NO! This has no rhythm and Mitch Mitchell was an integral foundation of The Experience. There's gotta be rhythm." So when I started playing the repertoire I always kept it rhythmic or at least, in Little Wing or suchlike, with a heartbeat pulse. Rhythm is what enabled Jimi's guitar to fly, structure, wings can't be made of jelly. No beat = jelly. Structure = beat = wings = no jelly!

It was with this in mind that I went on a snotty[46] kids' live Saturday morning TV show and played 'Purple Haze'. At that point I didn't know that Hendrix was going to become a commitment of mine on a level with Bach etc., but a geezer from The Hendrix Foundation heard/saw the TV transmission and asked me to do a Hendrix project. There were one or two classical or jazz versions of Jimi's stuff going on but they were innocuous in their limitations of remaining within a narrow genre concept. Jazz guys were doing it jazzy, classical guys were doing it clarse-y ... horrible! The rock guys were also a bit limited by pre-conceived genre definitions. The openness of Jimi's music was the key to making it worth doing.

I know that Hendrix on the violin (electric or acoustic) was probably more interesting than yet another guitarist doing it. But it was the approach from The Hendrix Foundation that made me realise my hands were the right ones for a project like that to fall into. All right, it might not have been suitable for a clarse-ico to play Jimi's music but with the rock and jazz sensibility I'd got from love and devotion to those areas of music I was, believe it or not, perfect for that particular endeavour. There was, also, Jimi's expressed desire to go towards jazz and symphonic. Yes, I was the guy ...

Two interesting strands of development then presented themselves. One was to record 'Fire' with Eddie Kramer, Jimi's original engineer/producer. 'Fire' is a fukkin great song, rock/soul grooves with blues overtones and an energetic narrative. It's a song I love interpreting and opening up, it's always killa with audiences. The recording was for a multi-artist collection called *Stone Free*, each invited muso contributing one track. As far as I recall there was a good diversity of contributors ranging from Seal and Jeff Beck to The Cure. It was a while back—can't remember the rest of them.

---

46 Opinion: Kids are nice if they're nice, not if they're snot. It's inane and dismissive to like all kids because they're kids. They are individuals with varying characters.

In addition to that the opportunity arose to go into the studio with John Leckie (of Stone Roses fame). For that session I chose to record 'Little Wing' and 'Purple Haze'. Meanwhile, Eddie Kramer was great, easy-going but super concentrated on working towards an end result. My idea of what I can do for Hendrix is not to do merely a carbon copy of the original with a Marcel Marceau mime on the top. Jimi's openness is so far-reaching that it's an insult to the song not to expand on the possibilities that he left behind him. Fukkin his stuff up with horrible 9th, 11th, 13th or even 7th complications à la jazz or clever jams on one chord with no consideration for structure also take, rather than give to his songs.

I approach Jimi's songs for the unique compositions they are, not from the guitar playing angle. It's easier for me as a violinist not to get infatuated by doing a mental monkey copy of all his riffs than it is for a guitar player. Eddie Kramer got the drift of that immediately and what he did in the mix with all his crazy panning and other stereo placements was just brilliant.

The sessions with Leckie were also fukkin' great. From him I learned a lot of stuff about setting up good trancy rocky grooves and I think from me he learned about the benefits of taking advantage of the mojo that a muso might have and recording them before they become a slowjo.

I remember in particular that I'd decided the drummer had to be Michael Lee. I'd met him because he was playing with Planty's band and his Bonham-esque deep sound and intelligent but no bullshit sensibility were muvvafukkin perfect for what I was after. He was also a lovely bloke, it's so sad that he was stolen from this planet at such a young age.

John Leckie got in some really talented and interesting people. Among them were the aforementioned Ravi (great on kora, shit on sitar) and Paul Inder who is an incredibly talented multifaceted muso and programmer. There were also that other lot, all great, called MORE...

The Leckie tracks and the one with Kramer, of 'Little Wing', 'Purple Haze' and 'Fire', have got something special. They are exactly the right direction for Hendrix. I'll put them out as a mini bastard LP soon. Don't watch this space, watch another space.

I did an acoustic album of Jimi's stuff called *The Kennedy Experience*. My septet recorded the album (after quite a long North American tour of the same repertoire) in Bryan Adams' studio in Vancouver. My engineer went a bit AWOL on the mix but there are parts of the album which are very, very good ... and parts which aren't. The sound quality is more tinny than we actually sounded.

Hendrix and I are spiritual brothers and there'll hardly ever be a gig where I won't play something of his. I have yet to make my definitive recording of his compositions. I'll be doing it soon. Don't watch this space, watch another space.

WATCH OUT! Detour to Billy Connolly! It was on the aforementioned North American tour that I met Billy Connolly in the lobby of our New York hotel. It transpired that we were going to be in LA at the same time so I invited him and his wife Pamela to my Hendrix gig there in Royce Hall. They are both huge stars but, as like many happy people who are great at what they do, no airs and graces, friendly. In fact, considerate to the extreme. When I checked with the box office that everything had gone all right with their tickets the answer was affirmative. Not only that, but they'd absolutely insisted on paying for them. As Mr Connolly put it to me after the gig, no artist could survive if the audience solely comprised people availing themselves of complimentary tickets. Lesson learned. I now always try and pay if someone nice has left me comps, the problem now is that the ever so clever modern technology often doesn't allow for this.

Don't worry, muvvafukkas. If I've left you a comp I'm really, really NOT trying to get your fukkin dosh.

Please relax and enjoy the gig, see you after. I don't take cheques.

The Doors Concerto
2000

When I was approached by Jaz Coleman (of Killing Joke fame) to play a concerto he was writing based on and inspired by the music of The Doors. I thought profoundly to myself:

"Eh, wot?"

And after a bit more even deeper deep, deeper than deep deliberation I thought:

"Ummm, why not?"

As it turned out, Jaz Coleman had written a masterpiece. When I received the violin part with nothing else to hear, just a bunch of written violin notes, it looked pretty difficult but with no context it was impossible to tell what I had in my hands. I practised it anyway to make sure I could play the notes. It was only the day before recording that I got to hear what I was recording those notes with. Yeah, man. Coleman had written a masterpiece. Depending on your taste it's either better or worse than The Doors originals. How I see it is that Jaz Coleman has done wizardry with the orchestra and the addition and assimilation of indigenous Vietnamese instruments. Such enlightened orchestration has produced something so brilliant that it doesn't need to be compared to anything. Even someone who had never heard The Doors would love this concerto. How Jaz has written it the orchestra hovers, glides, swoops, embraces, awakens, caresses and opens the heart of the listener and I play some hot shit soulful fiddle as well.

We recorded it in Abbey Road Studio No. 2. It has the famous recording room downstairs and the 'control' room upstairs. The great thing about the session was that Jaz had broken his leg and was on crutches. This meant that when I was downstairs recording he could only cripple down the stairs with great pain and difficulty, so I could get on with my playing undisturbed by too much talk about how to do it. I was able to zone in and that's what always gets the best results.

Check this fukkin' album. Jaz has written a masterpiece.

It's fukkin' fukkin' good.

Interlude
Jazz Summers—Summertime

Special mention has to go to Jazz Summers. I worked with him for a bit and it was immediately evident that he was a great manager. We worked together on a tour of Japan and Australia, my Doors Concerto recording and my Bach concertos recording with the Berliner Philharmoniker.

He was a real personality, I wouldn't call him old school, he was modern thinking and non-conformist, but he had a good bit of old time menace underneath a charming debonair exterior. He instilled fear into record companies, and like John Stanley, he wouldn't waste time on record company underlings. When EMI Classics were pulling their feet about giving me what I was worth for a new contract he just went way above their heads to the 'head of the world' and then waved the contract under Classics' nose after.

He was into alternating Zen with intimidating and frightening people-ish creatures like record company promotion types. He was a bit of a The Limey type of guy but even my very proper 'classical music only' mum loved him. A few quotes of his sum him up completely:

"I've never burned a venue to the ground. I've never even hit an A&R man. I locked one in a cupboard once, as punishment for some racism and sexism."

I love the use of the word even! Despite the muvva success he had managing Wham!, The Verve, Yazz, Badly Drawn Boy, The Scissor Sisters, Lisa Stansfield, Soul to Soul, The Orb and more something else he said resonates with his love of music.

"For me success is simple: if I really love a piece of music, get it recorded, get it released and it sells one copy—that's a success. It means you've created something. You've added something to the world. You've contributed a piece of music to life."

Despite being a master of the art of confrontation his underlying humility and lack of bullshit shone through in that last quote and in the next.

"I went from being a wanker to being a genius, as you can in the music industry—though you're normally a wanker again by the following week."

In these most boring of grey days in the history of the music business one misses the character and hutzpah of Jazz Summers more than ever. When compared to other managers I've worked with, John Stanley and Jazz Summers were like fully sighted people living in The Land of the Blind, everyone else fumbling in the darkness. Present company excepted of course! Maybe!

East Meets East
Featuring Tomasz Kukurba's Kroke Band
2003

For me, particularly after being through two types of schooling which indulge and encourage excessive note playing, melody has established itself in my mind as being the most valuable element of music. This value is proven to be more than just an opinion when one becomes aware of all the beautiful melodies handed down from generation to generation without them ever being written down or recorded. Why do people remember these melodies hundreds of years later? Because they are fukkin' GOOD and melody is what matters. Great artists can play a melody, lesser artists have big problems with that.

My love of and ability with melody found me ready to make this album. This work was made possible by two lasting friendships. After recording his beautiful *Doors Concerto* I was lucky that Jaz Coleman could come in and produce for me, he definitely gave this album some balls so that it wasn't only airy fairy melodies. A new and strong friendship had evolved between Tomasz Kukurba and myself. He is a spiritual and talented viola player, singer and let's face it, muvva multi-instrumentalist. We had a killa connection immediately, combining his amazing imagination with my good sense of focus and line.

Working with the serious heritage of Klezmer and Balkan melodies was something I'd wanted to do for a long time and now I had the ideal partnership to share that vision. Inspired by these timeless melodies we wrote some originals as well.

Favourite tracks of mine could be 'Ajde Jano', 'T 4.2', 'Ederlezi', 'Kazimierz' and 'One Voice' (for which I invited the greater than great Palestinian violinist Aboud Abdel Aal to share this melody of mine with me and Tomasz Kukurba. Jewish and Palestinian together in peace).

When I was at school my musical mentor Yehudi Menuhin had made an album with Ravi Shankar very aptly called *East Meets West*. Because the majority of us on this album were from Eastern Europe playing music from Eastern Europe with extra influences from the Middle East and from further East in Northern Africa I very, very cleverly decided to call the album *East Meets East*.

The title caused quite a few problems during my publicity rounds for the album with many interviewers completely unable to say the name. I was verbally assaulted by 'East Meets West' so many times that I had to look in the mirror to double check that I wasn't, indeed, Yehudi Menuhin or Ravi Shankar. Other spluttering abuses of the name included *East Meets Yeast, Yeast Meets East, Yeast Meets Yeast, East Yeasts Meat* (not veggie), *Yeasts Meats Eat, Eat Yeast Meat, Meet Eats Yeasts, Eeeeezzzt Meatzzzzz Syeeeeeeeeezzszzszztz* which loosened some dentures.

My advice, learn to pronounce or spell it before you buy it.

The Blue Note Sessions
2006

Sorry I done it!... I did a whole chapter on the Aristocracy of Rock. This album is the aristocracy of jazz. As you might know, my involvement in jazz started for real when I was 13 and was playing regularly with Stéphane Grappelli. Later I was playing pretty regularly with Jimmy Rowles in Bradley's. It's funny that people from both of these guys' camps thought I was selling out whenever I let them know when I was going off to do some classical gigs. They literally dismissed it as a class thing that I was choosing instead of life values. Maybe they were right in a way but I was just pleased to be asked to play any type of good music, jazz however, has always been around me and in my life. Frequently I've been jamming after a gig for five, six, seven hours—'til everybody drops!

I've always loved the comradery of jazz and the inclusiveness of it as an environment. In a jazz club the audience and musicians are on the same social level, in other areas of music it's very unlikely to find the musos sitting around together with the punters before, during and after the gig.

With classical music, as you've probably gathered, it's all a bit too uptight for me and in pop or rock it's a bit like football, often they're stars who don't like hanging out with the proletariat who paid for all their swimming pools. In the good days jazz wasn't about a social divide, it was about a social coming together. I like to think that I've brought some of the spontaneity and love of the moment from jazz onto the classical stages I've played on. From classical I've brought dynamic changes and possibly a greater sense of structure and pacing onto jazz stages.

It had taken a while so it was a great moment for me when discussions started with Blue Note about finally making an album of proper jazz.

Nicolas Pflug got me a muvva of a band to play with, a true Aristocrats of Jazz line up. Ron Carter (bass), Jack DeJohnette (drums), J. D. Allen (sax), Joe Lovano (sax), Lucky Peterson (Hammond), Kenny Werner (piano) and Danny Sadownick (percussion).

The way that Ron Carter worked with Jack DeJohnette was fascinating and turned out to be an inspired choice of rhythm section. Ron, capable technically of playing anything but never tempted to play a note too many, and everything with perfect timing, laid back microscopically behind the beat, made it possible for Jack to be free—because Ron provided the strong foundations that a 'sound' architectural structure needs. Perfect. Jack never repeats himself and was able to be as free as he wanted, each take different and not one drum fill repeated. J. D. Allen played a spacious wistful solo on my song 'Stranger in a Stranger Land', Kenny Werner played beautiful tasteful piano on any repertoire he touched, Lucky Peterson was killa in the more blues inflected songs (Hammond and fiddle go great, both have endless sustain if one wants that) and Joe Lovano played great in the couple of Duke Pearson songs I arranged, very soulful.

There were two signposts to the future which became clear to me while recording this album. Firstly, that I was going to enjoy searching through Duke Pearson's work to find more of his fantastic songs, I've since been doing that and the journey's not over yet. Secondly, that if great musicians of this incomparable level enjoyed playing my compositions as much as they did I should carry on writing much more, I've since been doing that and that journey isn't over yet either.

My three favourite songs on this album are 'Stranger in a Stranger Land' (subtle and beautiful work from Kenny Werner and Danny Sadownick), 'I Almost Lost My Mind' and 'After the Rain'.

Go on you bastard[47], check this shit.

NKQ
A Very Nice Album/Shhh!
2008/2010

The title of *A Very Nice Album* came into my head when I thought of an old grandma waiting at the bus stop talking to her friend who would've been another nursing home escapee.

"So nice to see you Mavis, it's been a long time, all of five minutes."

"Yes, Ethel, do you think a bus will come? It would be so very lovely to see a bus."

"I saw a bus pass by here in 1946 soon after the war, there might be another one in a year or two, that's how it works under our very lovely Tory government, Mavis."

"Ethel, you know, between my knitting sessions I like really nice things and things which are lovely? Well, I got something today which is really lovely and nice…"

"What did you get, Mavis, which is very lovely and nice?"

"Well, you know that lovely punk violinist called Nigel Kennedy, or sometimes Kennedy, or sometimes Nigel or sometimes Noige?"

"Yes, was he on TV before the First World War? He's lovely, isn't he?"

"Yes, he's very young as well, only 50 or something."

"Oh, lovely."

"Well, he's made a new plastic recording."

"Spastic?"

"No, I don't think so or he wouldn't be able to play that lovely violin of his."

"So he's still OK, then?"

"I think he's lovely, so lovely and never causing too much trouble…."

---

47 Dear sensitive politically correct one, please don't cry. I am not questioning or attaching any importance to your parents' marital state. In my mind all bastards are kool. Having been born out of wedlock I'm one myself.

"Rubble?"

"Ermmm. Anyway, Ethel, he's lovely so I've got his new plastic recording … it's a very nice album...."

So the title *A Very Nice Album* was born.

Another conversation between the same members of the intelligentsia could have been:

"Hello Ethel, have you got *A Very Nice Album* by Nigel Kennedy?"

"No, Mavis, all the ones I've got of his are horrible...."

Then there's *Shhh!* The silly title came around because of dunderheads and ignorance within EMI. I originally had a decent title for the album … *OY!* But one of the cloth ear wool brains came up with the theory that *OY!* had Nazi connotations and would be deemed offensive or anti-Semitic by various people. I'm not anti-Semitic against any Jewish or Arab person.

A well-known strategy of record companies is to pick a seemingly unresolvable argument in order to delay a payment due on the formal delivery of an album. If that's what they were attempting it didn't work. For once, I wasn't in an argumentative mood, I was in a very short mellow phase so I agreed with their ignorance.

I'm part Jewish and using the word *OY!* didn't fill my mind with pictures of loathsome Nazis. I use the word regularly to catch people's attention or to get them off my land without even a hint of any mishap. The EMI ditherers hadn't figured that it's not a bad idea for the name of an album to catch people's attention! Because of their self-indulgence we ended up with a name which was unpronounceable, unspellable, and unrecognisable on the radio.... Nice one, marketing team!... OY! Wake up! I'd like to reiterate that I'm not anti-Semitic against any Semite. Anti-Semitic behaviour against Arabic and Jewish people still goes on and it's a disgusting reflection of our society. I've still to find any evidence that OY! is an anti-Semitic word in any of the countries I play in or sell albums in. What I do know is that introducing gratuitous pseudo-concerns like the one above only belittle the real problems that others are actually facing.

Both *A Very Nice Album* and *OY!* (OOOPS! *Shhh!*) Feature my Polish Jazz Quintet NKQ (The Nigel Kennedy Quintet). I met the players through hanging and jamming in the Kraków jazz clubs, the best of which is Jazz Club u Muniaka. Tomasz Grzegorski and Krzysztof Dziedzic deserve special mention for not only their considerable talent on their instruments but also their ability to learn from some of my basic musical objectives. I have four very simple and essential ways of communicating effectively through music. If these are respected (in any genre) then music becomes a story, not just a lot of clever notes. 1. Dynamic contrast. 2. Contrast of energy levels. 3. Don't play two notes where one is necessary, if one note isn't necessary DON'T PLAY. 4. No mannerisms like automatic over-complication. Jazz complications are mainly just habitual mannerisms. The proof being that if you ask most jazzers to play harmonies without 7ths or not to play too many notes almost invariably they can't do it. In my view one doesn't communicate through mannerisms, one hides behind them. Our job is to tell a story, not hide behind musical nervous tics.

I learned plenty from playing with my colleagues in NKQ but all forward momentum had to come from me and that's not the way for a band to progress.

Nevertheless, two albums from one band on a major record label (in name only) is pretty good and *OY!* is a proper good album. All of the songs (except for the Boy George Riverman version horribly wasted by the EMI wallies) are mine and I'm pleased with the results.

Favourite tracks:

A Very Nice Album—'Nice Bottle of Beaujolais, Innit?', 'Invaders', '15 Stones', 'Father and Son'.

OY! (*Shhh!*)—'Transfiguration', 'Riverman', 'Silver Lining', 'Shhh!'

While My Guitar Gently Weeps
British Rock Symphony
2013

When I was asked to play on an album called *British Rock Symphony* my initial reaction was suspicion. Symphony orchestras have bad rhythm and in the past have crapped so much shit on Rock in their unkool attempts to be kool that this could've been another attempt on the toilet.

However, when I found out the song being asked of me was 'While My Guitar Gently Weeps' the idea seemed better. It's not primarily a rock 'n' roll number, the rhythmic aspect of a ballad wasn't going to be so crucial. I was told that Zak Starkey was on drums so the idea of lame rhythm was put right to bed.

I was on tour in my beloved Germany at the time of recording but I had a day off in Hannover so it was possible to go into Mousse T's studio and record my bit as an over dub.

What with George Harrison's melodic style of playing I decided to play the verses and choruses on acoustic violin and the solos on electric. Apart from the climax in one of the solos I kept it well melodic out of respect for Mr Harrison.

The result is a fukkka and I've had loads of positive reaction to it. I'm glad to have done George Harrison proud, I love his music.

Chekkit.

P.S. I dragged my long, long time friend Pieter Daniel into the studio and he played too. Piet, mate—what the fukk were you doing?

My World
2017

I returned to my own compositions for this album, hence the title. The first half was a collection of songs called Dedications, the most important of which were songs in honour of musicians to whom I owed the enjoyment and understanding of music.

'Solitude' was for Yehudi Menuhin because of his open-minded but sometimes solitary views on humanity and world politics.

'Fallen Forest' was for Isaac Stern because in my eyes my melody reflected Stern's unremitting honesty.

These guys were important but it was Stéphane Grappelli who was the breath of fresh air which pointed me away from the written page and towards that moment called NOW. We might have important memories, we might have important plans for the future, but in all kinds of music and many other ways of life that really magic NOW moment seems to have been largely forgotten. Technical information like "Oh dear, I've got some fast notes coming up which might impress people, particularly if I look serious enough" is of little consequence in the grand scheme of things but seems to have replaced that moment of shared inspiration which is the important part of music (for me). Menuhin, Stern but in particular Grappelli tapped into the magic moment. I do that too. Stéphane was my biggest inspiration when I needed one so I resurrected Melody in the Wind (which I wrote for him) in his honour. Nowadays I play that song with Mostafa Saad, I like seeing it reach a brilliant new generation violinist after the brilliant old generation violinist.

The second part of the album is incidental music that I wrote for my wife Agnieszka's production and translation of Chekhov's *The Three Sisters*.

Normally when I write it comes from within, this time I was stimulated by a masterpiece from someone else. It was an inspirational experience. At first I thought I had no interest in the bourgeoisie characters that Chekhov was portraying, but human values were what Chekhov was interested in and his radiant view of things was relevant to anybody. Playing live for the performances was also memorable. Responding to what came from the actors was a three-dimensional version of what merely came off the page. It was also kool to share in that kind of energy without being centre stage.

After the performances it became clear that the music was self-sufficient so I recorded it for this album. The sense of destiny unfolding is still there.

It's a very nice album, oh, no it isn't. It's some aspects of My World.

Gershwin
2018

George Gershwin was born in Brooklyn and was of Jewish Ukrainian ancestry. His music paved the way forward in jazz for such luminaries of the school of Jewish life as Artie Shaw, Benny Goodman, Dave Brubeck and many more people. All of his music has his own fingerprint on it, a unique one consisting of jazz, classical and Klezmer influences. I feel uniquely placed to play his music, not just because he is a famous composer, but because I have pursued each of his three main influences individually with dedication and love. I also had incomparable experience playing his songs at a young age.

I started playing those songs as a 13 year old with Stéphane Grappelli without even knowing who they were by. 'Lady Be Good', 'The Man I Love', 'How Long Has This Been Going On?' and others were regularly on Steff's set list so I got to know the songs and Gershwin's song writing style by working with a master. None of that knowledge came out of a book, it was deeper than that. I was also listening to proper good versions of Gershwin by Miles Davis, Satchmo and the deep but angst free Ella Fitzgerald.

One of the great things about Gershwin's music is the bitter sweet thing, particularly in his ballads, but always overriding everything is that uplifting feeling. One thing though, please don't be put off by hearing one of his musicals. I agree that hearing those overdramatic pseudo-classical singers can make you feel nauseous unless you're drugged up to the nines, in which case you'd just shoot the stereo/computer and have done with the problem.

I decided to record Gershowitz—Gershwina—Gershvin—Gershwin (all of those name changes within two generations). My versions of the songs all relied to a certain extent on what I'd learned along the way from Grappelli, Menuhin, folk music in the Klezmer way and more importantly, perhaps, just being myself.

Because of the great times I'd had in clubs and concert halls all over the place with Grappelli in most of this repertoire I decided to go down the guitar route as far as the instrumentation of the band was concerned as did Stéphane. First on the list for this one was my long, long, long time friend Rolf 'Das Kobra' Bussalb, we play all types of music and he's a particularly great player in Hot Club music. The cultivated Tomasz Kupiec was also an automatic choice on bass. I got inspired and then invited the great swing aficionado Howard Alden over from America (we had enjoyed a killa jam a few years before), what a fukkin' artist. He really contributed special stuff. The icing on the cake was Beata Urbanek-Kalinowska. One of Poland's greatest 'cellists she played the parts I'd written for her with elegance, feel and grace. Her 'cello helped me portray the classical aspect of Gershwin which often goes missing in jazz orientated renditions of his music.

My favourite tracks on this one are my excerpts from 'Porgy & Bess' (intimate but sweeping melodies with real jazz feel), 'Summertime' (I take it down less expected roads) and 'You Can't Take That Away From Me' (which features my jazz piano recording debut, my way is Feel, not Spiel). Fukkit! I forgot to mention Dave Heath's flute solo in Summertime, it's worth getting the album for that alone.

Recital
2013

I forgot this one! I recorded it for Sony in Abbey Road Studio 2 and it comprised quite a few songs by the inimitable Fats Waller. I've always loved him because he showed us all that topper than top music making can be fun and he composed phenomenal songs. As it happened Dave Brubeck died during our recordings so I did a version of 'Take Five' for the album as well.

An argument developed between me and the head of Sony, a wanker called Bogdan who is from Serbia. Now, I have many friends in Serbia and was the first artist to play there after the United Nations' atrocities against the Belgrade people. I know things are black and white with Serbian people, that's one of the things I like about them. So when the Bogdan pillock said (purportedly) that my album would go out with that repertoire only over his dead body I thought that it was a shame he had to die, but no one was going to tell me what's what with my own album. The album was released exactly as I planned and the last I heard the wanker was still alive which was a bit of a relief. Even wankers should be allowed to live.

The album sounds great and I might have been able to put more repertoire on it if one of the Sony employees hadn't wasted so much studio time arguing with me about what I should have been recording.

The cover picture was painted by the wonderful creative free spirit Dora Holzhandler. We met on the street where I live and at eighty plus she was still a painter, a real hippie in the best sense of the word. Her work lives on and it makes me proud that one example is still around on this album cover.

If you want to know what the album sounds like CHEKKIT!

FRIENDS AND WORK FRIENDS

Pete Adams—One of that great line of English 'cellists, he follows the natural and musical ways of Jacqui du Pré. Actually he doesn't follow. He's his own man.

Andreas Adelhofer—Das Hof is a fantastic front of house sound engineer and we've worked together for yonks. We have strong and different opinions and learn from each other because of it. He'll always go that extra 100 miles to get a great result.

Howard Alden—This man is the master of swing. His love of music, his original solos, his wonderful rhythm playing, his unique approach, all mean I love every moment of playing with him.

Lizzie Ball—An amazing talent in any of the types of music she gets involved in, either as violinist or singer. The type of musician who when she says I might have been an influence makes me feel proud. She led my Orchestra of Life in a way no other person could have done.

Ernst Bier—What a killer drummer. A musician's musician. A monster fixture at the A-Trane in Berlin and I'm looking forward to our next noise.

Rolf Bussalb—Die Kobra (he hates it when I repeatedly call him Das Kobra and I'm not in the mood to annoy him right now) is one of the best, most versatile guitarists I've met. We've been friends and colleagues since before the dinosaurs and have played anything which moves.

Caleb (K-Leb) Clarke—We were best mates and used to play everywhere, airports, streets, pubs, concert stages and had muvvafukka times. A geezer who looks like Roger Waters now deals with his communication. Get a phone Caleb! My number's still the same.

Basia Dziewiecka—Another natural talent. Basia didn't improvise when I met her—she does now. And she improvises beautifully, honestly and is never tempted by the cliché.

John Etheridge—One of the English guitar greats. Together we can play anything. We met playing Hot Club stuff with Stéphane Grappelli but with his Soft Machine background we have been able to go on and do almost anything. NEGATIVE: eats all the rider blocking it with his long legs.

Dr. Barry Grimaldi and Hazel—Where would one be without a good doctor? The fact that I'm here is the case in point.

Michael Guttman—A wonderful musician. Another Juilliard escapee. Brilliant sense of humour and always fun to be with.

Kuba Haufa—A great violinist and orchestra leader from Poznań who led my orchestra for quite a while. Good times.

Huxley—Like every dog, four things keep Huxley happy. Food, exercise, games and companionship. The way he shows his happiness is unique and unlike any other dog. "A dog is a man's best friend" is a well worn cliché but not without reason. Huxley has given me so much happiness and comradeship during his life that I owe him bigtime and now it's payback. He is very, very old and cannot walk without being carried. I am devoted to him and all of my time is dedicated to Huxley being happy and having yet another wonderful day. Soft as fukk.

Jaworki—As with every community I've lived in I've put in more than I've taken out. 50 free concerts over 15 years, for instance, at Muzyczna Owczarnia. Loads of respect to Jaworki people. Everything was great until the construction of the new couple of houses which look as if on a burial mound. Since then we've had regular illegal trespass, regular vandalism and an attempted assault. Strange how one new nightmare neighbour can seem to completely change the vibe.

Jazz Klub u Muniaka—The best jazz club in Kraków by a long way. Started by the great saxophonist Janusz Muniak the unique standards of this place are being continued and maintained by my friends the Lunz family.

Dom Kelly—One of the greatest oboists and from the English tradition so no edgy sound to worry about. Intuitive muso and great guy. Also, if you need an orchestra his English Session Orchestra is the way to go.

Tomasz Kukurba—Great violist/singer/percussionist/composer. We met playing Klezmer and our spiritual musical partnership is taking us far beyond.

Piotr Kułakowski—Looks a bit like a football hooligan because he is. Beautiful (sonically) bass player. The bass sounds like wood (as it should but doesn't often do) and his timing and harmonic sense are A+.

Tomasz Kupiec—His bass playing is always accommodating to the musicians around him and whether I'm on piano or violin I always feel his musical generosity. Great sounds.

Stefan de Leval Jezierski—The best French horn player I've ever heard. We met when I was playing with the Berlin Philharmonic and he is one of the very, very, very few French hornists to be brilliant in the world of jazz. Hoping to make more music soon. He is really on de leval...

Cho-liang Lin—A giant of the violin. The first time I heard him play Mendelssohn Violin Concerto at age of 15—WOW! Impeccable taste, feeling and sound. I've never forgotten that. He is also a responsible, optimistic and caring friend.

Cora Lunny—She's a great person to make music with, and to hang with. She's the only one I know who has parties as good as mine. Cora could've been a leading violinist in classical, Balkan or both but she had a kid.

Azadeh Maghsoodi—I love listening to Azadeh play the violin. A story unfolds and the truth rings out through her beautiful sound.

Muzyczna Owczarnia—Wietek Kołodziejski's unique concept of a music club in the hills of Jaworki has produced a venue like no other. The building is a converted sheep barn and the musicians playing there are the best in the world. Keep shouting tourists from fukkin' it up and this club will be a jewel in the Polish crown forever!

Ola and Zbigniew Nowak—Every now and then someone is born on this planet who knows how to harness all the positive energy around us for the benefit of everyone else's better existence. Science finds some of the world's truths inexplicable but this generous friend of mine has cured the incurable on a regular basis. And even for the relatively healthy such as myself he produces an effect so positive that it would be cheapened by scientific explanation. Ola is the intelligent compassionate force who helps bring structure to Zbiggy's inspiration.

Orchestra of Life—Everyone in this orchestra is my friend. I started the orchestra with a view of playing every kind of music. Everyone duly obliged at a top level. As with the Polish Chamber Orchestra of which I was director before the Orchestra of Life, I introduced them to major record labels and got them into the most important concert venues worldwide.

James Pearson—We don't work together enough. His broad experience at Ronnie's has enabled him to do amazing and sympathetic work. Every time I see him he has something special and new to give.

Edd Richardson—A muvvafukka drummer. He can rock, he can do sophisticated jazz. I've been equally happy playing Hendrix, Komeda or my shit with him.

Orphy Robinson—A Blue Note artist who plays vibes, marimba, percussion, composes, produces, to name but a few. His technique and knowledge of music are second to none but it's his feel and love of all music which set him apart. He lights up the room when he walks in. He has played and recorded in my Orchestra of Life and produced my Gershwin album.

Ronnie Scott's—The best jazz club in the world. Looking forward to my next gig there.

Mostafa Saad—Mostafa is a great spokesperson for his people and for music. A wonderful charismatic musician he has a great chance to lead the people of Palestine to a better future.

Sonja Schebeck—Could be a major presence in the violin world but her other talents take up a lot of her time. Multi-genre performances' gain is violin music lovers' loss.

Manfred Seipt—It's not every agent (or manager) that loves music so much that you can sit all night with them talking about it. He's one of the tallest, smartest and most elegant people I've worked with and we have been involved in our work together now for some years.

Gabby Swallow—Another musician who sometimes says she was inspired by me. If that is the case I am honoured to have had anything to do with her musical direction. On stage she is super charismatic and has a killa positive influence on whatever music she plays.

Beata Urbanek-Kalinowska—OoL One of the leading 'cellists of Poland and larger areas. Her aristocratic, noble and sensitive approach light up the music she plays.

Cleveland Watkiss—What an artist. He can sing any form of music because it flows from his soul. We have done stuff ranging from Kashmir, jazz, gypsy, Hot Club and he's not a breadhead, loves to jam after a gig. We are going to make an album on inclusiveness to try and offer an alternative to the divisiveness which is presently dominating society.

Piotr Zalewski—He's done my stage monitoring brilliantly for years. His love of music in general and all the types of it that I play sets him apart. The world got lucky on the 28th of December because we both woke up in this world for the first time on that day.

OUTRO

Well, comrade, for indeed, if you have got this far you are indeed a comrade (in arms against the pseudo spielers that it has been my life's work to out and oust from what will be a better world without them), farewell!

Since the beginning of some cheap politicians' enforced schlockdown life hasn't been a total waste of time. I am writing these last words of my first book after also having finished writing my first violin concerto 'Für Ludwig Van'. I played it a few times last month and it went down muvvafukkin killadilla with the orchestras and audiences that I played it for.

Since my involvement in music (or music's involvement in me) I have been amazingly lucky, meeting and working with unique people and forging an indelible bond with you through concertizing or other forms of musical communication.

When I was in my 20s things were going brilliantly musically but on the normal British fees I found myself £15,000 overdrawn. I persevered because I had some mad dream that I could make a living playing music. That I am no longer in that position is down to you and other members of my audiences who found it within them to come to gigs of mine and listen to my music.

At the risk of sounding like one of those fearsomely banal award acceptance speeches (by stars who are pretending they didn't know they were going to win) I would like to give BIG thanks to you and anyone else who has checked my stuff. It's a muvvafukkin privilege to be doing a job I love so much and to still be able to improve at it. My aim is to give you better gigs than ever before.

Music is an incredible and uncharted journey of discovery towards which the destinations are in the moment and in unique unplanned realities. These unforeseeable special moments happen because of the life force of music—the audience combined with the performers. A real bit of music making can't happen without either component. If one of those were missing our beloved art form would only belong in a laboratory or on a factory line.

Thank you for your friendship. You have supported me and I will be forever grateful. See you soon during one of those special moments which only you and I can make and be part of.

All the best,

INDEX

EDITORIAL NOTE

Several chapters of this book include material from an interview Nigel Kennedy gave to Tom Müller, his German publisher, in July 2021.

The chapter On Tour with Nigel: Memories from Rolf, Das Kobra, Bussalb was written by Rolf Bussalb, Nigel Kennedy's friend and guitarist of more than 20 years, and is printed with permission. All rights reserved.